Hadoop Blueprints

Use Hadoop to solve business problems by learning from a rich set of real-life case studies

Anurag Shrivastava
Tanmay Deshpande

BIRMINGHAM - MUMBAI

Hadoop Blueprints

First published: September 2016

Production reference: 1270916

Published by Packt Publishing Ltd.
Livery Place
35 Livery Street
Birmingham
B3 2PB, UK.
ISBN 978-1-78398-030-7

www.packtpub.com

Credits

Authors

Anurag Shrivastava
Tanmay Deshpande

Reviewers

Dedunu Dhananjaya
Wissem El Khlifi
Randal Scott King

Commissioning Editor

Aron Lazar

Acquisition Editor

Smeet Thakkar

Content Development Editor

Deepti Thore

Technical Editor

Vivek Arora

Copy Editor

Safis Editing

Project Coordinator

Shweta H Birwatkar

Proofreader

Safis Editing

Indexer

Aishwarya Gangawane

Graphics

Disha Haria

Production Coordinator

Nilesh Mohite

About the Authors

Anurag Shrivastava is an entrepreneur, blogger, and manager living in Almere near Amsterdam in the Netherlands. He started his IT journey by writing a small poker program on a mainframe computer 30 years back, and he fell in love with software technology. In his 24-year career in IT, he has worked for companies of various sizes, ranging from Internet start-ups to large system integrators in Europe.

Anurag kick-started the Agile software movement in North India when he set up the Indian business unit for the Dutch software consulting company Xebia. He led the growth of Xebia India as the managing director of the company for over 6 years and made the company a well-known name in the Agile consulting space in India. He also started the Agile NCR Conference, which has become a heavily visited annual event on Agile best practices, in the New Delhi Capital Region.

Anurag became active in the big data space when he joined ING Bank in Amsterdam as the manager of the customer intelligence department, where he set up their first Hadoop cluster and implemented several transformative technologies, such as Netezza and R, in his department. He is now active in the payment technology and APIs, using technologies such as Node.js and MongoDB.

Anurag loves to cycle on the reclaimed island of Flevoland in the Netherlands. He also likes listening to Hindi film music.

I would like to thank my wife, Anjana, and daughter, Anika, for putting up with my late-night writing sessions and skipping of weekend breaks. I also would like to thank my parents and teachers for their guidance in life.

I would like to express my gratitude to colleagues at Xebia and Daan Teunissen, where I learned about the value of technical writing from colleagues, who inspired me to work on this book project. I would like to thank all the mentors that I've had over the years. I would like to express thanks and gratitude to Amir Arooni, my boss at ING Bank, who provided me time and opportunity to work on big data and, later on, this book. I also give thanks to the Packt team and the coauthor, Tanmay, who provided help and guidance in the whole process.

Tanmay Deshpande is a Hadoop and big data evangelist. He's interested in a wide range of technologies, such as Apache Spark, Hadoop, Hive, Pig, NoSQL databases, Mahout, Sqoop, Java, and cloud computing. He has vast experience in application development in various domains, such as finance, telecoms, manufacturing, security, and retail. He enjoys solving machine learning problems and spends his time reading anything he can get his hands on. He has a great interest in open source technologies and promotes them through his lectures. He has been invited to various computer science colleges to conduct brainstorming sessions with students on the latest technologies. Through his innovative thinking and dynamic leadership, he has successfully completed various projects. Tanmay is currently working with Schlumberger as the lead big data developer. Before Schlumberger, Tanmay worked with Lumiata, Symantec, and Infosys.

Tanmay is the author of books such as *Hadoop Real World Solutions Cookbook-Second Edition*, *DynamoDB Cookbook*, and *Mastering DynamoDB*, all by Packt Publishing.

I would like to thank my family and the Almighty for supporting me throughout my all adventures.

About the Reviewers

Dedunu Dhananjaya is a senior software engineer in personalized learning and analytics at Pearson. He is interested in data science and analytics. Prior to Pearson, Dedunu worked at Zaizi, LIRNEasia, and WSO2. Currently, he is reading his masters in applied statistics at the University of Colombo.

Wissem El Khlifi is the first Oracle ACE from Spain and an Oracle Certified Professional DBA with over 12 years of IT experience.

He earned his computer science engineering degree from FST Tunisia and master's in computer science as well as in big data science analytics and management from UPC Barcelona. His areas of interest are Linux system administration, high availability Oracle databases, big data NOSQL database management, and big data analysis.

His career has included the following roles: Oracle and Java analyst/programmer, Oracle DBA, architect, team leader, and big data scientist. He currently works as a senior database and applications engineer for Schneider Electric/APC. He writes numerous articles on his website, `http://www.oracle-class.com`, and his Twitter handle is `@orawiss`.

Randal Scott King is the managing partner of Brilliant Data, a consulting firm specializing in data analytics. In his years of consulting, Scott has amassed an impressive list of clientele, from mid-market leaders to Fortune 500 household names. In addition to Hadoop Blueprints, he has also served as technical reviewer for other Packt Publishing books on big data and has authored the instructional videos Learning Hadoop 2 and Mastering Hadoop. Scott lives just outside Atlanta, GA, with his children. You can visit his blog at `http://www.randalscottking.com`.

www.PacktPub.com

For support files and downloads related to your book, please visit www.PacktPub.com.

Did you know that Packt offers eBook versions of every book published, with PDF and ePub files available? You can upgrade to the eBook version at www.PacktPub.com and as a print book customer, you are entitled to a discount on the eBook copy. Get in touch with us at service@packtpub.com for more details.

At www.PacktPub.com, you can also read a collection of free technical articles, sign up for a range of free newsletters and receive exclusive discounts and offers on Packt books and eBooks.

https://www.packtpub.com/mapt

Get the most in-demand software skills with Mapt. Mapt gives you full access to all Packt books and video courses, as well as industry-leading tools to help you plan your personal development and advance your career.

Why subscribe?

- Fully searchable across every book published by Packt
- Copy and paste, print, and bookmark content
- On demand and accessible via a web browser

Table of Contents

Preface

This book covers the application of Hadoop and its ecosystem of tools to solve business problems. Hadoop has fast emerged as the leading big data platform and finds applications in many industries where massive datasets or big data has to be stored and analyzed. Hadoop lowers the cost of investment in the storage. It supports the generation of new business insights, which was not possible earlier because of the massive volumes and computing capacity required to process such information. This book covers several business cases to build solutions to business problems. Each solution covered in this book has been built using Hadoop and HDFS and the set of tools from the Hadoop ecosystem.

What this book covers

Chapter 1, *Hadoop and Big Data*, goes over how Hadoop has played a pivotal role in making several Internet businesses successful with big data from its beginnings in the previous decade. This chapter covers a brief history and the story of the evolution of Hadoop. It covers the Hadoop architecture and the MapReduce data processing framework. It introduces basic Hadoop programming in Java and provides a detailed overview of the business cases covered in the following chapters of this book. This chapter builds the foundation for understanding the rest of the book.

Chapter 2, *A 360-Degree View of the Customer*, covers building a 360-degree view of the customer. A good 360-degree view requires the integration of data from various sources. The data sources are database management systems storing master data and transactional data. Other data sources might include data captured from social media feeds. In this chapter, we will be integrating data from CRM systems, web logs, and Twitter feeds to build the 360-degree view and present it using a simple web interface. We will learn about Apache Sqoop and Apache Hive in the process of building our solution.

Chapter 3, *Building a Fraud Detection System*, covers the building of a real-time fraud detection system. This system predicts whether a financial transaction could be fraudulent by applying a clustering algorithm on a stream of transactions. We will learn about the architecture of the system and the coding steps involved in building the system. We will learn about Apache Spark in the process of building our solution.

Chapter 4, *Marketing Campaign Planning*, shows how to build a system that can improve the effectiveness of marketing campaigns. This system is a batch analytics system that uses historical campaign-response data to predict who is going to respond to a marketing folder. We will see how we can build a predictive model and use it to predict who is going to respond to which folder in our marketing campaign. We will learn about BigML in the process of building our solution.

Chapter 5, *Churn Detection*, explains how to use Hadoop to predict which customers are likely to move over to another company. We will cover the business case of a mobile telecom provider who would like to detect the customers who are likely to churn. These customers are given special incentives so that they can stay with the same provider. We will apply Bayes' Theorem to calculate the likelihood of churn. The model for churn detection will be built using Hadoop. We will learn about writing MapReduce programs in Java in the process of building our solution.

Chapter 6, *Analyze Sensor Data Using Hadoop*, is about how to build a system to analyze sensor data. Nowadays, sensors are considered an important source of big data. We will learn how Hadoop and big-data technologies can be helpful in the Internet of Things (IoT) domain. IoT is a network of connected devices that generate data through sensors. We will build a system to monitor the quality of the environment, such as humidity and temperature, in a factory. We will introduce Apache Kafka, Grafana, and OpenTSDB tools in the process of building the solution.

Chapter 7, *Building a Data Lake*, takes you through building a data lake using Hadoop and several other tools to import data in a data lake and provide secure access to the data. Data lakes are a popular business case for Hadoop. In a data lake, we store data from multiple sources to build a single source of data for the enterprise and build a security layer around it. We will learn about Apache Ranger, Apache Flume, and Apache Zeppelin in the process of building our solution.

Chapter 8, *Future Directions*, covers four separate topics that are relevant to Hadoop-based projects. These topics are building a Hadoop solutions team, Hadoop on the cloud, NoSQL databases, and in-memory databases. This chapter does not include any coding examples, unlike the other chapters. These fours topics have been covered in the essay form so that you can explore them further.

What you need for this book

Code and data samples have been provided for every chapter. We have used Hadoop version 2.7.x in this book. All the coding samples have been developed and tested on the stock (Apache Software Foundation) version of Hadoop and other tools. You can download these tools from the Apache Software Foundation website. In Chapter 2, *A 360-Degree View of the Customer*, we have used Hortonworks Data Platform (HDP) 2.3. HDP 2.3 is a bundle of Hadoop and several other tools from the ecosystem in a convenient virtual machine image that can run on VirtualBox or VMWare. You can download this virtual image from the website of Hortonworks at http://hortonworks.com/downloads/#data-platform. Due to the fast-evolving nature of Hadoop and its ecosystem of tools, you might find that newer versions are available than the ones used in this book. The specific versions of the tools needed for the examples have been mentioned in the chapters where they are first introduced.

Who this book is for

This book is intended for software developers, architects, and engineering managers who are evaluating Hadoop as a technology to build business solutions using big data. This book explains how the tools in the Hadoop ecosystem can be combined to create a useful solution, and therefore, it is particularly useful for those who would like to understand how various technologies can be integrated without understanding any particular tool in depth.

Conventions

In this book, you will find a number of text styles that distinguish between different kinds of information. Here are some examples of these styles and an explanation of their meaning.

Code words in text, database table names, folder names, filenames, file extensions, pathnames, dummy URLs, user input, and Twitter handles are shown as follows: "You can also run the transmodel.py program using the Python command-line interpreter pyspark."

A block of code is set as follows:

```
#!/bin/bash
while [ true ]
do
echo 1 2 $RANDOM
sleep 1
done
```

Any command-line input or output is written as follows:

```
>>> from pyspark.mllib.clustering import KMeans, KMeansModel
>>> from numpy import array
```

New terms and **important words** are shown in bold.

Warnings or important notes appear in a box like this.

Tips and tricks appear like this.

Reader feedback

Feedback from our readers is always welcome. Let us know what you think about this book-what you liked or disliked. Reader feedback is important for us as it helps us develop titles that you will really get the most out of.

To send us general feedback, simply e-mail feedback@packtpub.com, and mention the book's title in the subject of your message.

If there is a topic that you have expertise in and you are interested in either writing or contributing to a book, see our author guide at www.packtpub.com/authors.

Customer support

Now that you are the proud owner of a Packt book, we have a number of things to help you to get the most from your purchase.

Downloading the example code

You can download the example code files for this book from your account at `http://www.packtpub.com`. If you purchased this book elsewhere, you can visit `http://www.packtpub.com/support` and register to have the files e-mailed directly to you.

You can download the code files by following these steps:

1. Log in or register to our website using your e-mail address and password.
2. Hover the mouse pointer on the **SUPPORT** tab at the top.
3. Click on **Code Downloads & Errata**.
4. Enter the name of the book in the **Search** box.
5. Select the book for which you're looking to download the code files.
6. Choose from the drop-down menu where you purchased this book from.
7. Click on **Code Download**.

Once the file is downloaded, please make sure that you unzip or extract the folder using the latest version of:

- WinRAR / 7-Zip for Windows
- Zipeg / iZip / UnRarX for Mac
- 7-Zip / PeaZip for Linux

The code bundle for the book is also hosted on GitHub at `https://github.com/PacktPublishing/hadoop-blueprints`. We also have other code bundles from our rich catalog of books and videos available at `https://github.com/PacktPublishing/`. Check them out!

Errata

Although we have taken every care to ensure the accuracy of our content, mistakes do happen. If you find a mistake in one of our books-maybe a mistake in the text or the code-we would be grateful if you could report this to us. By doing so, you can save other readers from frustration and help us improve subsequent versions of this book. If you find any errata, please report them by visiting http://www.packtpub.com/submit-errata, selecting your book, clicking on the **Errata Submission Form** link, and entering the details of your errata. Once your errata are verified, your submission will be accepted and the errata will be uploaded to our website or added to any list of existing errata under the Errata section of that title.

To view the previously submitted errata, go to https://www.packtpub.com/books/content/support and enter the name of the book in the search field. The required information will appear under the **Errata** section.

Piracy

Piracy of copyrighted material on the Internet is an ongoing problem across all media. At Packt, we take the protection of our copyright and licenses very seriously. If you come across any illegal copies of our works in any form on the Internet, please provide us with the location address or website name immediately so that we can pursue a remedy.

Please contact us at copyright@packtpub.com with a link to the suspected pirated material.

We appreciate your help in protecting our authors and our ability to bring you valuable content.

Questions

If you have a problem with any aspect of this book, you can contact us at questions@packtpub.com, and we will do our best to address the problem.

1
Hadoop and Big Data

Hadoop has become the heart of the big data ecosystem. It is gradually evolving into a full-fledged data operating system. While there is no standard definition of big data, it is generally said that by big data we mean a huge volume of data, typically several petabytes in size, data arriving at huge velocity such as several thousand clickstreams per second, or data having variety in combination with volume such as images, click data, mails, blogs, tweets and Facebook posts, and so on. A big data-processing system will have to deal with any combination of volume, velocity and variety. These are also known as the 3Vs of big data and are often used to characterize the big data system. Some analysts and companies, most notably IBM, have added a fourth V that stands for veracity, to signify the correctness and accuracy problems associated with big datasets that exists at much lower levels in the enterprise datasets.

In this chapter, we will introduce you to the explosive growth of data around the turn of the century and the technological evolution that has led to the development of Hadoop. We will cover the following topics in this chapter:

- The technical evolution of Hadoop
- The rise of enterprise Hadoop
- Hadoop design and tools
- Developing a program to run on Hadoop
- The overview of solution blueprints
- Hadoop architectural patterns

The beginning of the big data problem

The origin of Hadoop goes back to the beginning of the century, when the number of Internet searches started growing exponentially and Google emerged as the most popular Internet search engine. In 1998, when Google started offering an Internet search service, it was receiving only 10,000 search queries per day. By 2004, when Google did its IPO, it was serving 200 million queries per day. By the year 2006, Google users were submitting 10,000 queries per second to this popular search engine. One thousand computers processed a search query in just 0.2 seconds. It should be fairly obvious, by the massive numbers of queries and 50% average year to year growth between 2002 and 2006, that Google could not rely upon traditional relational database systems for its data processing needs.

Limitations of RDBMS systems

A **relational database management system** (**RDBMS**) stores data in tables. RDBMSs are the preferred choice for storing the data in a structured form, but the high price and lower performance of RDBMSs becomes a limiting factor to support big data use cases where data comes both in structured and unstructured forms. RDBMSs were designed in the period when the cost of computing and data storage was very high, and data of business relevance was generally available in a structured form. Unstructured data such as documents, drawings and photos were stored on LAN-based file servers.

As the complexity of queries and the size of datasets grow, RDBMSs require investment into more powerful servers whose costs can go up to several hundred thousand USD per unit. When the size of data grows, and the system still has to be reliable, then businesses invest in Storage Area Networks' which is an expensive technology to buy. RDBMSs need more RAM and CPUs to scale up. This kind of upward scaling is called vertical scaling. As the size of RAM and the number of CPUs increase in a single server, the server hardware becomes more expensive. Such servers gradually take the shape of a proprietary hardware solution and create a severe vendor lock-in.

Hadoop and many other NoSQL databases meet higher performance and storage requirements by following a scale out model, which is also called horizontal scaling. In this model, more servers are added in the cluster instead of adding more RAM and CPUs to a server.

Scaling out a database on Google

Google engineers designed and developed Bigtable to store massive volumes of data. Bigtable is a distributed storage system, which is designed to run on commodity servers. In the context of Hadoop, you will often hear the term commodity servers. Commodity servers are inexpensive servers that are widely available through a number of vendors. These servers have cheap replaceable parts. There is no standard definition for commodity servers but we can say that they should cost less than 7000 to 8000 USD per unit.

The scalability and performance of Bigtable and the ability to linearly scale it up made it popular among users at Google. Bigtable has been in production since 2005, and more than 60 applications make use of it, including services such as Google Earth and Google analytics. These applications demand very different size and latency requirements from Bigtable. The data size can vary from satellite images to web page addresses. Latency requirements involve batch processing of bulk data at one end while real-time data serving at the other end of the spectrum. Bigtable demonstrated that it could successfully serve workloads requiring a wide range of class of service.

In 2006, Google published a paper titled Bigtable: A Distributed Storage System for Structured Data (Fay Chang, 2015), which established that it was possible to build a distributed storage system for structured data using commodity servers. Apache HBase, which is a NoSQL key value store on the top of **Hadoop Distributed File System** (**HDFS**), is modeled after Bigtable, which is built on the top of **Google File System** (**GFS**). The goal of the HBase project is to build a storage system to store billions of rows and millions of columns with real-time querying capabilities.

Parallel processing of large datasets

With the growing popularity of Google as the search engine preferred by Internet users, the key concern of engineers at Google became keeping its search results up to date and relevant. As the number of queries exponentially grew together with the searchable information on the World Wide Web, Google needed a fast system to index web pages. In 2004, Google published a paper titled MapReduce: Simplified Data Processing on Large Clusters (Dean & Ghemawat, 2004). This paper described a new programming model named MapReduce to process large data sets. In MapReduce, data processing is mainly done in two phases, which are known as Map and Reduce. In the Map phase, multiple intermediate key/values are created using a map function specified by the user from a key/value pair. In the Reduce phase, all intermediate key/values are merged to produce the results of processing.

MapReduce based programming jobs can run on a single computer to thousands of commodity servers each costing few thousand dollars. Programmers find MapReduce easy to use because they can take the benefit of parallel processing without understanding the intricacies of complex parallel processing algorithms. A typical Hadoop cluster will be used to process from a few terabytes to several hundreds of petabytes of data.

Nutch project

From 2002 to 2004, Doug Cutting and Mike Cafarella were working on the Nutch project. The goal of the Nutch project was to develop an open source web scale crawler type search engine. Doug Cutting and Mike Cafarella were able to demonstrate that Nutch was able to search 100 million pages on four nodes. In 2004, after the publication of the MapReduce white paper, Cutting and Cafarella added a distributed file system (DFS) and MapReduce to Nutch. This considerably improved the performance of Nutch. On 20 nodes, Nutch was able to search several 100 millions of web pages but it was still far from web scale performance.

Building open source Hadoop

In 2006, Doug Cutting joined Yahoo in a team led by Eric Baldeschweiler (also known as eric14 or e14). This team had grid computing experts and users. Eric was in charge of figuring out how to build a next generation search grid computing framework for web searches. Here is a quote from a Yahoo employee at that time that described the situation prevailing at that time:

> *"Fortunately, and I remember the day well, Eric14 assembled the merry bunch of Grid (then called 'Utility Computing') engineers, and started down the path of rethinking the strategy – focussing on figuring out how to make Hadoop functional, featureful, and robust, instead." (Kumar, 2011)*

The new team split out of Hadoop from Nutch with the leadership of Doug Cutting and created an open source Hadoop Framework based upon Hadoop Distributed File System as its storage system, and the MapReduce paradigm as the parallel computing model. Yahoo put more than 300 person-years of effort into Hadoop projects between 2006 – 2011. A team of nearly 100 people worked upon Apache Hadoop, and related projects such as Pig, ZooKeeper, Hive, HBase and Oozie.

In 2011, Yahoo was running Hadoop on over 40,000 machines (>300 cores). Hadoop has over a thousand regular users who use Hadoop for search-related research, advertising, detection of spam and personalization apart from many other topics. Hadoop has proven itself at Yahoo in many revenue driving improvement projects.

Hadoop Timeline	
2003	Doug Cutting and Mike Cafarella build Nutch
Oct 2003	Google publishes Google File System (GFS) paper
Dec 2004	Google publishes MapReduce (MR) Paper
2006	Yahoo! Builds Hadoop based upon GFS and MR papers with Doug Cutting and team
2007	Hadoop scales out to 1000 nodes at Yahoo!
Jan 2008	Hadoop becomes an Apache Software Foundation (ASF) project
Jul 2008	Hadoop is tested successfully on a 4000 node cluster
2009	Hadoop demonstrates sorting of Petabytes of data
Dec 2011	Hadoop Version 1.0 is available
Aug 2013	Hadoop Version 2.0 is available
Apr 2015	Hadoop Version 2.7.0 is available
Aug 2016	Hadoop Version 2.7.3 is available
Sep 2016	Hadoop Version 3.0.0-alpha1 is available

Figure 1 Timeline of Hadoop evolution

Nowadays, Hadoop is a top-level project at Apache Foundation. Hadoop is a software library that contains programs that allow processing of very large datasets, also known as big data, on a large cluster of commodity servers using a simple programming model known as MapReduce. At the time of writing this book, Hadoop 2.7.1 is the latest stable version.

It should be evident from the history of Hadoop that it was invented to solve the problem of searching and indexing massive data sets in large Internet companies. The purpose of Hadoop was to store and process the information inside Yahoo. Yahoo decided to make Hadoop open source so that the Hadoop project could benefit from the innovative ideas and involvement of the open source community.

Enterprise Hadoop

Large enterprises have traditionally stored data in data warehouse systems for reporting and analysis. These data warehouse systems store data in the order of hundreds of gigabytes, but they rarely match the scale of the storage and processing challenge Hadoop intended to take. Enterprises spend a considerable part of their budget in procuring and running ETL systems, data warehousing software and hardware required to run it. Commercial vendors of Hadoop see the opportunity to grab a share of the data warehousing spending, and increase their market share by catering to the storage and processing of big data.

Let's examine, in the next two sections, the factors which have led to the rise of Hadoop in enterprises.

Social media and mobile channels

Social media and mobile channels have emerged as the prime media through which to conduct business, and to market products and services. This trend is evident across all sectors of industry. For example, airlines use mobiles for bookings and check-ins and banks use social media such as Facebook to inform customers about their latest offerings, and to provide customer support. These channels create new kinds of customer interactions with business that happens several times per week and contain valuable information about customer behavior and preference in raw form. Analyzing this data, with the help of Hadoop, is an attractive proposition for businesses because of the lower cost of storage, and the ability to analyze data quickly.

Data storage cost reduction

Enterprise Data Warehouse Systems procured from the software vendors bring the software license costs of DBMS software, ETL tooling and schedulers with them. A resilient and high performing Enterprise data warehouse hardware setup for a Fortune 500 company could cost several million dollars. Also, 10% to 20% of procurement cost would be paid in the form of annual support services and the salary cost of operational support personnel.

Enterprise Hadoop vendors aim to derive their revenues by expecting that Hadoop can take over the storage and workload of an Enterprise Data Warehouse system in part or full, and thereby it will contribute to the reduction of the IT costs.

Open source Hadoop was not designed keeping the requirements of large enterprises in mind. Business enterprises need fine-grained security and ease of integration with other enterprise systems in Hadoop. Availability of training, and round the clock service and support, when Hadoop supports important business processes, is considered very important in enterprise adoption. Hadoop vendors emerged to fill the gaps in the Hadoop ecosystem and developed a business model to sell service and support to enterprises. They are also working on strengthening the Hadoop ecosystem to make it appealing for the enterprise market. With the help of contributions to open source Hadoop, or by developing proprietary products to enhance the appeal of their specific offering to the enterprise customers, Hadoop vendors are trying to make in roads in enterprise.

At the time of writing this book, several vendors were active in the Hadoop market as described in the next section.

Enterprise software vendors

Enterprise software vendors such as IBM, Teradata, Oracle and SAS have adopted Hadoop as the standard platform for big data processing. They are promoting Hadoop as a complimentary offering in their existing enterprise data warehouse solutions.

IBM Infosphere Big Insights product suite is one such example that packages open source Hadoop with proprietary products such as Infosphere Streams for streaming analytics, and IBM Big Sheets as a Microsoft Excel-like spreadsheet for ad-hoc analysis of data from a Hadoop cluster. IBM leverages its long experience in Enterprise Data Warehouse systems to provide the solutions for security and data lineage in Hadoop.

SAS Visual Analytics is another example in which SAS packages Hadoop as the data store for their line of analytics and visualization products. SAP positions its in-memory analytics system, **SAP HANA**, as the storage for high-value, often used data such as customer master data, and Hadoop as a system to store information for archiving and retrieval of weblogs, and other unstructured and unprocessed data, because storing such data in-memory on the system would be expensive, and not of much direct value.

Pure Play Hadoop vendors

Pure Play Hadoop vendors have emerged in the past six years. Vendors such as Cloudera, MapR, and Hortonworks fall in this category. These vendors are also very active contributors to open source Hadoop and its ecosystem of other tools. Despite falling into the same category, these vendors are trying to carve out their own niche in Hadoop business.

These vendors do not have a long record of accomplishment in developing and supporting enterprise software where large vendors such as IBM, SAS or SAP enjoy superiority. The familiarity of Enterprise Software vendors with complex integration and compliance challenges in large enterprises bestows on them an edge over Pure Play Hadoop vendors in the lucrative market where Pure Play vendors are relatively inexperienced.

Pure Play Hadoop vendors have a different revenue and growth model. Hortonworks, which is a spinoff company from Yahoo, focuses upon providing services on the Hadoop framework to enterprise, but also to Enterprise Software Vendors such as Microsoft, who have bundled Hadoop in their offering. Hortonworks has repackaged Apache Hadoop and related tools in a product called Hortonworks Data Platform.

Pure Play Hadoop vendor Cloudera is No. 2 in the market in terms of revenue. Cloudera has developed proprietary tools for Hadoop monitoring and data encryption. They earn a fee for licensing these products and providing support for their Hadoop distribution. They have more than 200 paying customers as of Q1 2014, some of who have deployments as large as 1,000 nodes supporting more than a petabyte of data. (Olavsrud, 2014)

MapR is another Pure Play Hadoop player. MapR lacks the aggressive marketing and presence that Hortonworks and Cloudera have. They started early on enhancing the enterprise features of Hadoop when Hadoop implementations were in their infancy in enterprises. MapR has introduced performance improvements in HBase and support for the network filesystem in Hadoop.

Pure Play Hadoop vendors may not be as dominant in enterprises as they would like to be, but they are still the driving force behind Hadoop innovations and making Hadoop a popular data platform by contributing to training courses, conferences, literature, and webinars.

Cloud Hadoop vendors

Amazon was the first company to offer Hadoop as a cloud service with Amazon EMR (Elastic MapReduce). Amazon is very successful with the EC2 service for in-cloud computing and S3 for in-cloud storage. EMR leverages the existing services of Amazon and offers to pay for actually using the model. In addition, Amazon also has Amazon Kinesis as a streaming platform and Amazon RedShift as a data warehousing platform on a cloud, which are the part of the Amazon big data roadmap.

The hosted Hadoop provided by Amazon EMR allows you to instantly provision Hadoop with the right capacity for different workloads. You can access Amazon EMR by using the AWS Management Console, Command Line Tools, SDKS, or the EMR API, which should be familiar to those who are already using the other Amazon cloud services.

Microsoft HDInsight is a Hadoop implementation on the Microsoft Azure cloud. In terms of service offering, like Amazon it leverages existing Azure services and other Microsoft applications. BI Tools such as Microsoft Excel, SQL Server Analysis Services, and SQL Server Reporting Services integrate with HDInsight. HDInsight uses the **Hortonworks Data Platform** (**HDP**) for Hadoop distribution.

These cloud-based Hadoop solutions require little setup and management effort. We can upscale or downscale the capacity based upon our workload. The relatively lower cost of initial setup make this offering very attractive for startups and small enterprises who would like to analyze big data but lack the financial resources to set up their own dedicated Hadoop infrastructure.

Despite the benefits of cloud-based Hadoop in terms of lower setup and management costs, the laws of various legal jurisdictions restrict the kind of data that can be stored in the cloud. The laws of the land also severely restrict the kind of analytics permitted on data sets if they involve customers' personal data, healthcare records or financial history. This restriction does not affect the choice of cloud-based Hadoop vendors alone, but all other Hadoop vendors too. However, storing data on a cloud outside the data center of the enterprise and in different legal jurisdictions makes compliance with privacy laws the foremost concern. To make cloud-based Hadoop successful in enterprise, t vendors need to address the compliance-related concerns in various legal jurisdictions.

The design of the Hadoop system

In this section, we will discuss the design of Hadoop core components. Hadoop runs on a Java platform. Hadoop has the Hadoop Distributed File System or HDFS in its core as the distributed data storage system, and Map Reduce APIs that make possible distributed parallel processing of distributed data on HDFS. In addition to the Hadoop core components, we will cover the other essential components that perform crucial process coordination among the cluster of computers. The Hadoop ecosystem is undergoing a rapid change driven by community-based innovation.

 This book is on Hadoop 2.x and therefore Hadoop refers to Hadoop 2.x releases in this book. If we refer to the older versions of Hadoop then we will make it explicit.

The Hadoop Distributed File System (HDFS)

The Hadoop Distributed File System, or HDFS, enables data storage over a cluster of computers. The computers in the HDFS cluster are regular commodity servers, which are available from hardware vendors such Dell, HP and Acer through their published hardware catalog. These servers come with hard disk drives for data storage. HDFS does not require RAID configuration because it manages the failover and redundancy in the application layer. HDFS is essentially a distributed file system designed to hold very large amounts of data (terabytes or even petabytes), and provide high-throughput access to this information. Files are split into blocks and stored in a redundant fashion across multiple computers. This ensures their durability to failure and high availability to parallel applications.

Another example of a distributed file system is the **Network File System** (**NFS**). The NFS allows a server to share its storage in the form of shared directories and files on other client machines connected to the network. With the help of NFS, the other machines access the files over the network as if they were stored on a local storage. A server that intends to share its files or directories defines the names of the file and directories in a file. This file is called /etc/exports on Unix systems.

The client machine mounts the exported file system, which enables users and programs to access the resources in the file system locally. The use of NFS lowers data storage costs because the data does not have to be replicated on several machines for multiple users to get access. However, accessing the files over the network leads to heavy data traffic over the network so it requires a good network design in order that the network can deliver optimum performance when several users access the shared file system over the network.

In spite of similarities between HDFS and NFS, the most striking difference between them is the lack of built-in redundancy in NFS. NFS shares the filesystem of one server. If for any reason the server fails or the network goes down, then the file system becomes immediately unavailable to the client machine. If the client machine was in the middle of processing a file from an NFS-based server when the failure took place, then the client program must respond appropriately in the program logic to recover from the failure.

HDFS has the following characteristics, which give it the upper hand in storing a large volume of data reliably in a business critical environment:

- It is designed to run on commodity servers with **just a bunch of disks (JBOD)**. JBOD is a name for multiple hard drives either separately or as one volume without a RAID configuration.
- It is designed to minimize seek attempts on disks that are suitable for handling large file sizes.
- It has a built-in mechanism to partition and store data on multiple nodes in a redundant fashion.
- It has built-in data replication to available nodes when one node fails.
- It is a write-once-read-many access model for files that enables high throughput data access.

The design of the HDFS interface is influenced by the Unix filesystem design but close adherence to Unix file system specification was abandoned in favor of improved performance of applications.

Like any other filesystem, HDFS should keep track of the location of data on a large network of computers. HDFS stores this tracking information on a separate system known as NameNode. Other computers in the network store the data and are known as DataNodes. Without NameNode, it is impossible to access the information stored on HDFS because there is no reliable way to determine how data has been distributed on the DataNodes.

When an application needs to process data on HDFS, then the computation is done closer to where the data is stored. This reduces congestion over the network and increases the over throughput. This is particularly useful when the datasets stored on HDFS are huge in size. Distributing processing over multiple nodes enables the parallel processing of data and thereby reduces the overall processing time.

Data organization in HDFS

The Unix file system organizes data into blocks. For example, the ext3 filesystem on Unix has a default block size of 4,096 bytes. Solaris uses a default block size of 8,192 bytes. HDFS also organizes data in blocks. The default block size for HDFS is 128 MB but this is also configurable. The block size is the smallest size a file occupies on a file system even if its size is less than the block size. For example, for a file of 1 MB, the HDFS will take a total of 128 MB storage space on a DataNode if the default block size is configured. A file larger than one block size will take more than one block to store. HDFS stores a whole block on a single machine. It never truncates a block to store it on two or more machines. HDFS sits on the top of a filesystem of an operating system, therefore the filesystem of the OS stores HDFS files in smaller chunks that correspond to the block size in the native filesystem.

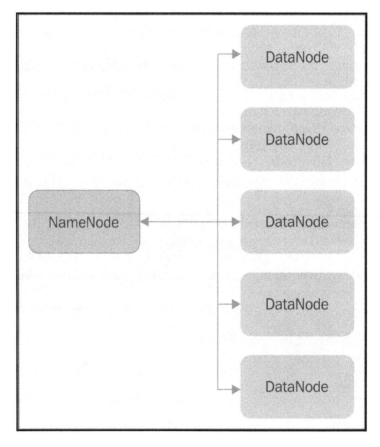

Figure 2 NameNode acts as master controlling the slave DataNodes

HDFS is designed to process huge volumes of data in an easy to scale out architecture. The choice of a relatively very large block size supports the intended use of HDFS.

Every block of data stored on HDFS requires a corresponding entry in the NameNode central metadata directory so that when a program needs to access a file on HDFS, the location of the blocks can be tracked to compose the full file as stored. The large block size means that there are fewer entries in the central metadata directory. This speeds up file access when we need to access large files on HDFS.

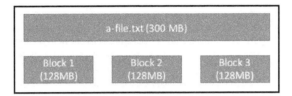

Figure 3 HDFS splits files in blocks of fixed size

HDFS is a resilient filesystem, which can withstand the failure of a DataNode. A DataNode may experience failure caused by a defective hard disk drive, system failure or network failure. HDFS keeps multiple copies of the same block on different nodes as a backup to cope with failures. HDFS uses these backup copies of the block in the event of failure to reconstruct the original file. HDFS uses a default replication factor of three, which implies that each block of a file in HDFS in stored on three different nodes if the cluster topology so permits.

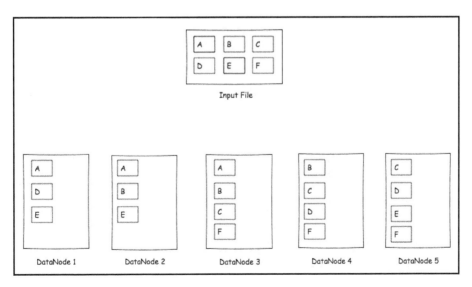

Figure 4 A block is replicated on three DataNodes

The HDFS coherency model describes visibility of data on the file system during reads and writes of a file. Data distribution and replication on multiple nodes for large files introduces a lag between writing the data and its visibility to other programs.

When a file is created in HDFS, it becomes visible in the namespace of HDFS. However, it is not guaranteed that the contents of the file will be visible to other programs. So the file might appear to have zero length even after flushing the file stream for some time until the first block is written.

The first block of file data becomes visible to other programs when more than one block of data has been already written. The current block, which is still being written, is not visible to the other programs. HDFS provides a method to synchronize the data buffers with the data nodes. After successful execution of the synchronization method, the data visibility is guaranteed up to that point.

The HDFS coherency model has some important implications in application design. If you do not synchronize your buffers with DataNodes then you should be prepared to lose buffered data in case of client or system failure. Synchronization comes at the cost of reduction in throughput. Therefore, synchronization intervals should be tuned by measuring the performance on the application at different sync intervals.

HDFS file management commands

The basic commands of the file management on HDFS should appear similar to the file management commands on the Unix operating system. We cover a small selection of the commonly used HDFS commands here. In order to try out these commands, you will need a single node Hadoop installation:

1. Create a directory on HDFS:

   ```
   hadoop fs –mkdir /user/hadoop/dir1
   ```

2. Copy a local file `weblog.txt` to HDFS:

   ```
   hadoop fs –put /home/anurag/weblog.txt /user/hadoop/dir1/
   ```

3. List an HDFS directory contents:

   ```
   hadoop fs –ls /user/hadoop/dir1
   ```

4. Show the space utilization on HDFS:

```
hadoop fs -du /user/hadoop/dir1
```

5. Copy an HDFS file to a file `weblog.txt.1` in the local directory:

```
hadoop fs -get /user/hadoop/dir1/weblog.txt
/home/anurag/weblog.txt.1
```

6. Get help on HDFS commands:

```
hadoop fs -help
```

The preceding examples demonstrate that HDFS commands behave similarly to Unix file management commands. A comprehensive list of HDFS commands is available on the Hadoop page of The Apache Software Foundation website at `http://hadoop.apache.org /`. (The Apache Software Foundation, 2015).

Hadoop Installation

To get started quickly, you can use the Hadoop Sandbox from Hortonworks, which is available from the link `http://hortonworks.com/ products/sandbox/`. Hortonworks Sandbox is a fast way to get started with many tools in the Hadoop ecosystem. To run this sandbox on VirtualBox or VMWare, you need a good PC with 16 GB or more RAM to get a decent performance.

You can also set up Hadoop from scratch on your PC. This, however, requires you to install each tool separately while taking care of compatibility of those tools on JVM versions and dependencies on various libraries. With a direct installation of Hadoop on the PC, without a virtualization software, you can get a better performance on less RAM. You can also pick and choose which tools you will install. Installation from scratch is a time consuming process. Hadoop installation instructions are available under this link: `https://hadoop.apache.org/docs/r2.7.2/had oop-project-dist/hadoop-common/SingleCluster.html`

In the examples given in this book, we have used both Hadoop Sandbox and the bare metal installation of Hadoop from scratch on a Linux server. In both cases, the system had 8 GB RAM.

NameNode and DataNodes

NameNode and DataNodes are the most important building blocks of Hadoop architecture. They participate in distributed data storage and process coordination on the Hadoop cluster. NameNode acts as the central point that keeps track of the metadata of files and associated blocks. NameNode does not store any of the data of the files stored on HDFS. Data is stored on one or more DataNodes.

In an HDFS cluster, NameNode has the role of a master that controls multiple DataNodes acting as workers. The main responsibility of NameNode is to maintain the tree structure of a file system and directories in the tree, and the file system namespace. The NameNode keeps a list of DataNodes for each file where the block of files is stored. This information is kept in the RAM of NameNode and it is reconstructed from the information sent by the DataNodes when the systems starts.

During the operation of a cluster, DataNodes send the information about the addition and deletion of blocks, as a result of file write or delete operations, to the NameNode as shown in *Figure 5*. NameNode determines which blocks will be stored in which DataNode. DataNodes perform tasks such as block creation, block deletion, and data replication when they are instructed to do so by the NameNode.

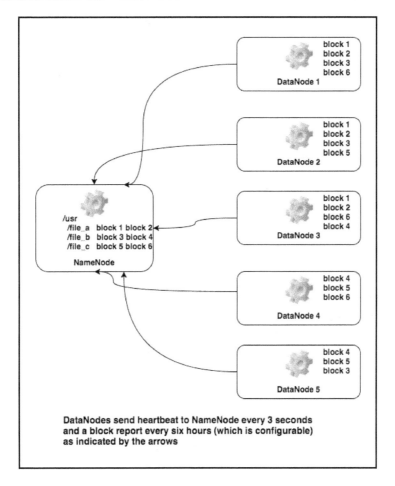

Figure 5 DataNodes and NameNode communication

NameNode and DataNode are open source software written in Java, which run on commodity servers. Generally, HDFS clusters are deployed on Linux-based servers. Hadoop software components run in the number of instances of Java Virtual Machine. Java Virtual Machines are available for all major operating systems. As a result, HDFS software can run on many operating systems, but Linux is the most common deployment platform for HDFS. It is possible to run several instances of DataNode on a single machine. It is also possible to run NameNode and DataNode on a single machine. However, the production configuration of HDFS deploys each instance of DataNode on a separate machine, and NameNode on a separate machine that does not run DataNode.

A single NameNode simplifies the architecture of HDFS, as it has the metadata repository and the role of master. DataNodes are generally identical machines operating under a command from NameNode.

A client program needs to contact NameNode and the DataNodes where the data is stored to access the data stored on an HDFS file. The HDFS exposes a POSIX-like filesystem to the client program, so the client programs do not have to know about the inner workings of NameNode and DataNodes in order to read and write data on HDFS. Because HDFS distributes file contents in blocks across several data nodes in the clusters, these file are not visible on the DataNodes local file system. Running ls commands on DataNodes will not reveal useful information about the file or directory tree of HDFS. HDFS uses its own namespace, which is separate from the namespace used by the local file system. The NameNode manages this namespace. This is why we need to use special HDFS commands for file management on HDFS.

Metadata store in NameNode

HDFS namespace is similar to namespace in other filesystems wherein a tree-like structure is used to arrange directories and files. Directories can hold other directories and files. NameNode keeps the information about files and directories in inode records. Inode records keep track of attributes such as permissions, modification and access times, namespace and diskspace quotas. Metadata such as nodes and the list of blocks that identifies files and directories in the HDFS, are called the image. This image is loaded in the RAM when NameNode starts. The persistent record of the image is stored in a local native file of the NameNode system known as checkpoint. The NameNode uses a write-ahead log called a journal in its local file system to record changes.

When a client initiates sending a request to NameNode, it is recorded in the journal or editlog. Before NameNode sends a confirmation to the client about the successful execution of their request, the journal file is flushed and synced. Running an `ls` command on the local file system of the NameNode where the checkpoint and journal information is stored shows the following:

```
$ ls -l
total 28
-rw-r--r-- 1 hduser hadoop 201 Aug 23 12:29 VERSION
-rw-r--r-- 1 hduser hadoop  42 Aug 22 19:26
edits_0000000000000000001-0000000000000000002
-rw-r--r-- 1 hduser hadoop  42 Aug 23 12:29
edits_0000000000000000028-0000000000000000029
-rw-r--r-- 1 hduser hadoop 781 Aug 23 12:29
fsimage_0000000000000000027
-rw-r--r-- 1 hduser hadoop  62 Aug 23 12:29
```

```
fsimage_0000000000000000027.md5
-rw-r--r-- 1 hduser hadoop 781 Aug 23 12:29
fsimage_0000000000000000029
-rw-r--r-- 1 hduser hadoop  62 Aug 23 12:29
fsimage_0000000000000000029.md5
```

The files with the `fsimage_` prefix are the image files and the files with the `edit_ prefix` are the edit log of the journal files. The files with the `.md5` extension contain the hash to check the integrity of the image file.

The image file format that is used by NameNode is very efficient to read but it is not suitable for making small incremental updates, as the transactions or operations are done in HDFS. When new operations are done in HDFS, the changes are recorded in the journal file instead of the image file for persistence. In this way, if the NameNode crashes, it can restore the filesystems to its pre-crash state by reading image files and then by applying all the transactions stored in the journal to it. The journal or edit log comprises a series of files, known as edit log segments, that together represent all the namespace modifications made since the creation of the image file. The HDFS NameNode metadata such as image and journals (and all the changes to them) should be safely persisted to a stable storage for fault tolerance. This is typically done by storing these files on multiple volumes and on remote NFS servers.

Preventing a single point of failure with Hadoop HA

As Hadoop made inroads into Enterprise, 24/7 availability, with near zero downtime of Hadoop clusters, became a key requirement. Hadoop HA or Hadoop High Availability addresses the issue of a single point of failure in Hadoop.

NameNode in Hadoop forms a single point of failure, if it is deployed without the secondary NameNode. A NameNode contains metadata about the HDFS and it also acts as the coordinator for DataNodes. If we lose a NameNode in a Hadoop cluster, then even with functioning DataNodes the cluster will fail to function as a whole. Before Hadoop 2.x, the NameNode risked this single point of failure. Moreover, it reduced the uptime of the cluster because any planned maintenance activity on NameNode would require it to be taken down in the maintenance window.

The secondary NameNode is a second NameNode, which is used in the Hadoop **High Availability** (**HA**) setup. In the HA setup, two NameNodes are deployed in the active-passive configuration in the Hadoop cluster. The active NameNode handles all the incoming requests to Hadoop cluster. The passive NameNode does not handle any incoming requests but just keeps track of the state of the active NameNode, so that it can take over when the active NameNode fails. To keep the state of the active NameNode synchronized with the passive NameNode, a shared file system such as NFS is used. Apart from the shared filesystem, Hadoop also offers another mechanism known as Quorum Journal Manager to keep the state of both NameNodes synchronized.

The DataNodes are aware of the location of both the NameNodes in the HA configuration. They send block reports and heartbeats to both of them. This results in a fast failover to the passive NameNode when the active NameNode fails. (Apache Software Foundation, 2015).

Checkpointing process

The primary role of an HDFS NameNode is to serve client requests that can require the creation of new files or directories on the HDFS, for example, a NameNode can have two other roles in which it can act either as a CheckpointNode or a BackupNode.

A journal file log entry can be 10 to 1,000 bytes in size, but these log entries can quickly grow to the size of journal file. In some cases, a journal file can consume all the available storage capacity on a node, and it can slow down the startup of a NameNode because the NameNode applies all the journal logs to the last checkpoint.

The checkpointing process takes a checkpoint image and a journal file and compacts them into a new image. During the next startup of the NameNode, the state of the file system can be recreated by reading the image file and applying a small journal file log. (Wang, 2014).

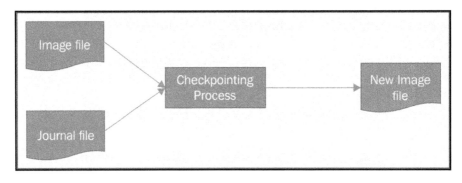

Figure 6 The checkpointing process

Data Store on a DataNode

The DataNode keeps files on the native filesystem for each block replica. The first file contains the actual block data of the file. The second file records the metadata of the block including the checksums to ensure data integrity of the block and the generation stamp. A sample listing of a file using `ls -l` on the data directory of DataNode is shown in the next listing:

```
$ ls -l
total 206496
-rw-r--r-- 1 hduser hadoop      37912 Aug 22 19:35 blk_1073741825
-rw-r--r-- 1 hduser hadoop        307 Aug 22 19:35
blk_1073741825_1001.meta
-rw-r--r-- 1 hduser hadoop      37912 Aug 22 19:36 blk_1073741826
-rw-r--r-- 1 hduser hadoop        307 Aug 22 19:36
blk_1073741826_1002.meta
-rw-r--r-- 1 hduser hadoop 134217728 Aug 22 19:44 blk_1073741827
-rw-r--r-- 1 hduser hadoop    1048583 Aug 22 19:44
blk_1073741827_1003.meta
-rw-r--r-- 1 hduser hadoop  75497472 Aug 22 19:44 blk_1073741828
-rw-r--r-- 1 hduser hadoop     589831 Aug 22 19:44
blk_1073741828_1004.meta
```

The size of the data file is equal to the actual block length. If you suppose a file needs less than a single block space, then it doesn't pad it with extra space to fill the full block length.

Handshakes and heartbeats

Before a DataNode is registered in a Hadoop cluster, it has to perform a handshake with the NameNode by sending its software version and namespace ID to the NameNode. If there is a mismatch in either of these with the NameNode, then the DataNode automatically shuts down and does not become part of the cluster.

After the successful completion of a handshake, the DataNode sends a block report to the NameNode containing information about the data blocks stored on the DataNode. It contains crucial information such as the block ID, the generation stamp and length of block copy that the DataNode has stored.

After DataNode has sent the first block report, it will keep sending block reports to the NameNode every six hours (this interval is configurable) with up to date information about the block copies stored on it.

Once DataNode is part of a running HDFS cluster, it sends heartbeats to the NameNode to confirm that the NameNode is alive and the block copies stored on it are available. The heartbeat frequency is three seconds by default. If the NameNode does not receive a heartbeat from a DataNode for 10 minutes, then it assumes that the DataNode is not available any more. In that case, it schedules the process of creation of additional block copies on other available DataNodes.

The NameNode does not send special requests to DataNodes to carry out certain tasks but it uses the replies to heartbeats to send commands to the DataNodes. These commands can ask the DataNode to shut down, send a block report immediately and remove local block copies.

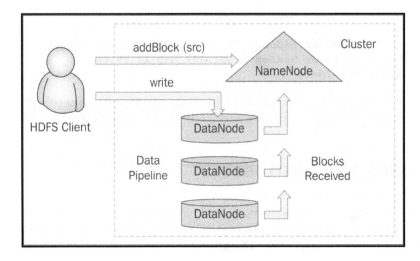

Figure 7 Writing a file on HDFS involves a NameNode and DataNodes (Source: http://www.aosabook.org/en/hdfs.html)

Figure 7 shows how the NameNode and several DataNodes work together to serve a client request.

The NameNode and DataNodes play a crucial role in data storage and process coordination on the HDFS cluster. In the next section, we will discuss Map/Reduce, which is a programming model used by HDFS clusters to process the data stored on them.

MapReduce

MapReduce is a programming model used to process and generate large data sets in parallel across multiple computers in a cluster using a distributed algorithm. In the case of Hadoop, the MapReduce programs are executed on a cluster of commodity servers, which offers a high degree of fault tolerance and linear scalability.

MapReduce libraries are available in several programming languages for various database systems. The open source implementation of MapReduce in Hadoop delivers fast performance, not just because of the MapReduce, but also because Hadoop minimizes the expensive movement of data on a network by performing data processing close to where the data is stored.

Until the launch of Apache YARN, MapReduce was the dominant programming model on Hadoop. Though MapReduce is simple to understand at conceptual level, the implementation of MapReduce programs is not very easy. As a result, several higher order tools, such as Hive and Pig, have been invented which let users take advantage of Hadoop's large data set processing capabilities without knowing the inner workings of MapReduce. Hive and Pig are open source tools, which internally use MapReduce to run jobs on Hadoop cluster.

The introduction of Apache **YARN (Yet Another Resource Negotiator)**, gave Hadoop the capability to run jobs on a Hadoop cluster without using the MapReduce paradigm. The introduction of YARN does not alter or enhance the capability of Hadoop to run MapReduce jobs, but MapReduce now turns into one of the application frameworks in the Hadoop ecosystem that uses YARN to run jobs on a Hadoop cluster.

From Apache Hadoop version 2.0, MapReduce has undergone a complete redesign and it is now an application on YARN, and called MapReduce version 2. This book covers MapReduce Version 2. The only exception is the next section, where we discuss MapReduce Version 1 for background information to understand YARN.

The execution model of MapReduce Version 1

In this section, we will discuss the execution model of MapReduce Version 1 so that we can better understand how Apache YARN has improved it.

MapReduce programs in Hadoop essentially take in data as their input and then generate an output. In MapReduce terminology, the unit of work is a job which a client program submits to a Hadoop cluster. A job is broken down into *tasks*. These tasks perform map and reduce functions.

Hadoop controls the execution of jobs with the help of a *JobTracker* and a number of TaskTrackers. JobTrackers manage resources and all the jobs scheduled on a Hadoop cluster. Several TaskTrackers run tasks and periodically report the progress to the JobTracker, which keeps track of the overall progress of a job. The JobTracker is also responsible for rescheduling a task if it fails.

In Hadoop, data locality optimization is an important consideration when scheduling map tasks on nodes. Map tasks are scheduled on the node where the input data resides in the HDFS. This is done to minimize the data transfer over the network.

Hadoop splits the input to MapReduce jobs into fixed size chunks. For each chunk, Hadoop creates a separate map task that runs the user-defined map function for each record in the chunk. The records in each chunk are specified in the form of key-value pairs.

An overview of a MapReduce processing stage is shown in *Figure 8*:

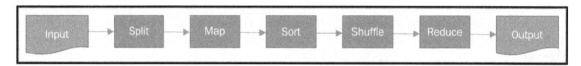

Figure 8 MapReduce processing stages

Apache YARN

Apache YARN provides a more scalable and isolated execution model for MRv2. In MRv1, a singular JobTracker handled resource management, scheduling and task monitoring work. To keep the backwards compatibility, the MRv1 framework has been rewritten so that it can submit jobs on top of YARN.

In YARN, the responsibilities of the JobTracker have been split into two separate components. These components are as follows:

- ResourceManager
- ApplicationMaster

ResourceManager allocates the computing resources to various applications running on top of Apache YARN. For each application running on YARN, ApplicationMaster manages the lifecycle of the application. These two components run as two daemons on a cluster.

YARN architecture also introduces the concept of the NodeManager that manages the Hadoop processes running on that machine.

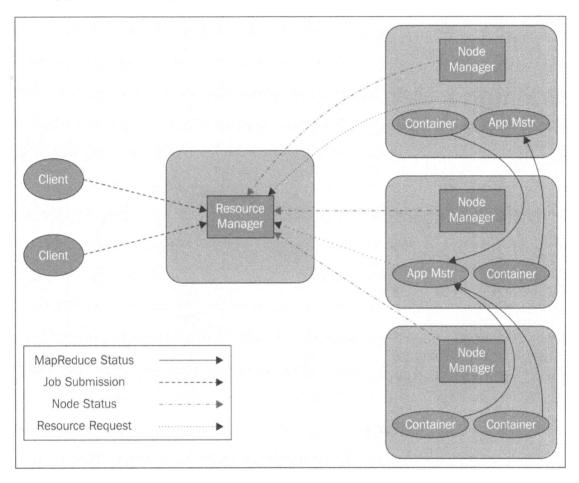

Figure 9 The design of Apache YARN (Source: http://hadoop.apache.org/docs/current/hadoop-yarn/hadoop-yarn-site/YARN.html)

The ResourceManager runs two main services. The first service is a pluggable Scheduler service. The Scheduler service manages the resource scheduling policy. The second service is the ApplicationsManager, which manages the ApplicationMasters by starting, monitoring, and restarting them in case they fail.

A container is an abstract notion on the YARN platform representing a collection of physical resources such as the CPU cores and disk, along with the RAM. When an application is about to get submitted into the YARN platform, the client allocates a container from the ResourceManager, where its ApplicationMaster will run.

Figure 9 (The Apache Software Foundation, 2015) explains the execution model of Hadoop with YARN.

Readers who are interested to learn about YARN in detail can find elaborate information on the Cloudera blog. (Radwan, 2012)

Building a MapReduce Version 2 program

We have done sufficient groundwork to understand the Hadoop data storage and computation model in previous sections. Now we can write our first MapReduce program to put our knowledge in practice.

Problem statement

In this problem, we will calculate the yearly average stock price of IBM from the daily stock quotes.

Publicly traded companies have fluctuating stock prices. The stock prices are available on various finance portals where you can track day-by-day movement in stock prices. Such datasets are in the public domain. We will download one such dataset that contains the historical daily stock price of IBM (Symbol: IBM). The historical stock price of IBM is available on Yahoo Finance in various formats on this URL: `http://finance.yahoo.com/q /hp?s=IBM`. The historical price dataset covers the stock prices from 2nd Jan 1962 until today.

Solution workflow

We will divide the solution to stock averaging into a problem in several small steps as follows:

1. Get the dataset
2. Study the dataset
3. Cleanse the dataset
4. Load the dataset on the HDFS
5. Code and build a MapReduce program
6. Run the MapReduce program
7. Examine the result
8. Further processing of the results

Each small step will help bring us closer to the final solution. Note that we are running a single node Hadoop cluster on an Ubuntu machine installed on Virtual Box. The Virtual Box itself is running on OS X Yosemite version 10.10.2.

On my Ubuntu machine, I can check the OS version as follows:

```
hduser@anurag-VirtualBox:~$ uname -a
Linux anurag-VirtualBox 3.19.0-25-generic #26~14.04.1-Ubuntu SMP Fri Jul 24
21:16:20 UTC 2015 x86_64 x86_64 x86_64 GNU/Linux
```

Getting the dataset

You can see the historical stock price of IBM on Yahoo Finance by visiting its URL at `http://finance.yahoo.com/q/hp?s=IBM`. You can view the prices on your browser as shown in *Figure 10*. We are interested in daily stock prices so that we can create a yearly average.

We will first get the dataset from Yahoo's finance website using the `wget` command, and then save the results in a file called `ibmstockquotes.txt`:

```
hduser@anurag-VirtualBox:~$ wget -O ibmstockquotes.txt
http://real-chart.finance.yahoo.com/table.csv?s=IBM
--2015-08-24 19:52:51--
http://real-chart.finance.yahoo.com/table.csv?s=IBM
Resolving real-chart.finance.yahoo.com (real-chart.finance.yahoo.com)...
188.125.66.140
Connecting to real-chart.finance.yahoo.com (real-
chart.finance.yahoo.com)|188.125.66.140|:80... connected.
HTTP request sent, awaiting response... 200 OK
Length: unspecified [text/csv]
Saving to: 'ibmstockquotes.txt'

    [ <=>                              ] 861,145     1.67MB/s   in
0.5s

2015-08-24 19:52:52 (1.67 MB/s) - 'ibmstockquotes.txt' saved [861145]
```

Now we have downloaded the historical stock price data of IBM going back to January 02, 1962 in a file. The file `ibmstockquotes.txt` contains this data. This file has 13,504 lines in this file, as of August 24, 2015, but none of these lines would depend on when you downloaded this data:

```
hduser@anurag-VirtualBox:~$ wc -l ibmstockquotes.txt
13504 ibmstockquotes.txt
```

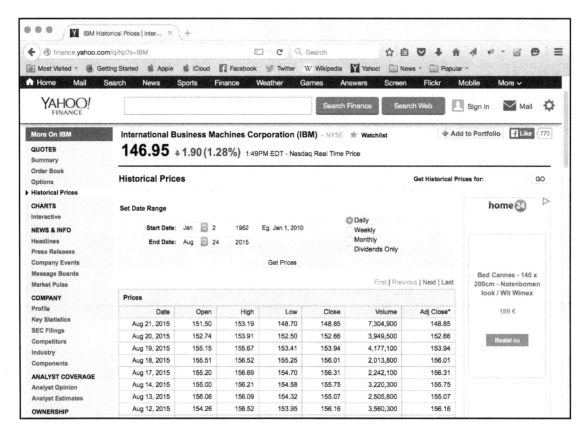

Figure 10 The historical stock price of IBM on Yahoo! Finance

Studying the dataset

Let's open the dataset using the `head` command and examine its contents:

```
hduser@anurag-VirtualBox:~$ head ibmstockquotes.txt
Date,Open,High,Low,Close,Volume,Adj Close
2015-08-21,151.50,153.190002,148.699997,148.850006,7304900,148.850006
2015-08-20,152.740005,153.910004,152.50,152.660004,3949500,152.660004
2015-08-19,155.149994,155.669998,153.410004,153.940002,4177100,153.940002
2015-08-18,155.509995,156.520004,155.25,156.009995,2013800,156.009995
2015-08-17,155.199997,156.690002,154.699997,156.309998,2242100,156.309998
2015-08-14,155.00,156.210007,154.580002,155.75,3220300,155.75
2015-08-13,156.059998,156.089996,154.320007,155.070007,2505800,155.070007
2015-08-12,154.259995,156.520004,153.949997,156.160004,3560300,156.160004
2015-08-11,155.960007,155.990005,154.860001,155.509995,3143300,155.509995
```

In this dataset, we have the date, the opening stock quote, the day's high, the day's low, the traded volume and the closing price. The fields are separated by a comma and the first line in the dataset is the header. We will use the opening stock quote to calculate the average. Except for the date and the opening quote, all other fields in this dataset will not be used in the solution.

Cleaning the dataset

If the quality of the dataset is not very good, then it should be cleansed before we load it on our single node Hadoop cluster. A good quality dataset is a must for processing. In a bad quality dataset, you might find problems such as missing data fields, data field header mismatches, missing entries and missing delimiters such as commas.

For very large datasets, it is time-consuming to visually scan the data line by line to check its quality. Therefore, we can cleanse the datasets using common Unix tools such as `awk`, `sed`, and `grep`, or commercial tools such as Talend Open Studio for Data Quality.

Our dataset `ibmstockquote.txt` is a clean and well-structured dataset, which does not require much cleansing. The first row in the dataset is the header data, which need not be processed. Using a text editor tool such as vieditor, we will remove the first line containing the header from this dataset. We can also remove the first line using the Unix stream editor `sed` as follows:

```
$sed '1d' ibmstockquote.txt > ibmstockquote.clean.txt
```

We also notice that this file contains additional data such as the day's low, day's high, the volume and the closing price, which we do not need to process. We can either remove this data from this dataset, or just leave it as it is, in case we need it for other problems. In this case, we just leave the additional data in the dataset.

At the end of this step, our dataset ibmstockquote.txt has the header line removed, and now it is ready to be loaded on the Hadoop cluster in the next step.

Loading the dataset on the HDFS

We will use the Hadoop filesystem command to put our dataset on the HDFS. We will first create a directory structure on the HDFS to store our dataset. We will use this directory structure to put the dataset ibmstockquote.txt from our local filesystem on the HDFS.

Let's list the root directory of our Hadoop cluster:

```
hduser@anurag-VirtualBox:~$ hadoop fs -ls /
Found 2 items
drwx------    - hduser supergroup        0 2015-08-24 11:53 /tmp
drwxr-xr-x    - hduser supergroup        0 2015-08-24 10:50 /user
```

We will make a new directory structure for our examples, which will be /hbp/chapt1:

```
hduser@anurag-VirtualBox:~$ hadoop fs -mkdir /hbp
hduser@anurag-VirtualBox:~$ hadoop fs -mkdir /hbp/chapt1
```

We will copy our dataset in the new directory /hbp/chapt1:

```
hduser@anurag-VirtualBox:~$ hadoop fs -put ibmstockquotes.txt /hbp/chapt1
```

Let's examine the contents of the directory /hbp/chapt1 to see if our file is on the Hadoop filesystem:

```
hduser@anurag-VirtualBox:~$ hadoop fs -ls /hbp/chapt1
Found 1 items
-rw-r--r--    1 hduser supergroup    861145 2015-08-24 21:00
/hbp/chapt1/ibmstockquotes.txt
```

We can also check the contents of the directory by using the web interface of the HDFS on the URL `http://localhost:50070/explorer.html#/hbp/chapt1` as shown in *Figure 11*. We are running a single node Hadoop cluster locally on the PC. In a production environment, typically the name localhost will be replaced with the hostname or IP address of the NameNode.

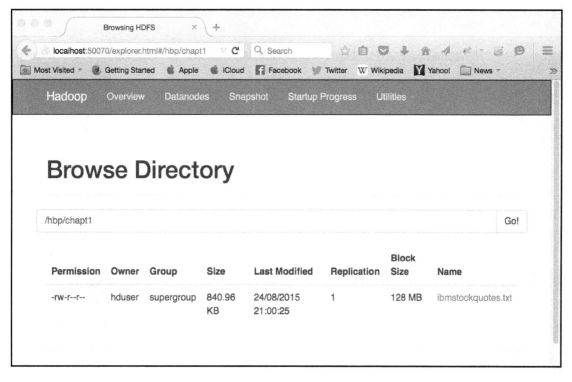

Figure 11 Browsing an HDFS directory using a web interface

Click on the link `ibmstockquotes.txt`. We can see that the block size for this dataset is 128 MB, and it has occupied exactly one block on the HDFS. If you click the filename link then you will see the additional information such as the block ID and generation stamp, as shown in *Figure 12*.

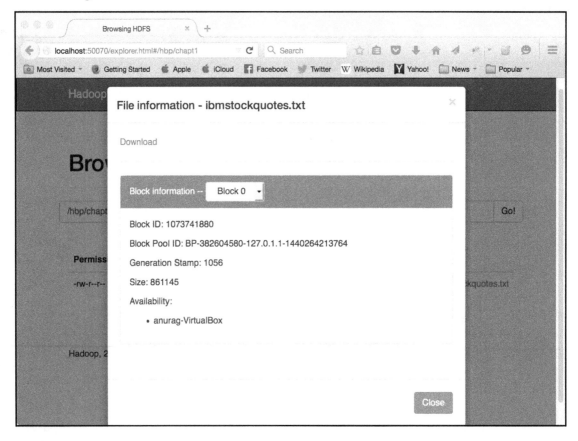

Figure 12 Additional block information

Starting with a MapReduce program

In this example, we will write a MapReduce program using the Java programming language. For Java programming, we will make use of the Eclipse IDE to build and package the programs.

Installing Eclipse

You can download Eclipse from https://www.eclipse.org/downloads/.

 We have used Eclipse Java EE IDE, 64 bit, for Web Developers Mars Release (4.5.0) in the examples used in this book.

I am using a MacBook Pro to run Eclipse. After installing of Eclipse, launch it by clicking on the Eclipse icon.

The Eclipse select workspace dialog should pop up. This indicates that Eclipse has been successfully installed.

Let's create a new workspace in Eclipse in the directory <your directory>/workspace/hbp/chapt1 and go to the Eclipse workbench by clicking the workbench icon.

We will now install the Hadoop Development tools. You can download the Hadoop Development Tools from http://hdt.incubator.apache.org/download.html.

After downloading, unzip and untar the file in your local directory. Now go to **Eclipse Help** | **Install New Software**. In the pop-up dialog, as shown in *Figure 13 Adding Hadoop Development Tools in Eclipse*, click on the **Add**. button. You will see another dialog box. In this dialog box, specify the local repository in the directory where you have untared the downloaded file.

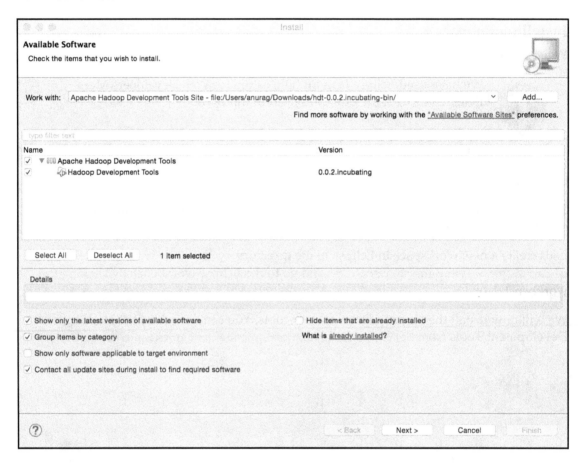

Figure 13 Adding Hadoop development tools in Eclipse

We have now set up the environment to start creating our MapReduce project in Eclipse.

Creating a project in Eclipse

We will create a Maven project in Eclipse. Navigate to **File** | **New** | **Maven Project**. We will see the window shown in the following screenshot:

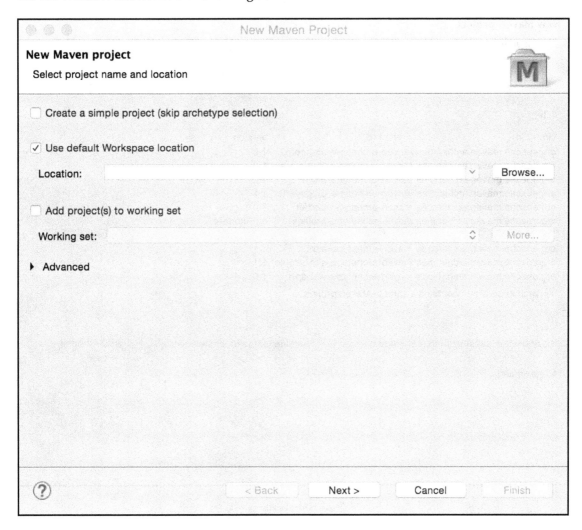

Figure 14 File | New | Maven Project

Check the default workspace location and click on the **Next** button. In the next window, shown in *Figure 15*, we choose `archetype-quickstart` and click on the **Next** button.

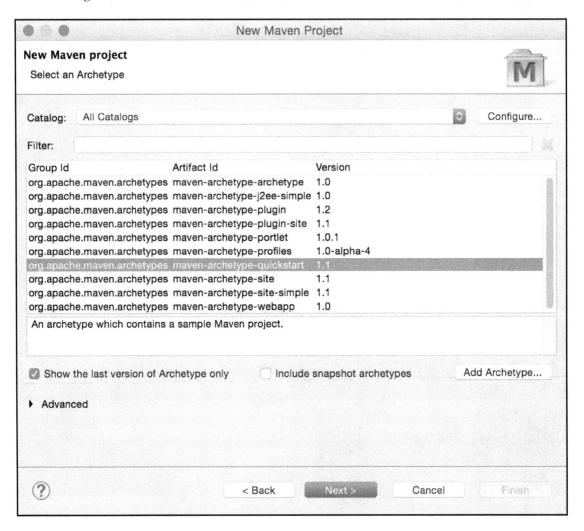

Figure 15 Select an archetype

We will see the window shown in *Figure 16*. In this window, we will specify the GroupID and ArtifactId as show in the window. Now click on the **Finish** button. This will trigger the creation of a Maven project in Eclipse. Eclipse will create the file pom.xml which contains build dependencies and the basic directory structure for the project. It will also create an App.java file. We will not use this file, so you can delete it from your project.

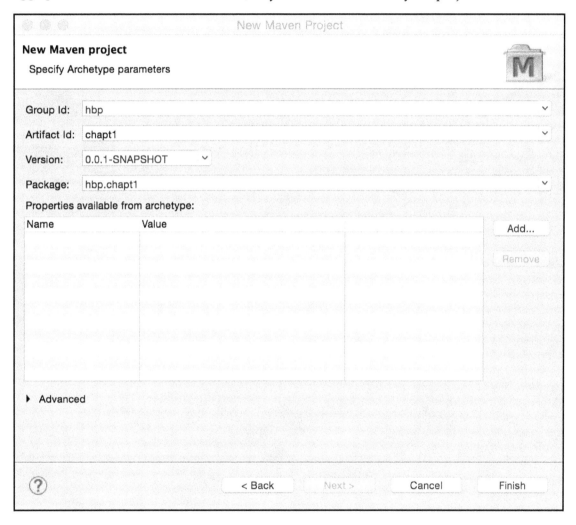

Figure 16 Specify GroupId and ArtifactId

We will need to specify the dependency on the Hadoop libraries in the `pom.xml` of Maven so that we can build our programs. To do so, you should open the `pom.xml` file in your newly created project. Add the following lines in the dependencies section of the `pom.xml` file as shown in *Figure 17*:

```
<dependency>
<groupId>org.apache.hadoop</groupId>
<artifactId>hadoop-client</artifactId>
<version>2.7.1</version>
</dependency>
```

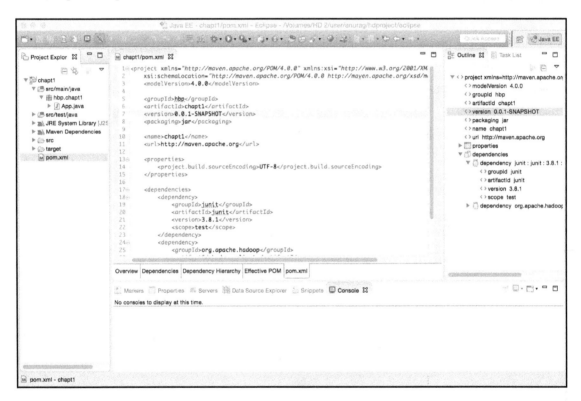

Figure 17 Project dependencies in the pom.xml file

Coding and building a MapReduce program

We are building a simple MapReduce program in Java. This program has three Java files:

- Mapper : StockAverageMapper.java
- Reducer: StockAverageReducer.java
- Driver: StockAverageDriver.java

We will first create our Mapper file by navigating to **File** | **New** | **Other** in Eclipse. Locate Hadoop in the dialog that has just popped up, as shown in *Figure 18*. Click on the **Next** button.

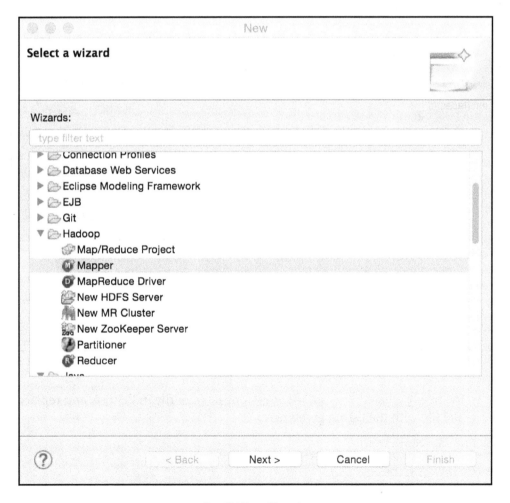

Figure 18 Add a new Mapper class

On the next screen, specify the name of your `Mapper` class, which is `StockAverageMapper`, as shown in *Figure 19*.

Figure 19 Specify the Mapper class name

Now open the newly created `StockAverageMapper.java` file in Eclipse, and replace the contents of the file with the listing given here:

```
package hbp.chapt1;

import java.io.IOException;
import org.apache.hadoop.io.DoubleWritable;
import org.apache.hadoop.io.LongWritable;
```

```
import org.apache.hadoop.io.Text;
import org.apache.hadoop.mapreduce.Mapper;

public class StockAverageMapper extends Mapper<LongWritable, Text,  Text,
DoubleWritable> {
  private DoubleWritable quote = new DoubleWritable(1);
    private Text word = new Text();
  public void map(LongWritable key, Text value, Context context)    throws
IOException, InterruptedException {
    //Extract the tokens from the line text
    String line = value.toString();
    String[] tokens = line.split(",");
    //Extract the year value from date
    String year = tokens[0].split("-")[0];
    //Extract the stock quote and convert it into a number
    String quoteStr = tokens[1];
    double quoteVal = Double.parseDouble(quoteStr);
    //Set the key
        word.set(year);
        //Set the value
        quote.set(quoteVal);
        context.write(word, quote);
  }
}
```

Using steps similar to the ones described in the `Mapper` class creation, you will now create the `Reducer` class. Replace the contents of the newly created class with the following listing:

```
package hbp.chapt1;

import java.io.IOException;

import org.apache.hadoop.io.DoubleWritable;
import org.apache.hadoop.io.Text;
import org.apache.hadoop.mapreduce.Reducer;

public class StockAverageReducer extends Reducer<Text, DoubleWritable,
Text, DoubleWritable> {

  public void reduce(Text key, Iterable<DoubleWritable> values,    Context
context)
      throws IOException, InterruptedException {
    double quoteAverage = 0;
    double quoteTotal = 0;
    int quoteCount = 0;
    for (DoubleWritable value : values) {
      quoteTotal += value.get();
```

```
        System.out.println("Reducer: " + key + " "+ quoteTotal);
        quoteCount++;
    }
    quoteAverage = quoteTotal/quoteCount;
    context.write(key, new DoubleWritable(quoteAverage));
  }


}
```

Using steps similar to the ones described in the `Mapper` class creation, you will now create the `Driver` class. Replace the contents of the newly created class `StockAverageDriver` with the following listing:

```
package hbp.chapt1;

import java.io.IOException;

import org.apache.hadoop.fs.Path;
import org.apache.hadoop.io.DoubleWritable;
import org.apache.hadoop.io.Text;
import org.apache.hadoop.mapreduce.Job;
import org.apache.hadoop.mapreduce.lib.input.FileInputFormat;
import org.apache.hadoop.mapreduce.lib.output.FileOutputFormat;

public class StockAverageDriver {

  public static void main(String[] args) throws IOException,
  InterruptedException, ClassNotFoundException {
    Job job = Job.getInstance();
    job.setJarByClass(StockAverageMapper.class);
    job.setJobName( "First Job"  );
    FileInputFormat.setInputPaths(job, new Path(args[0]));
    FileOutputFormat.setOutputPath(job, new Path(args[1]));
    job.setMapperClass(StockAverageMapper.class);
    job.setReducerClass(StockAverageReducer.class);
    job.setOutputKeyClass(Text.class);
    job.setOutputValueClass(DoubleWritable.class);
    boolean success = job.waitForCompletion(true);
    System.exit(success ? 0 : 1);
  };


}
```

Run the MapReduce program locally

We are now ready to run our MapReduce program. We will first run this program locally on our Unix file system before running it on HDFS. In Eclipse, click on **Run | Run Configurations**…. We will see the dialog shown in *Figure 20 Input file and output directory for MapReduce job*. We go to the **Arguments** tab and specify these two values in the **Program arguments** field:

- Input filename: `ibm-stock.csv`
- Output directory name: `output`

Make sure that the file `ibm-stock.csv` exists in your local project directory. Click on the **Run** button now. Congratulations. Now you are running your MapReduce program.

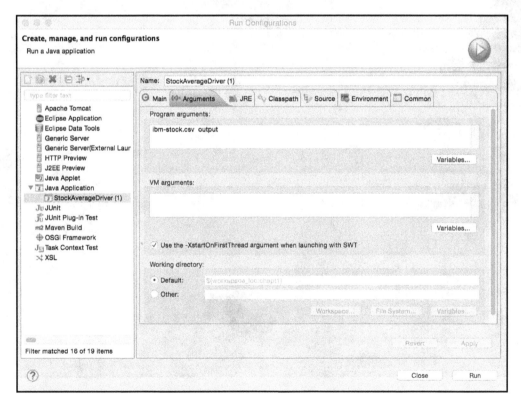

Figure 20 Input file and output directory for MapReduce job

Examine the result

After running the program, go to the project directory using a terminal window. Run an `ls -l` command in your shell. You will see a new directory `output`. This directory has been created by running your MapReduce program. Run the directory listing for the output directory using an `ls -l output` command.

In the output directory, you will see two files. The first file is `_SUCCESS` which indicates that our program has run successfully. The second file is `part-r-00000` which contains the results of our MapReduce execution.

```
                                1. bash
Anurags-MacBook-Pro:chapt1 anurag$ ls -l
total 1696
-rw-r-----@ 1 anurag   staff   861103 Sep   8 21:14 ibm-stock.csv
drwxr-xr-x  6 anurag   staff      204 Sep   8 21:38 output
-rw-r--r--  1 anurag   staff      850 Sep   8 19:08 pom.xml
drwxr-xr-x  4 anurag   staff      136 Sep   8 19:07 src
drwxr-xr-x  4 anurag   staff      136 Sep   8 19:07 target
Anurags-MacBook-Pro:chapt1 anurag$ ls -l output/
total 8
-rw-r--r--  1 anurag   staff        0 Sep   8 21:38 _SUCCESS
-rw-r--r--  1 anurag   staff     1273 Sep   8 21:38 part-r-00000
Anurags-MacBook-Pro:chapt1 anurag$ head output/part-r-00000
1962     433.3511795396825
1963     448.48554415139404
1964     489.16551569960467
1965     480.82985311111105
1966     408.9866005873015
1967     499.4905379123505
1968     425.8838481415928
1969     328.94249967600007
1970     297.1336121732284
1971     321.8779635454545
Anurags-MacBook-Pro:chapt1 anurag$ []
```

Figure 21 Examine the results of the program execution

Run the MapReduce program on Hadoop

We have successfully run the MapReduce program on our desktop. We used this program to process the files stored on our local file system Now, let's run this program on our Hadoop server on a file stored on the HDFS.

Create a JAR file for your program. To do so, right-click on the `pom.xml` file and go to **Run As** | **Maven build**. You will see the **Edit Configuration** window. Type `package` in the **Field Goals** and click on the **Run** button. You have now created a JAR file called `chapt1-0.0.1.SNAPSHOT.jar`.

First let's copy the file `MapReduce.jar` file onto our Hadoop system, where we have the correct environment and libraries to run this program. We have copied this file to our Hadoop system using the `scp` command:

```
$ pwd
/Users/anurag/hdproject/eclipse/chapt1
$ ls
ibm-stock.csv   pom.xml      target
output      src
$ ls target
chapt1-0.0.1-SNAPSHOT.jar   maven-status
classes           surefire-reports
maven-archiver       test-classes
$ scp chapt1-0.0.1-SNAPSHOT.jar hduser@192.168.2.120:/home/hduser
hduser@192.168.2.120's password:
chapt1-0.0.1-SNAPSHOT.jar                      100% 5095      5.0KB/s
00:00
```

You will recall that you have already copied `ibm-stock.csv` onto the HDFS in the HDFS directory `/hbp/chapt1`. You can verify this by running the following command:

```
hduser@anurag-VirtualBox:~$ hadoop fs -ls /hbp/chapt1
Found 1 items
-rw-r--r--    1 hduser supergroup      861145 2015-08-24 21:00
/hbp/chapt1/ibmstockquotes.txt
```

Now we will run our program on the Hadoop system using the following command:

```
hduser@anurag-VirtualBox:~$ hadoop jar chapt1-0.0.1-SNAPSHOT.jar
hbp.chapt1.StockAverageDriver /hbp/chapt1/ibmstockquotes.txt
/hbp/chapt1/output
```

Let's examine the contents of the output directory:

```
hduser@anurag-VirtualBox:~$ hadoop fs -ls /hbp/chapt1/output15/09/12
Found 2 items
-rw-r--r--   1 hduser supergroup          0 2015-09-12 19:16
/hbp/chapt1/output/_SUCCESS
-rw-r--r--   1 hduser supergroup       1273 2015-09-12 19:16
/hbp/chapt1/output/part-r-00000
```

We can see the `part-r-00000` file on the HDFS that contains the output of our MapReduce job.

Further processing of results

We have successfully run our MapReduce job but our results are still stored on the HDFS. Now we can use the HDFS copy command to copy the results file to the local filesystem for further processing using other tools such as Microsoft Excel:

```
hduser@anurag-VirtualBox:~$ hadoop fs -get  /hbp/chapt1/output/part-r-00000
/home/hduser/results.csv
```

Let's view the contents of the file:

```
hduser@anurag-VirtualBox:~$ head results.csv
1962    433.3511795396825
1963    448.48554415139404
1964    489.16551569960467
1965    480.82985311111105
1966    408.9866005873015
1967    499.4905379123505
1968    425.8838481415928
1969    328.94249967600007
1970    297.1336121732284
1971    321.8779635454545
```

We have averaged the stock prices by year using Hadoop.

Hadoop platform tools

We have successfully run our first MapReduce program on Hadoop written in Java. The Hadoop ecosystem offers a rich set of tools to perform various activities on the Hadoop cluster. The rich tool set is a mix of open source tools and commercial tools available from vendors. The Hadoop ecosystem of tools improves continuously through the very active open source community and commercial vendors who actively contribute to improvements.

In this section, we cover some of the popular tools that we will use to build solutions from Chapter 2, *A 360-Degree View of Customer*, onwards in this book. A very comprehensive list of tools is available on a website known as Hadoop Illuminated at this URL: http://hadoop illuminated.com/hadoop_illuminated/Bigdata_Ecosystem.html.

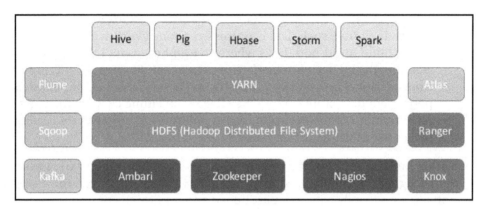

Figure 22 Hadoop: The ecosystem of tools

In the following sections, we will cover a brief overview of the tool after having learned what HDFS, MapReduce v2 and YARN are capable of. In the upcoming chapters, we will cover the installation and usage of these tools as we start using them.

Data ingestion tools

Data ingestion is the process of reading data from a source outside the HDFS and loading them onto the HDFS for storage and further processing. The data can come from flat files, relational database management systems, and through live data feeds. Three common tools to ingest incoming data in Hadoop are as follows:

- **Sqoop**: Hadoop usually coexists with other databases in the enterprise. Apache Sqoop is used to transfer the data between Hadoop and relational database systems or mainframe computers that are ubiquitous in enterprises of all sizes. Typically, you can use Sqoop to import the data from Oracle or SQL Server, transform it using MapReduce, or other tools such as Hive and Pig, and then export the data back to other systems. Sqoop internally uses MapReduce to import data into the Hadoop cluster. Relational database management systems are used to store operational data such as point of sale transactions, orders and customer master data. Apache Sqoop offers fast data loading in HDFS by running data loading tasks in parallel.

- **Flume**: Often we have to load data coming from streaming data sources in HDFS. Streaming data sources delivers data in the form of events, which arrive at random or fixed time intervals.

  Flume is used to ingest large volumes of data coming from sources such as web logs, click stream logs, twitter feeds and livestock feeds in the form of events. In Flume, such data is processed as one event at a time. Flume allows you to build multi-hop flows where an event can travel through before it is stored in the HDFS. Flume offers reliable event delivery. Events are removed from a channel only if they are stored in the next channel, or persisted in a permanent data store such as the HDFS. The Flume channel manages the recoverability of the events in case of failure by using a durable channel that makes use of the local filesystem.

- **Kafka**: Kafka is a messaging system based on a publish subscribe (pubsub) model of messaging commonly used by JMS and ActiveMQ. However, the design of Kafka is akin to a distributed, partitioned and replicated commit log service. Kafka maintains message feeds, which are classified using categories known as topics. Producers are the processes that publish the messages to the topics so that Consumers can consume them. In the pubsub model, a published message gets broadcast to all the consumers. Kafka also supports a queuing model in which a published message gets picked by exactly one consumer who is part of a consumer group.

  Between producers and consumers, Kafka acts as a broker running on a cluster of servers. Typical use cases for Kafka are log aggregation, website activity monitoring and stream processing. Despite its similarity to Flume, Kafka is a general purpose commit-log service suitable for Hadoop, but also for many other systems, while Flume is a solution designed for Hadoop alone. It is not uncommon to see Kafka and Flume working together to build a data ingestion flow for the HDFS.

Data access tools

With the help of data access tools, you can analyze the data stored on Hadoop clusters to gain new insights from the data. Data access tools help us with data transformation, interactive querying and advanced analytics. In this section, we will cover commonly used open source data access tools available from the Apache Software Foundation:

 In addition to open source tools, several commercial tools are available from vendors such as Datameer, IBM, and Cloudera

- **Hive**: SQL is a widely understood query language. Hive provides an SQL-like query language known as Hive Query Language(HQL). Though HQL is limited in features compared to SQL language, it is still very useful to developers who are familiar with running SQL queries on relational database management systems. A bigger group of database programmers can be engaged in the Hadoop ecosystem, using Hive. The Hive service breaks down HQL statements into MapReduce jobs, which execute on the Hadoop cluster like any other MapReduce job. From the Hive 1.2 release, we can take advantage of Apache Tez. Apache Tez is a new application framework built on top of YARN. Using Apache Tez instead of MapReduce solves some of the inefficiencies associated with the planning and execution of queries. This makes Hive perform faster.

- **Pig**: Apache Pig is another tool for analyzing large data sets that consists of a high-level language for expressing data analysis programs, coupled with an infrastructure for evaluating these programs. Pig uses a special language called Pig Latin. This programming language uses high-level constructs to shield the programmers from the complexity of coding MapReduce programs in Java. Pig comes with its own command line shell. You can load HDFS files into Pig and perform various transformations, and then store the results on the HDFS. Pig translates transformation tasks into MapReduce jobs. Once Pig scripts are ready they can be run with the help of a scheduler without any manual intervention to perform routine transformations.

- **Hbase**: Apache Hbase is a NoSQL database that works on top of the HDFS. Hbase is a distributed and non-relational column-oriented data store modeled after Google's Bigtable. It gives you random, real-time, read and write access to data, which is not possible in HDFS. It is designed to store billions of rows and millions of columns. Hbase uses HDFS to store data but it is not limited to HDFS alone. Hbase delivers low access latency for a small amount data from a very large data set.

- **Storm**: Apache Storm is a distributed near real-time computation system. Similarly to how Hadoop provides a set of general primitives for doing batch processing, Storm provides a set of general primitives for performing real-time computation. It defines its workflows in **Directed Acyclic Graphs (DAG's)** called topologies. These topologies run until they are shut down by the user or until they encounter an unrecoverable failure. Storm can read and write data from the HDFS. In its original form, Storm did not natively run on Hadoop clusters but it used Apache Zookeeper and its own master/ minion worker processes to coordinate topologies with a master and worker state. Now Storm is also available on YARN, bringing real-time streamed data-processing capabilities in Hadoop.

- **Spark**: Apache Spark is the newest kid on the block. It performs the memory processing of data stored in the HDFS. Hadoop is inherently a batch-oriented data processing system. In order to build a data pipeline, we have to read and write data several times on the HDFS. Spark addresses this issue by storing the data in memory, which makes low latency data processing possible after the initial load of data from the HDFS into the RAM. Spark provides an excellent model for performing iterative machine learning and interactive analytics. However, Spark also excels in some areas similar to Storm's capabilities, such as near real-time analytics and ingestion. Apache Spark does not require Hadoop to operate. However, its data parallel paradigm requires a shared file system for the optimal use of stable data. The stable source can range from Amazon S3, NFS, MongoDB or, more typically, HDFS. (Ballou, 2014). Spark supports a number of programming languages such as Java, Python, R, and Scala. Spark supports relational queries using a Spark SQL, machine learning with Mlib, graph processing with GraphX, and streaming with Spark Streaming.

Monitoring tools

Hadoop monitoring tools monitor its infrastructure and resources. This information is useful to maintain the quality of service as per the service level agreements, and monitor them over and under the utilization of deployed resources for financial charging and capacity management. Ambari is the most popular open source tool for Hadoop monitoring. Hadoop vendor Cloudera has a proprietary tool, called Cloudera Manager, which is also used to monitor Cloudera Hadoop installations

Cloudera Manager has been positioned as the Enterprise Hadoop Admin System by Cloudera. It helps in the deployment and management of Hadoop clusters. Monitoring is just a subset of many other features offered by it.

In this section, we will cover Ambari.

Apache Ambari is a monitoring tool for Hadoop. It also covers the provisioning and management of Hadoop clusters. Ambari has a REST interface that enables the easy integration of Hadoop provisioning, management, and monitoring capabilities to other applications in the enterprise. You can get an instant insight into the health of a running Hadoop cluster by looking at the web-based dashboard of Ambari (Zacharias, 2014). Ambari can collect the operational metrics of a Hadoop cluster for analysis later. Using the alert framework of Ambari, you can define the rules to generate alerts that you can act upon.

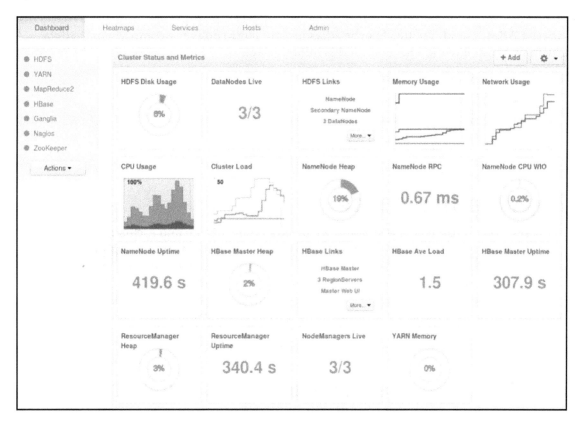

Figure 23 Ambari dashboard

Data governance tools

Data governance (DG) refers to the overall management of the availability, usability, integrity, and security of the data employed in an enterprise. The data governance architecture of Hadoop is evolving, and is still very underdeveloped. Presently, there is no comprehensive data governance within the Hadoop stack, and integration with the external governance frameworks is lacking.

Industry is responding to the need to build a comprehensive data-governance architecture, because Hadoop is becoming the central building block of big data processing systems in enterprises.

Apache Atlas: The aim of the Apache Atlas initiative is to deliver a comprehensive data governance framework. The goals of this initiative are:

- Support for data classification
- Support for centralized auditing
- Proving a search and lineage function
- Building a security and policy engine

Big data use cases

In the previous sections of this chapter, we discussed the design and architecture of Hadoop. Hadoop and its powerful ecosystem of tools provides a strong data platform to build data-driven applications. In this section, you will get an overview of the use cases covered in this book. These use cases have been derived from real business problems in various industry sectors, but they have been simplified to fit a chapter in this book. You can read from `Chapter 2`, *A 360-Degree View of the Customer*, onwards in any order because each chapter is complete in itself.

Creating a 360 degree view of a customer

A 360 degree view of a customer combines information about a customer's attitude, behavior, preferences and static data such as date of birth, and presents it as a single integrated view. Call center agents and field sales agents use this information to better understand the customer's needs and to offer better services or sell the right product.

Large financial institutions operating in the retail market have millions of customers. These customers buy one or more financial products from such institutions.

Large enterprises use master data-management systems to store customer data. The customer data includes key details about the customers such as their name, address and data of birth. Customer service processes use this information to identify a customer during the processing of service requests. Marketing processes use this information to segment customers for direct mailings. The data stored in the MDM systems remain static for several months, if not for several years, because a change in customer addresses does not happen too often, and the other data, such as the name or date of birth, remains unchanged in the lifetime of the customer. The information stored in the MDM systems is very reliable because it undergoes multiple levels of checks before it is stored in the system. Many times, the information in the MDM system is directly taken from the customer data form filled in by the customers.

Despite the high quality of data in the MDM systems or other enterprise data stores, the data in these systems does not create a complete view of the customers. The views created from the static data lack information about what is happening currently that might define the nature of the product or service required by the customer. For example, if a customer is deeply unsatisfied with a product then trying to sell them another accessory will be counterproductive. A 360-degree view should attempt to capture the information about the products in the customer's possession, but also information about his recent experience with the product.

In Chapter 2, *A 360-Degree View of the Customer*, we will build a 360 degree view of a customer by combining information available in the enterprise data store and information available via social media. We will use Hadoop as the central data warehouse to create the 360-degree view.

Fraud detection systems for banks

According to a report published in Forbes in 2011 (Shaughnessy, 2011), merchants in the United States lose $190 billion per year owing to credit card fraud. Most of this credit card fraud originates from online channels. Banks lose $11 billion to fraud. With the proliferation of digital channels, online fraud is on the rise, and therefore timely fraud detection makes a strong business case for the banks. A solid fraud detection system helps banks in two ways:

- By reducing financial loss, lowering the risk exposure, and reducing the capital tied to indemnify customers against the fraud
- By strengthening the safe image of the bank and thereby growing its market share

Spending behavior of bank customers usually follows a pattern that repeats based upon events such as a credit of their salary into the bank account or the payment of utility bills. Any significant deviations from the spending pattern could point to a potential fraudulent activity. Such potential fraudulent activity should trigger an alert so that the bank can take timely action to limit or prevent the financial loss.

In Chapter 3, *Building a Fraud Detection System*, we will cover a transaction screening system. The goal of this system is to screen every transaction for a potential fraud and generate real-time fraud notifications, so that we can block the transaction and alert the prey. A big data based fraud detection system uses transaction data and enriches it with other static and location data to predict a possible fraud. In this use case, we will focus upon real-time fraud detection as opposed to detecting frauds in a historical data set.

A real-time fraud detection system is a very effective way to fight transaction fraud because it can prevent the movement of funds immediately when a fraud is detected. This prevention mechanism can be built into the transaction approval process. Batch-processing based fraud detection also has value because some types of frauds cannot be detected in real time owing to intensive computing power requirements. However, by the time a fraud is detected using the batch-processing mechanism the money might be irrecoverably lost, and the criminal might have fled, which is why a real-time fraud detection system is more useful.

Marketing campaign planning

You will be familiar with promotional folders that get delivered to your mailboxes by post or with newspapers and magazines. These promotional folders are sent as a part of a campaign run by the marketing departments of companies. A campaign is typically part of a project with a well-defined objective. Often these objectives are related to the successful sale of a product, or a customer visiting a store in response to a campaign. The rewards of the employees in the marketing department are linked to the success of the campaign. Promotional campaigns have a lot of waste associated with them because they target the wrong customers, who are unlikely to respond to a promotional folder, but they still get them because there is no way of knowing who the right and wrong customers are.

 For example, if you send offers for meat products to a person who is a vegetarian then it is very unlikely that it will result in a sale of your product

As a result, the promotional folders are sent to everyone.

In `Chapter 4`, *Marketing Campaign Planning*, we will build a system to decide which customers are more likely to respond to a promotional folder by using an example of a fictitious company. We will build a predictive model from the historical campaign response data. We will use the predictive model to create a new target list of customers who are more likely to respond to our promotional campaign. The aim of this exercise is to increase the success of marketing campaigns. We will use a tool called BigML to build a predictive model and Hadoop to process the customer data.

Churn detection in telecom

Customer churn or customer attrition refers to the loss of clients to competitors. This problem is acute among technology service providers such as Internet service providers, mobile operators and vendors of software as a service. As a result of customer churn, the companies lose a source of revenue. In very competitive markets where vendors outdo each other by slashing the prices, the cost of acquiring new customers is much more than retaining customers. In these saturated markets, with little or no room for growth, customer retention is the only strategy to maintain market share and revenue. A customer churn detection system is a very compelling business case in the telecom sector.

In the telecom business, a customer might defect to another provider at the end of a contract period. If a telecom company knows in advance, which customer is likely to move to a new provider, then they can make a suitable offer to the customer that will increase the likelihood that the customer will stay with them after the end of the existing contract period.

To predict customer churn, we should examine what kind of signal we can derive from the data. Just by examining the static data about the customer, we will not be able to conclude much about an upcoming churn event. Therefore, a churn-detection system should look into customer behavior such as the calling patterns, social interactions and contacts with the call center. All this information, when analyzed properly, can be put to use for building a churn-detection model.

The churn-detection problem is also well suited for large-scale batch analytics, which Hadoop excels at. We can start shortlisting the customers who are likely to churn a few months before the contract end date. Once we have this list, we have a way that we can target the customers with both inbound and outbound marketing campaigns to increase the chances that customer will stay with the company after the end of the existing contract period.

In Chapter 5, *Churn Detection*, we will build a system to predict customer churn. We will use customer master data, and other master data, to build a customer-churn model. We will use this model to predict customers who are likely to churn. We will use batch processing to generate the list that will be used by inbound sales staff and outbound campaign managers to target customers with tailor made offers.

Analyzing sensor data

Nowadays sensors are everywhere. GPS sensors are fitted in taxis to track their movement and location. Smartphones carry GPS, temperature and speed sensors. Even large buildings and factory complexes have thousands of sensors that measure the lighting, temperature, and humidity. The sensor data is collected, processed and analyzed in three distinct steps using a big data system. The first step involves the detection of events that generate data from the sensor. The sensor transports this data using a wire or wireless protocol to a centralized data-storage system. In the second step, the sensor data is stored in a centralized data-storage system after data cleansing, if necessary. The third step involves analyzing and consuming this data by an application. A system capable of processing sensor data is also called an **Internet of Things (IOT)** system. However, sometimes we might need to analyze the sensor data in near real time. For example, the temperature or the humidity in a large factory complex, if not monitored or controlled in real time, might lead to perished goods or loss of human productivity. In such cases, we need a near real-time data analytics solution. Although the HDFS is suitable for batch analytics, other tools in the Hadoop ecosystem can support near real-time analytics very well.

Sensor data usually takes the form of time series, because data sent by a sensor is a measurement at a specific moment in time. This measurement might contain information about temperature, voltage, humidity or some other physical parameter of interest. In the use case covered in Chapter 6, *Analyze Sensor Data Using Hadoop*, we will use sensor data to build a batch and real-time data analytics system for a factory.

Building a data lake

The term data lake has gained popularity in recent years. The main promise of a data lake is to provide access to large volumes of data in a raw form for analytics of an entire enterprise and to introduce agility into the data-warehousing processes.

Data Lakes are challenging the traditional enterprise data-warehousing paradigm. Traditional data warehousing is based upon the **Extract-Transform-Load** (**ETL**) paradigm. The ETL based data-warehousing processes have a long cycle time because they require a well-defined data model where the data should be loaded. This process is called transformation because the data extracted from the operational systems is transformed for loading into the enterprise data warehouse. It's only when the data is loaded into the data warehouse that it becomes available for further analysis.

Hadoop supports the Extract-Load-Transform ELT paradigm. The data files in their raw format can be loaded into the HDFS. It does not require any kind of knowledge of the data model. Once the data has been loaded on the HDFS, then we can use a variety of tools for ad-hoc exploration and analytics. The transformation of data to facilitate structured exploration and analytics can continue, but users already get access to the raw data for exploration without waiting for a long time.

The data lake use case opens up new frontiers for businesses because data lakes give access to data to a large group of users. The lower cost of data storage in the HDFS makes this an attractive proposition because data with no immediate use does not have to be discarded to save the expensive storage space in the Enterprise Data Warehouse. The data lake stores all the data for an enterprise. It offers an opportunity to break the data silos in enterprises that made data analysis using cross-departmental data a very slow process owing to interdepartmental politics and boundaries created by different IT systems.

The data lake use case opens up a new set of questions about data governance and data security. Once all the enterprise data is stored in the data lake, fine-grained access to datasets becomes crucial to ensure that data does not get into the wrong hands. A system containing all the enterprise data becomes a valuable target for hackers too.

In Chapter 7, *Build a Data Lake*, we will build a basic data lake and see how we can keep it secure by using various tools available in the Hadoop ecosystem.

The architecture of Hadoop-based systems

After covering the various use cases covered in this book, we will discuss the architecture that forms the basis of the solutions that we will create in the following chapters. Lambda architecture is a good architecture pattern that we can refer to while designing a big data system. Lambda architecture is a generic architecture in which Hadoop and its ecosystem of tools fit nicely.

Lambda architecture

Nathan Marz is an ex-Twitter engineer who gained significant experience in building real-time distributed data-processing systems. He went on to design Lambda architecture, which is a generic architecture for big data systems. This architecture addresses the requirements of batch and real-time analytics.

The underlying thoughts behind building a generic architecture for big data systems are as follows:

- The system should be fault tolerant and capable of coping with hardware failures.
- The system should be able to run a variety of workloads. In some workloads, low latency is required such as interactive queries.
- It should support linear scalability. This means that adding more servers should scale up the processing capacity of the system linearly.

From a high-level perspective, this system has the following building blocks:

- A data ingestion block, which dispatches data to the batch and the speed layer for processing.
- The batch layer, which is an immutable, append-only data store. This computes the batch views.
- The serving layer, which indexes batch views for consumption by interactive queries and applications.

- The speed layer, which processes the data in real time and compensates for the delay introduced in the batch layer.
- Any interactive query can be answered by merging the results from the serving layer and batch layer.

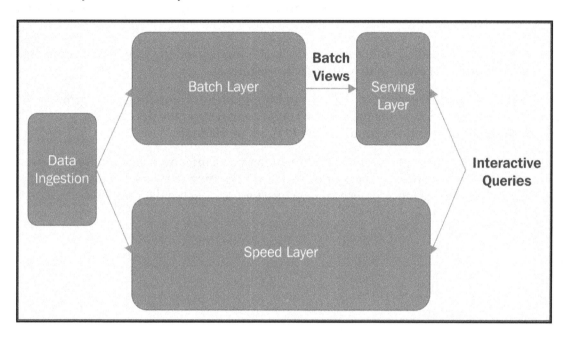

Figure 24 The Lambda architecture for big data systems

As a reader, you will quickly recognize how Hadoop and the HDFS fit in the batch layer. Technologies such as MapReduce and Pig are suited for the creation of batch views. In the serving layer, we can use tools such as Hbase or MongoDB, which support both interactive queries and full CRUD operations on the datasets. In the speed layer, we can use tools such as Apache Storm and Apache Spark Streaming.

Lambda architecture is a reference model. In our use cases, we should make good choices about which components of this reference model are used in our solution architecture. For example, a use case that does not require a near real-time response or interactive queries will not need components to build the speed layer and serving layer.

Summary

In this chapter, we started by learning about the origins of big data problems. We learned how Google publications gave rise to the development of Hadoop and its ecosystem of tools and how the engineering teams at Yahoo were the main driving force behind the evolution of Hadoop.

We covered how industrial scale use of Hadoop at Yahoo paved the way for the commercial scale of adoption of Hadoop in diverse industry segments.

We learned about the design of the HDFS and MapReduce as computing paradigms followed by an overview of the tools in the Hadoop ecosystem. We developed a MapReduce program and also studied how to run it on Hadoop.

The latter part of this chapter was devoted to giving you a brief overview of cases covered in this book, which we will learn in our projects in the coming chapters. We also covered Lambda architecture as the reference architecture for building big data systems.

2
A 360-Degree View of the Customer

In this chapter, we will take the example of a fictitious company called Cosmetica Inc. This company was founded in 1983, when the web commerce was invented. From its humble start as a small shop in Uden, it has now more than 300 shopping outlets. The company also runs a web shop where customers can buy products 24×7. The company is planning to launch a personalized shopping service where the customer will get assistance in choosing the right product.

This company is interested in building a 360-degree view of customers who often visit their web shop, and who are also active on social media. To build a 360-degree view, we will follow the following steps in this chapter:

- Understanding the data required in the 360-degree view
- Setting up the technology stack
- Engineering the solution
- Presenting the solution using a web interface

Capturing business information

Like any other mid-sized retailer, the information technology needs of Cosmetica have grown with times. Previously, most customers visited their shopping outlets and did most of their purchasing during the weekends. During the festival seasons, the sales used to be brisk. In late 90s, Cosmetica introduced a loyalty card to boost customer loyalty. This loyalty card allowed customers to collect loyalty points at the time of making a purchase in the shop. The customers could redeem those loyalty points to buy products that were on special offer.

Since the year 2005, Cosmetica has a good presence on the World Wide Web through their webshop; customers can browse their products online and buy them. Cosmetica is planning to offer a personalized cosmetic shopping service. A customer can call the Cosmetica call center in order to approach a human shopping assistant and get personalized advice.

In order to do this, Cosmetica wants to have a 360-degree view of customers, which will help the human shopping assistants better understand customer needs, and respond accordingly.

In a traditional sense, Cosmetica customers are physically less present in their shops nowadays, but customer interactions with Cosmetica are taking place more often. Social media platforms capture much more information about customer preferences and behavior than ever before. Creating a 360-degree view of a customer is a technique to combine the information from various data sources, and present it in a format that can be used to provide better service to customers, or to spot opportunities to maximize revenue.

Collecting data from data sources

To create a 360-degree view of a customer, the following kinds of data are available to us:

- Customer master data
- Access logs from the web shop of Cosmetica
- Twitter feeds

Customer master data is stored in the CRM system of the company. The CRM system is a software package, which uses a MySQL based RDBMS to store customer information. The access logs from the web shop are available in the form of text files. Cosmetica collects tweets that contain the keyword "Fragrances." These tweets are available in a file containing the tweets as JSON documents.

Online customer behavior

Customers are online and always connected. This has resulted in a major shift in how customers interact with an enterprise when they want to buy a product or request after-sales services for certain products. The value of physical channels such as high street shops and bank branches is diminishing at a faster pace than ever before as the preferred channel for customers. At the end of the last century, bank customers often visited bank branches for activities such as cashing cheques or collecting debit cards. Banks took advantage of these visits to better understand customer's preferences to upsell or cross-sell products. Explosive growth of digital channels such as web interfaces and mobile apps has reduced the need to be physically present at a shop or branch. As a consequence, the enterprises started losing access to valuable information about their customers, which had the potential to service customers better or spot potential upsell and cross-sell opportunities.

Traditional enterprises were challenged in their established territories and market segments by the new e-commerce entrants who were better prepared to take advantage of new opportunities created by ever-growing digital interactions with the customers. These interactions happen more often and leave a valuable trail of information that can be used to spot opportunities to drive higher customer satisfaction.

Nowadays, customers spend a lot of time on social media platforms such as Facebook, Twitter, and Foursquare. A customer's social network and his or her behavior on these platforms may reveal interesting information about their product preferences and dislikes.

We have chosen a fictitious company in this example. In a real life scenario, tens or hundreds of data sources might be involved in creating the 360-degree view. Data sources such as customer relationship management systems, order management systems, fulfilment systems, and web logs may be used to compile the 360-degree view. *Figure 1* shows IBM's vision of an enhanced 360-degree view of the customer (IBM, 2015) and the data sources associated with it as an example.

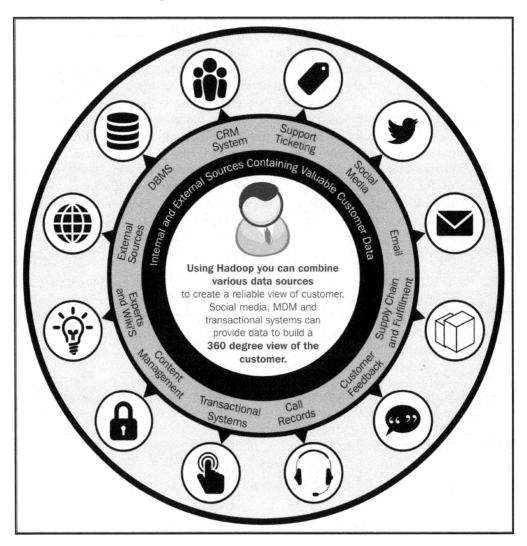

Figure 1 Enhanced 360-degree view of customers by IBM

Creating a data processing approach

The data processing approach in this chapter will use the **extract, load, and transform (ETL)** paradigm, which is the preferred paradigm for analyzing data using Hadoop. As you might recall from `Chapter 1`, *Hadoop and Big Data*, we can store data on HDFS without caring much about the schema, at the time of loading the data. Once the data has been loaded on HDFS, it is directly available for ad-hoc analysis, using tools such as Hive and MapReduce. This type of analysis is also called exploratory analytics because it leads to the discovery of patterns in data, which might uncover new business opportunities or generate insights that cannot be generated by questions known to the business.

However, the ad-hoc analysis may not be sufficient in many cases because many users might be unfamiliar with ad-hoc analysis techniques. Certain business processes require us to present data in a structured form to the users, so they can quickly take decisions based upon the information presented to them.

The creation of a 360-degree view of the customer is one such process where we have to distil out the useful data about a customer from the datasets, and present it in a format which can be used and understood by the online shopping assistants who will advice the customers through web-based chat sessions, or on the phone.

Our data processing steps will be as follows:

1. Load data from data sources in HDFS.
2. Perform a data inspection and decide what is the relevant data.
3. Create tables in Hive to store the data in tabular format.
4. Query and join the tables to create a 360-degree view.
5. Export the data contained in the 360-degree view.

Presenting the results

A 360-degree view can be presented in a number of ways. We can use a web interface to present the data to the shopping. We might integrate the view with the call center software so that it pops up to help shopping assistants when a customer contacts the call center on the phone, or via the chat function.

The presentation of the results is also sometimes referred to as the consumption of data. In this chapter, we will use a simple web application to present the results. However, we should keep in mind that, once the view is available on a database management system, a wide variety of tools can present it.

Setting up the technology stack

In Chapter 1, *Hadoop and Big Data*, we covered various tools in the Hadoop ecosystem. In this chapter, we will use some of those tools to set up the technology stack for building a 360-degree view of a customer. Setting up all the tools in the Hadoop ecosystem can be cumbersome and a fault-prone process, owing to multiple dependencies on the libraries. The tools in the Hadoop ecosystem have evolved over a period of time by contributions from the open source community. Therefore, these tools lack an integrated installation and configuration approach. The Pure Play Hadoop vendors have made good progress in easing the installation of Hadoop by offering Hadoop sandboxes and RPM packages. One such vendor is Hortonworks who offer the Hortonwork Data Platform or HDP. HDP is a pure open source platform built upon open source Hadoop, and several tools from the Hadoop ecosystem.

HDP is available on a CentOS-based virtual machine such as a VirtualBox image. We will deploy this image on VirtualBox and then spin the machine. It will give us access to a single node Hadoop cluster and the associated ecosystem of tools.

Note that the performance of your HDP depends a lot upon the RAM available to your virtual machine. A Hadoop sandbox system, such as HDP, is good to learn about Hadoop and tools, but it never reflects the production environment configuration of a Hadoop cluster. In a production environment, NameNodes and DataNodes will be deployed on separate nodes. Typically the NameNodes will be deployed on slightly more robust servers than the DataNodes. A minimal production configuration without Hadoop HA will have one NameNode and five DataNodes.

Tools used

We will import data from various data sources to build a customer 360-degree view. Our customer relationship database runs on a MySQL server, which is a relational database management system. A CRM system is an operational system in the company where customer master records, as well as customer interactions, are recorded. A typical in-house CRM system will use a relational database as the persistent store for the data. A CRM system is highly suited for managing the customer data, but not for combining data from the different sources to create new insights. Here is where we can use Hadoop to process and combine data from multiple sources.

We will use Sqoop to read the database from MySQL tables, store it on HDFS, and build a Hive table from it. Sqoop will allow us to connect with source RDBMS directly using JDBC, and import the data in HDFS. Our website access log file is a flat text file. We will use the HDFS copy command to store this file on HDFS. Tweets from Twitter represent a kind of semi-structured data that will need some transformation to become useful for further analysis. We will use Hive to do these transformations in Hadoop after loading raw tweets in HDFS.

Finally, we will use Hive to run queries using HiveQL. HQL is a powerful query language modeled after SQL. HQL will allow us to write queries to join various tables and build the 360-degree view without the need for a lower level programming language such as Java.

Installing Hortonworks Sandbox

You can download Hortonworks Sandbox by visiting the download link `http://hortonwor ks.com/products/hortonworks-sandbox/#install`. At the time of writing this chapter, we downloaded HDP 2.3, which is available as a VirtualBox image running CentOS. You will also find an installation guide on the same website. HDP stands for Hortonworks Data Platform, which is a name given by Hortonworks to their bundle of the most important tools in the Hadoop ecosystem. Note that all the tools included in HDP are pure open source tools. They can also be individually downloaded from the website of the Apache Software Foundation. However, using the sandbox saves us lot of time compared to time taken in installing Hadoop tools from scratch.

HDP 2.3 comes with Hadoop 2.7.1 and many other tools such as Hive and Sqoop are included in the bundle (Hortonworks, 2015). Figure 2 shows the components included in HDP 2.3 and
their version numbers.

Hortonworks is not the only Hadoop sandbox available on the market. Other Hadoop vendors such as Cloudera and MapReduce have similar offerings available for download.

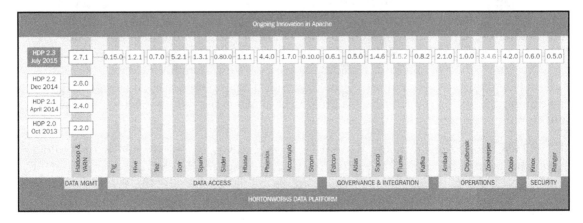

Figure 2 Hortonworks Data Platform bundles several Hadoop open source innovations

Creating user accounts

HDP comes with a Unix root account. The password of this account is displayed after you boot the VirtualBox image. You can use the user root and password to log on to the sandbox. Once you see the command prompt, you will be able to create new users on the system. In my HDP instance, I have created a user named hduser, which I will use to run the examples in this chapter.

Exploring HUE

HUE, or Hadoop User Experience, provides a web-based interface for many Hadoop tools. It has been created by Cloudera. HUE comes with a lightweight web server, which lets you connect with Hadoop using a web interface. HUE is just a view on top of any Hadoop distribution, which is HDP in our case. HUE comes preinstalled in the HDP version that we use in the examples in this chapter. Unlike many other tools covered in this book, HUE is not a tool from the Apache Software Foundation; it is an open source tool supported by Cloudera. In Chapter 7, *Building a Data Lake*, we will cover another similar tool called Zeppelin, which is from the Apache Software Foundation.

You can run HUE by visiting `http://<ip address of HDP Sandbox>: 8000` on your browser.

Hortonworks Sandbox is running on the IP address 192.168.2.104 in my LAN as you can see on the home page of HUE, as shown in *Figure 3*, when I visit: `http://192.168.2.104:8000`.

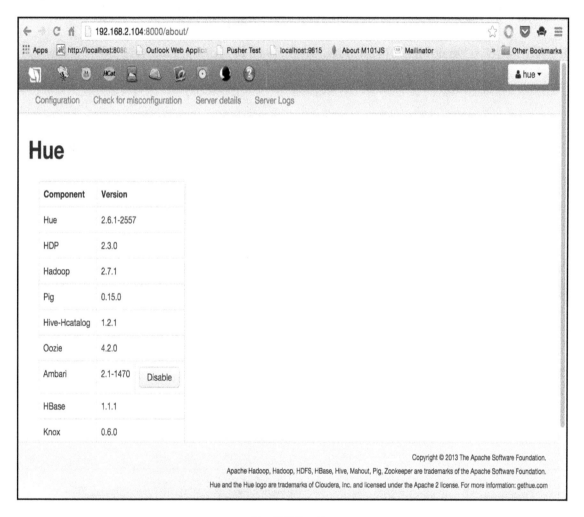

Figure 3 HUE Home Page

Clicking on the HCat icon gives you access to the HCatalog page, which shows the names of databases and tables in the Hive metastore. Clicking the Beeswax icon gives you a screen to enter and run Hive queries using Hive Query Language. You can also browse the files and directories on HDFS by clicking the File Browser Icon as shown in Figure 4.

You can also set up batch processing jobs using Oozie and Job Designer. We will discuss these tools later in this book. In addition, you can manage users and groups in Hue. You will notice that Hue comes with several pre-configured users and groups.

In HDP 2.3, Hue version 2.6.1 is included. At the time of writing, Hue version 3.8 is the latest version of Hue offering basic data visualization features.

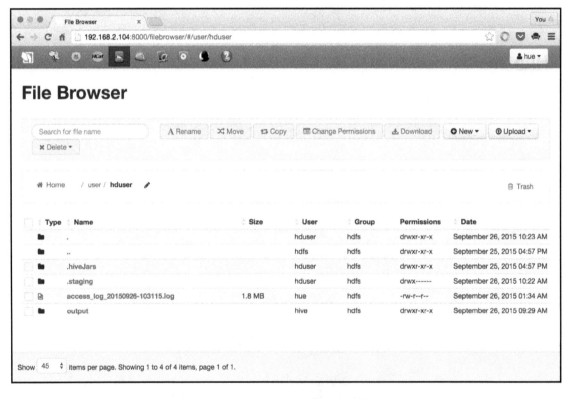

Figure 4 HDFS file browser in Hue

Exploring MYSQL and the HIVE command line

After exploring Hadoop with Hue, we can explore MySQL and Hive on the command line. Please open a new terminal window. I generally use the SSH command to open a new terminal session from my laptop to the server where my Hadoop virtual machine is running.

```
[hduser@sandbox ~]$ mysql -u root
Welcome to the MySQL monitor.  Commands end with ; or \g.
Your MySQL connection id is 18215
Server version: 5.1.73 Source distribution

Copyright (c) 2000, 2013, Oracle and/or its affiliates. All rights
reserved.

Oracle is a registered trademark of Oracle Corporation and/or its
affiliates. Other names may be trademarks of their respective
owners.

Type 'help;' or '\h' for help. Type '\c' to clear the current input
statement.

mysql> show databases;
+--------------------+
| Database           |
+--------------------+
| information_schema |
| hive               |
| mysql              |
| ranger             |
| ranger_audit       |
| test               |
+--------------------+
6 rows in set (0.00 sec)
```

We see that HDP has already created a database with the name `hive`. This is the metastore database created for Hive in the MySQL database.

In Mysql, we will create a new database named `crm` as follows:

```
mysql> create database crm;
Query OK, 1 row affected (0.21 sec)
```

The database `crm` has been created successfully. This database will contain the customer master data. Please note that in this step we have only defined the database. We will create a customer table and populate it with data when we engineer the solution.

HiveServer and HiveServer2

HDP 2.3 comes with HiveServer and HiveServer2. Using command line tools, you can connect with one of these servers. From the end user perspective, the availability of authentication support in HiveServer2 is the major difference between HiveServer2 and the original HiveServer. The original HiveServer lets you access data if you have access to the host and port where HiveServer is running, and no further authentication is necessary. This will be undesirable when Hive is being used by a large group of users where the access to Hive has to be restricted and logged. HiveSever2 supports authentication schemes such as Kerberos, LDAP, and custom authentication plugins. The JDBC and ODBC drivers also support these authentication models, which connect to Hive using HiveServer2. In this chapter, we will also use HiveServer2, which uses a client named Beeline to run Hive QL queries.

We will connect to Hive using Hive CLI and list the databases defined in Hive as follows:

```
[hduser@sandbox ~]$ hive
logging...........
hive> show databases;
OK
default
xademo
Time taken: 4.864 seconds, Fetched: 2 row(s)
```

You will notice that by default the Hive instance in HDP has two databases in it.

We will use Hive to filter and join the data from various datasets to create the 360-degree view. For this purpose, we will define a new database in Hive using the following command:

```
hive> create database customer360;
OK
Time taken: 22.495 seconds
```

We have created a new database called `customer360`. In this database, we will transform the datasets obtained from various data sources.

To connect with HiveServer2, we will use the `beeline` command. This command where we can run HiveQL queries. HiveServer2 supports multiple authentication schemes. In our case, HiveServer2 uses the Java **Simple Authentication and Security Layer (SASL)** protocol to establish a security layer between the client and the server.

 You can read about various authentication schemes available in HiveServer2 on this page: `http://docs.hortonworks.com/HDPDocuments /HDP2/HDP-2.3./bk_dataintegration/content/beeline-vs-hive-cli. html`.

We will login using SASL:

```
[hduser@sandbox ~]$ beeline
Beeline version 1.2.1.2.3.0.0-2557 by Apache Hive
beeline>  !connect jdbc:hive2://localhost:10000/default
Connecting to jdbc:hive2://localhost:10000/default
Enter username for jdbc:hive2://localhost:10000/default: hduser
Enter password for jdbc:hive2://localhost:10000/default: ******
Connected to: Apache Hive (version 1.2.1.2.3.0.0-2557)
Driver: Hive JDBC (version 1.2.1.2.3.0.0-2557)
Transaction isolation: TRANSACTION_REPEATABLE_READ
0: jdbc:hive2://localhost:10000/default> show databases;
+-----------------+--+
| database_name   |
+-----------------+--+
| customer360     |
| default         |
| xademo          |
+-----------------+--+
3 rows selected (6.36 seconds)
```

Notice that to connect with HiveServer2, we have used a username and password on CentOS.

HiveCLI and Beeline both keep track of the command history. By using the up arrow on your keyboard, you can retrieve a command from the command history and run it again.

We can see that Hive has a default database. When we connected to Hive using Beeline or HiveCLI, we specified the name of this database in the connection string. If we want to use a different database, then we have to switch to that database using the `use` command as illustrated here:

```
0: jdbc:hive2://localhost:10000/default> use customer360;
No rows affected (0.614 seconds)
0: jdbc:hive2://localhost:10000/default> show tables;
+------------+--+
```

```
| tab_name  |
+-----------+--+
+-----------+--+
No rows selected (0.456 seconds)
```

Notice that at this moment, the database `customer360` contains no tables defined in it.

Exploring Sqoop at the command line

To build a 360-degree view, we will use Sqoop to copy data from the relational database management system, MySql, to HDFS. Sqoop is a command line utility that comes with many options.

We can invoke Sqoop at the command line to verify its presence on HDP as illustrated here:

```
[hduser@sandbox ~]$ sqoop help
2015-10-02 16:37:05,682 INFO  - [main:] ~ Running Sqoop version:
1.4.6.2.3.0.0-2557 (Sqoop:92)
usage: sqoop COMMAND [ARGS]

Available commands:
  codegen            Generate code to interact with database records
  create-hive-table  Import a table definition into Hive
  eval               Evaluate a SQL statement and display the results
  export             Export an HDFS directory to a database table
  help               List available commands
  import             Import a table from a database to HDFS
  import-all-tables  Import tables from a database to HDFS
  import-mainframe   Import datasets from a mainframe server to HDFS
  job                Work with saved jobs
  list-databases     List available databases on a server
  list-tables        List available tables in a database
  merge              Merge results of incremental imports
  metastore          Run a standalone Sqoop metastore
  version            Display version information

See 'sqoop help COMMAND' for information on a specific command.
```

Test driving Hive and Sqoop

In the previous section, we verified that MySQL, Hive, and Sqoop were available on our Hadoop Sandbox. We will now test drive Hive and Sqoop.

Querying data using Hive

We run Hive queries to select data from tables. Hive has two types of tables:

- Managed tables
- External tables

Hive creates managed tables by default. To create external tables, we specify the keyword `external` during table creation.

In the case of managed tables, the table lifecycle is completely managed by Hive. If you drop a managed table, then the associated data and metadata are also deleted by Hive. The external table reads data from an HDFS file. This file is not deleted when the table is dropped by Hive. Other tools can also access the HDFS file while at the same time we can run Hive queries on the HDFS by defining an external table for the file.

In `Chapter 1`, *Hadoop and Big Data*, of this book, we used a dataset containing the historical stock price of IBM to run a MapReduce job that calculated the yearly average stock price for IBM stock.

We will take the same dataset and run queries on it using Hive. The dataset is contained in the file `ibmstockquotes.txt`.

The first step in this process is uploading this file on HDFS:

```
[hduser@sandbox ~]$ hadoop fs -mkdir /hbp
[hduser@sandbox ~]$ hadoop fs -mkdir /hbp/chapt2
[hduser@sandbox ~]$ hadoop fs -put ibmstockquotes.txt /hbp/chapt2
```

We have now stored our dataset on HDFS.

The second step in this process is to create an external table in Hive. Before we can create an external table, we need to know the following:

- The full path of the dataset in HDFS
- The structure of the data
- The field and row delimiters

If we examine the first few rows of the file `ibmstockquotes.txt` then we can get some information about the structure of data and delimiters:

```
[hduser@sandbox ~]$ head ibmstockquotes.txt
Date,Open,High,Low,Close,Volume,Adj Close
2015-10-01,145.309998,145.669998,141.589996,143.589996,3815000,143.589996
```

The first row in this file specifies the field names. A comma (,) has been used as the field delimiter in the rows, and the rows are separated by a new line (\n) delimiter.

The following command creates the external table in Hive:

```
create external table if not exists t_ibm_stocks (
Value_Date DATE,
Open FLOAT,
High FLOAT,
Low FLOAT,
Close FLOAT,
Volume INT,
Adj_Close FLOAT)
row format delimited fields terminated by ','
location '/hbp/chapt2;
```

Note that we have modified the name of the first `field` date to `value_date` so that it does not conflict with the datatype DATE. Hive defaults to a new line as the row delimiter for the text, so we have not specified it. The row field delimited has been specified.

Let's create this table in the database `default`. We will open a `beeline` session and run the commands as illustrated here:

```
0: jdbc:hive2://localhost:10000/default> create external table if not
exists t_ibm_stocks ( value_Date DATE, Open FLOAT, High FLOAT, Low FLOAT,
Close FLOAT, Volume INT,Adj_Close FLOAT ) row format delimited fields
terminated by ',' location '/hbp/chapt2';
No rows affected (21.525 seconds)

0: jdbc:hive2://localhost:10000/default> describe t_ibm_stocks;
```

col_name	data_type	comment
value_date	date	
open	float	
high	float	
low	float	
close	float	
volume	int	
adj_close	float	

```
+-------------+-------------+----------+--+
```
7 rows selected (4.037 seconds)

We have created the table `t_ibm_stocks` successfully. The describe command shows the table column names and data types. We have not used comments while creating the table so it is empty.

Let's explore some HiveQL commands to retrieve the data from the newly created table.

- The following select query will return 10 rows from the table:

  select * from t_ibm_stocks limit 10;

- The following query will return the number of rows in the table:

  select count(*) from t_ibm_stocks;

The output of the preceding query is as follows:

```
0: jdbc:hive2://localhost:10000/default> select count(*) from t_ibm_stocks;
INFO  : Session is already open
INFO  : Status: Running (Executing on YARN cluster with App id
application_1443276402154_0019)
INFO  : Map 1: 0/1    Reducer 2: 0/1
INFO  : Map 1: 0/1    Reducer 2: 0/1
INFO  : Map 1: 0/1    Reducer 2: 0/1
INFO  : Map 1: 0/1    Reducer 2: 0/1
INFO  : Map 1: 0(+1)/1  Reducer 2: 0/1
INFO  : Map 1: 0(+1)/1  Reducer 2: 0/1
INFO  : Map 1: 0(+1)/1  Reducer 2: 0/1
INFO  : Map 1: 0(+1)/1  Reducer 2: 0/1
INFO  : Map 1: 0(+1)/1  Reducer 2: 0/1
INFO  : Map 1: 1/1    Reducer 2: 0/1
INFO  : Map 1: 1/1    Reducer 2: 0(+1)/1
INFO  : Map 1: 1/1    Reducer 2: 1/1
+----------+--+
|   _c0    |
+----------+--+
| 13532    |
+----------+--+
1 row selected (38.545 seconds)
```

You will notice that the preceding query triggers the MapReduce before the results are returned.

The following select query demonstrates the aggregation in HiveQL:

```
select MAX(Open), YEAR(Value_Date) a from t_ibm_stocks group by
YEAR(Value_Date);
```

The preceding query finds the maximum opening stock price for each year in the dataset. We use two functions from Hive. The MAX function finds the maximum value in the column. The YEAR function extracts the date from the full date in YYYY-MM-DD format.

The following select query will return the average stock prices for each year in the dataset:

```
select YEAR(Value_Date) as yr, AVG(Open) as av from t_ibm_stocks group by
YEAR(Value_Date);
```

You will notice that the output of this query is similar to the output of the Java MapReduce program in Chapter 1, *Hadoop and Big Data*. However, with the help of HiveQL, we are able to calculate the average without any need for cumbersome Java programming.

The Hive query language offers many more features, some of which will be covered in this book. A simple Hive cheat sheet is available at http://hortonworks.com/blog/hive-cheat-sheet-for-sql-users/.

Importing data in Hive using Sqoop

Apache Sqoop™ is a tool designed for efficiently transferring bulk data between Apache Hadoop and structured datastores such as relational databases. To test drive Sqoop, let's create a table called Persons in our relational database management system MySQL. We will use the database test where the table Persons will be created.

Download the file persons.sql, which contains the DDL and DML for the Persons table:

```
CREATE TABLE `Persons` (
  `id` mediumint(8) unsigned NOT NULL auto_increment,
  `Name` varchar(255) default NULL,
  `City` varchar(255),
  `AccountNo` varchar(34),
  PRIMARY KEY (`id`)
) AUTO_INCREMENT=1;
```

The `Person` table has three columns and one ID column. Source the file `Persons.sql` in MySQL as illustrated here:

```
mysql> use test
Reading table information for completion of table and column names
You can turn off this feature to get a quicker startup with -A
mysql> source persons.sql
Query OK, 0 rows affected (0.10 sec)
```

The table has 100 records that you can verify:

```
mysql> select count(*) from Persons;
+----------+
| count(*) |
+----------+
|      100 |
+----------+
1 row in set (0.00 sec)
mysql> select * from Persons limit 5;
+----+------------------+-------------------+----------------------------
----+
| id | Name             | City              | AccountNo
|
+----+------------------+-------------------+----------------------------
----+
|  1 | Jorden G. Soto   | Rotheux-Rimiï¿½re | AT785794993822733068
|
|  2 | Kyle U. Peterson | Burlington        | CZ1815524686851625092014
|
|  3 | Tanisha Z. Battle| Castle Douglas    | GR6139874299458461989160925
|
|  4 | Cynthia K. Carver| Rechnitz          |
PS1275823567164446962192013373  |
|  5 | Brock J. Cain    | Lisciano Niccone  |
MT27WSAN4610661252273913380567 4 |
+----+------------------+-------------------+----------------------------
----+
5 rows in set (0.00 sec)
```

We will now invoke Sqoop to import the data from the MySQL database into HDFS.

```
$ sqoop import --connect jdbc:mysql://localhost:3306/test --username root
--table Persons  --hive-table Persons --hive-import --split-by id --direct
```

When the run completes successfully, you will seeing something similar to the following output after logging:

```
Loading data to table default.persons
Table default.persons stats: [numFiles=4, totalSize=5627]
OK
Time taken: 3.805 seconds
```

We will now log on to Hive and see if our data has been imported successfully. Note that we are using `hive-cli` rather than Beeline to start the Hive session.

```
$hive

hive> select count(*) from persons;
Query ID = hduser_20151008210318_24fcc385-37f8-4004-aaae-1a78ce338fb0
Total jobs = 1
Launching Job 1 out of 1


Status: Running (Executing on YARN cluster with App id
application_1444336226319_0009)


---------------------------------------------------------------------------
-----
        VERTICES        STATUS  TOTAL  COMPLETED  RUNNING  PENDING  FAILED
KILLED
---------------------------------------------------------------------------
-----
Map 1 ..........        SUCCEEDED    1         1        0        0       0
0
Reducer 2 ......        SUCCEEDED    1         1        0        0       0
0
---------------------------------------------------------------------------
-----
VERTICES: 02/02  [==============================>>] 100%  ELAPSED TIME: 12.23 s
---------------------------------------------------------------------------
-----
OK
100
Time taken: 30.667 seconds, Fetched: 1 row(s)
```

We can see that Sqoop has created a new table called `Person` in the default database of Hive. This table contains 100 rows imported from the MySQL database.

Engineering the solution

We will engineer the solution by breaking down the problem into several parts. In each part, we will perform a step to import or transform the data. Finally, we will bring everything together to create the view. To engineer the solution, we will use Sqoop to load customer master data from MySql RDBMS into Hive. We will use HDFS copy commands to load the Apache Access logs and tweets in Hadoop.

In the 360-degree view of the customer, we will combine the information from the following sources:

- Full name, gender, userID, and e-mail from customer master data as the data from the system of records
- Brand names frequently visited on Cosmetica's web shop as the data from web logs
- Tweets on certain topics as the social media data

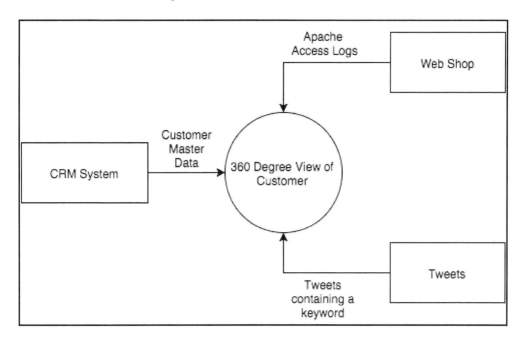

Figure 5 360-degree view combines data from various sources

You should bear in mind that we have taken a small set of data sources to create the 360-degree view. In practice, you should think of several data sources that can be used to build and enrich the 360-degree view of a customer. These data sources could be providing real-time location data from GPS sensors, or static and unstructured data such as e-mail archives in a company.

In our 360-degree view, we want to capture the following information:

- Full name of customer and gender
- User ID and E-mail address
- Recently visited brands on the web shop
- Relevant tweets
- Circle of influence

Datasets

In this example, we will use fabricated datasets, which have been generated with the help of data generation scripts. Getting access to good datasets, even in the trusted environments, is difficult, as a result of strict data governance and the politics of data.

Because we will be working with generated datasets, you should be aware of the limitations of such datasets. The data may look realistic but it is not real. It might contain certain discrepancies that may be obvious to a human observer, but not to a data generation program. You should also bear in mind that these datasets are miniscule by the standards of big data. The examples using these datasets demonstrate the technological capabilities of Hadoop and the solution-building approach.

We will now start loading the datasets from various sources into Hadoop.

Loading customer master data into Hadoop

Let's start setting up our MySQL database, which is the CRM database of Cosmetica Inc. This database was created when the company launched their loyalty program. Customers interested in joining the loyalty program registered themselves on a special campaign website. After successful registration, customers received a loyalty card, which was dispatched to their home address. During the loyalty card launch campaign, the initial customer data was captured and subsequently enriched with information available from other sources in the CRM system. The current customer master data table T_CUSTOMER consists of the columns shown in Figure 6.

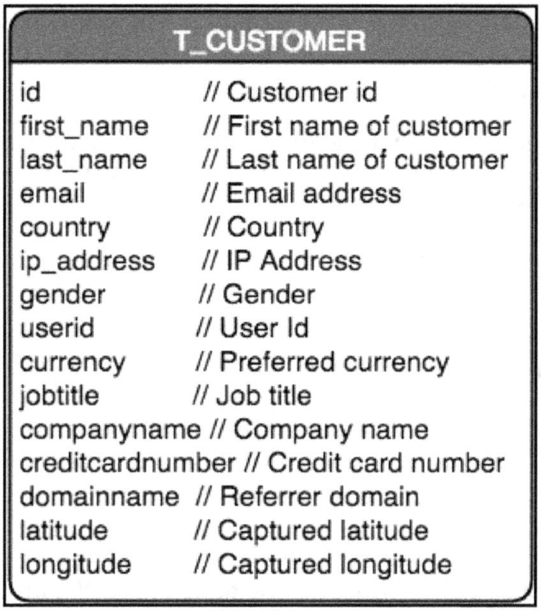

```
                    T_CUSTOMER
  id                  // Customer id
  first_name          // First name of customer
  last_name           // Last name of customer
  email               // Email address
  country             // Country
  ip_address          // IP Address
  gender              // Gender
  userid              // User Id
  currency            // Preferred currency
  jobtitle            // Job title
  companyname // Company name
  creditcardnumber // Credit card number
  domainname  // Referrer domain
  latitude            // Captured latitude
  longitude           // Captured longitude
```

Figure 6 Customer master data

You should download the following files:

- The t_customer.mysql file contains DDL for T_ CUSTOMER
- The t_customer_data.mysql file contains 1,000 customer master data records

Let's create the T_CUSTOMER table in MySQL and populate customer records after logging on to MySQL using the following commands:

```
mysql> use crm;
mysql> source t_customer.mysql
mysql> source t_customer_data.mysql
```

Note that we have already created a database called crm in MySQL, which stores customer master data and represents the database of our CRM system. After running the commands, check if the data has been imported correctly:

```
mysql> select count(*) from t_customer;
count(*)
1000
```

We will now import the data from the MySQL database into Hive using Sqoop. In Hive, we have already created a database known as `customer360` where we will build all the tables required for our 360-degree view:

```
$ sqoop import --connect jdbc:mysql://localhost:3306/crm --username root  -
-table t_customer  --hive-table customer360.t_customer --hive-import --
split-by id --direct
```

Note the following in the command line:

```
--hive-table customer360.t_customer
```

Target the database and table name in Hive:

```
--table t_customer
```

Source table in MySQL:

```
--split-by id
```

Split by row ID to distribute the values from the table across the mappers uniformly:

```
--direct
```

This uses a direct import fast path. This argument speeds up the import.

Loading web logs into Hadoop

We will first import the Apache Access logs in Hadoop. The access log contains the website visit log on a particular day within a small time window. You can download a file containing the access log `access_log_20151010-081346.log` here. Let's examine a single line in this log file to understand its structure:

```
173.216.153.220 - - [10/Oct/2015:08:22:50 ] "GET /Revlon HTTP/1.0" 200 4678
"http://www.google.com" "Mozilla/5.0 (Windows; U; MSIE 9.0; WIndows NT 9.0;
en-US))"
```

This file contains 10,000 lines. Each line signifies one HTTP request initiated by the client program when customers visit the Cosmetica web shop. Each row in this file has columns separated by a space and contains the following information:

Field 1	`173.216.153.220`	**IP Address of the Client**
Field 2	–	Not used
Field 3	–	Not used
Field 4	`[10/Oct/2015:08:22:50 ]`	Visit timestamp
Field 5	`"GET /Revlon HTTP/1.0"`	URL visited and protocol
Field 6	`200`	HTTP response code
Field 7	`4678`	Size of request
Field 8	`"http://www.google.com"`	Referrer URL
Field 9	`"Mozilla/5.0 (Windows; U; MSIE 9.0; WIndows NT 9.0; en-US))"`	Client program, operating system and locale.

This file contains much more data than we would need in building the 360-degree view so you might think that you should only import the information in Hadoop that you would need. However, by following the ELT paradigm, we will load all the access log data into Hadoop because, in the future, other use cases might require other data. The cost of storage on HDFS is low, which makes it a perfect candidate to store this type of data. Though this file is small, a web log of heavily visited websites can run into hundreds of gigabytes everyday.

To build a 360-view of the customer, only Field 1 and Field 5 are of relevance. All other fields can be ignored.

Let's make the following directory structure in HDFS:

```
$ hadoop fs -ls /hbp/chapt2/ex2
Found 2 items
drwxr-xr-x   - hduser hdfs          0 2015-10-10 07:40
/hbp/chapt2/ex2/apachelogs
drwxr-xr-x   - hduser hdfs          0 2015-10-10 10:15
/hbp/chapt2/ex2/tweets
```

I have already created two directories in HDFS as my directory listing shows. Let's copy the access log file `access_log_20151010-081346.log` in HDFS.

```
$ hadoop fs -copyFromLocal access_log_20151010-081346.log
/hbp/chapt2/ex2/apachelogs/
```

The file has been stored in HDFS, but Hive is not aware of the data schema of this file. We will define a table structure in Hive and link the access log file with it using the following command in Hive:

```
CREATE EXTERNAL TABLE t_accesslog (
            `ip`               STRING,
            `time_local`       STRING,
            `method`           STRING,
            `uri`              STRING,
            `protocol`         STRING,
            `status`           STRING,
            `bytes_sent`       STRING,
            `referer`          STRING,
            `useragent`        STRING
            )
    ROW FORMAT SERDE 'org.apache.hadoop.hive.contrib.serde2.RegexSerDe'
    WITH SERDEPROPERTIES (
    'input.regex'='^(\\S+) \\S+ \\S+ \\[([^\\[]+)\\] "(\\w+) (\\S+) (\\S+)"
(\\d+) (\\d+) "([^"]+)" "([^"]+)".*'
)
STORED AS TEXTFILE
LOCATION '/hbp/chapt2/ex2/apachelogs';
```

Let's examine the above DDL to create a table in Hive for the access log file:

```
CREATE EXTERNAL TABLE t_accesslog
```

Create a table `access_log` and tell Hive that the file for this table will not be managed by Hive. In other words, it is an external table:

```
`ip`               STRING,
`time_local`       STRING,
`method`           STRING,
`uri`              STRING,
`protocol`         STRING,
`status`           STRING,
`bytes_sent`       STRING,
`referer`          STRING,
`useragent`        STRING
```

This specifies the column names and column types in the table. We have defined all the columns of the type `STRING`. The definition of these columns is the same as in `Table 1`:

```
ROW FORMAT SERDE 'org.apache.hadoop.hive.contrib.serde2.RegexSerDe'
```

SerDe (Serializer, Deserializer) instructs Hive on how to process a record (Row). Hive enables semi-structured (XML, E-mail, and so on) or unstructured records (Audio, Video, and so on) to be processed also. In this case, we want Hive to process a file managed outside Hive as a table (external tables). SerDe, is a JAR file which Hive uses to translate data in files into records:

```
WITH SERDEPROPERTIES (
    'input.regex'='^(\\S+) \\S+ \\S+ \\[([^\\[]+)\\] "(\\w+) (\\S+) (\\S+)"
(\\d+) (\\d+) "([^"]+)" "([^"]+)".*'
)
```

Using SerDe, we read the data from a file stored on HDFS and then we use a regular expression to read the values of different fields, and map them with the columns in our table. This regular expression has been created using a web application available at http://rubular.com/:

```
STORED AS TEXTFILE
```

Here we specify that the access log file in HDFS is a text file:

```
LOCATION '/hbp/chapt2/ex2/apachelogs'
```

Here we specify the location of the directory in HDFS where our access log file is stored. Note that, if Hive finds data in the file that does not match the regular expression, then it will replace it with null values.

Now we are ready to run this command in Hive to create the t_accesslog table. After you have run this command successfully, let's examine the created table using the describe command:

```
hive> describe t_accesslog;
OK
ip                  string              from deserializer
time_local          string              from deserializer
method              string              from deserializer
uri                 string              from deserializer
protocol            string              from deserializer
status              string              from deserializer
bytes_sent          string              from deserializer
referer             string              from deserializer
useragent           string              from deserializer
Time taken: 1.195 seconds, Fetched: 9 row(s)
```

The `t_accesslog` table has been created. Let's count the rows in the table `t_accesslog` as follows:

```
hive> select count(*) from t_accesslog;
```

Let's select `ip` and `uri` from the table; these are the relevant columns for building the 360-degree view:

```
hive> select ip, uri from t_accesslog limit 5;
OK
181.3.249.130      /Store/cart.jsp?productID=1305
154.14.161.138 /Dior
179.203.132.160    /Gucci
20.149.200.80      /YSL
173.216.153.220    /Revlon
Time taken: 2.232 seconds, Fetched: 5 row(s)
```

Hive displays `ip` and `uri` from the table, confirming that we have successfully created an externally managed table in Hive.

So far, we have successfully created tables for customer master data and web logs. In the next section, we will import the tweets in HDFS.

Loading tweets into Hadoop

Cosmetica listens to all the tweets that contain the keyword "Fragrances." These tweets contain useful information about new product launches, special offers, and the tweets of users who like a certain fragrance product. The file `tweets01.json` contains all the tweets collected over a few days that contain the keyword *Fragrances* in them. We will load this file in HDFS, and then create a table in Hive to read these tweets using SQL queries.

Unlike Apache Access logs that we saw in previous sections, tweets come in the form of a nested data structure. Each tweet is a complete JSON document that contains not only the tweet text but much more information. *Figure 7* shows the Twitter website 's definition of a tweet.

Tweets

Tweets are the basic atomic building block of all things Twitter. Tweets, also known more generically as "status updates." Tweets can be embedded, replied to, favorited, unfavorited and deleted.

Brian Sutorius
@bsuto

♥ Follow

The "http://" at the beginning of URLs is a command to the browser. It stands for "head to this place:" followed by two laser-gun noises.

10:29 PM - 21 Feb 2012

↰   ⇄ 4,999   ★ 2,349

Figure 7 Twitter defines tweets

To build a 360-degree view of the customer, we are interested in the text contained in the tweet, the number of followers of a user, and the `screen_name` of the user where the tweet has originated. As discussed earlier, instead of importing the selected field out of this large JSON file, we will import the whole file in its raw format into HDFS.

If you are interested in knowing what a single JSON document representing a tweet contains then try the following command:

```
$ head -n 1 tweets01.json
```

This command will output one JSON document from the file. Now copy the output and paste it on a JSON formatter available at `http://jsonviewer.stack.hu/` . This will format the JSON document so that it is easier to read.

Let's copy the file `tweet01.json` into HDFS:

```
$ hadoop fs -copyFromLocal tweets01.json /hbp/chapt2/ex2/tweets/
```

In the next step, we will create the table definition in Hive:

```
CREATE EXTERNAL TABLE t_tweets (
   id BIGINT,
   created_at STRING,
   source STRING,
   favorited BOOLEAN,
   retweet_count INT,
   retweeted_status STRUCT<
      text:STRING,
      user:STRUCT<screen_name:STRING,name:STRING>>,
   entities STRUCT<
      urls:ARRAY<STRUCT<expanded_url:STRING>>,
      user_mentions:ARRAY<STRUCT<screen_name:STRING,name:STRING>>,
      hashtags:ARRAY<STRUCT<text:STRING>>>,
   text STRING,
   user STRUCT<
      screen_name:STRING,
      name:STRING,
      friends_count:INT,
      followers_count:INT,
      statuses_count:INT,
      verified:BOOLEAN,
      utc_offset:STRING,
      time_zone:STRING>,
   in_reply_to_screen_name STRING,
   year int,
   month int,
   day int,
   hour int
)
ROW FORMAT SERDE 'org.openx.data.jsonserde.JsonSerDe'
STORED AS TEXTFILE
LOCATION '/hbp/chapt2/ex2/tweets';
```

With the command shown earlier, we will create an external table named `t_tweets` in Hive. Note that we are using a JSON SerDe, which is not included in HDP 2.3. You can find the source code of this SerDe and its documentation on Github at `https://github.com/rcongiu/Hive-JSON-Serde`.

You will notice that, in the `create` table statement, we have defined the nested structures that will hold the nested data in the file. Consider the following fragment:

```
retweeted_status STRUCT<
   text:STRING,
   user:STRUCT<screen_name:STRING,name:STRING>>
```

This fragment defined a structure, which contains another structure in it.

Before creating the table in Hive, we need the SerDe JAR file, which is not included in HDP 2.3, as follows:

```
wget
http://www.congiu.net/hive-json-serde/1.3.6/hdp23/json-serde-1.3.6-jar-with
-dependencies.jar
```

Now we will add the JAR in Hive:

```
hive> ADD JAR json-serde-1.3.6-jar-with-dependencies.jar;
```

`user` is a SQL11-reserved word in Hive. To avoid conflict with our column name that `user`, we set the support for reserved keywords to false:

```
hive> set hive.support.sql11.reserved.keywords=false;
```

Let's run the create table command in Hive and then check the definition of the `t_tweets` table:

```
hive> describe t_tweets;
OK
id                      bigint              from deserializer
created_at              string              from deserializer
source                  string              from deserializer
favorited               boolean             from deserializer
retweet_count           int                 from deserializer
retweeted_status
struct<text:string,user:struct<screen_name:string,name:string>>    from
deserializer
entities
struct<urls:array<struct<expanded_url:string>>,user_mentions:array<struct<s
creen_name:string,name:string>>,hashtags:array<struct<text:string>>>    from
deserializer
text                    string              from deserializer
user
struct<screen_name:string,name:string,friends_count:int,followers_count:int
,statuses_count:int,verified:boolean,utc_offset:string,time_zone:string>
from deserializer
in_reply_to_screen_name string                 from deserializer
year                    int                 from deserializer
month                   int                 from deserializer
day                     int                 from deserializer
hour                    int                 from deserializer
Time taken: 1.148 seconds, Fetched: 14 row(s)
```

After the creation of the table, we can query the data contained in the tweets using regular SQL:

```
hive> select id, text, user.screen_name from t_tweets limit 2;
OK
652790148464119800    One Direction - "Between Us" Fragrance Commercial HD
http://t.co/OV7RqHhx39   nmfnh_
652790269184618500    RT @realinsan_deep: @Gurmeetramrahim Fragrance of
@MSGTheFilm is spreading all over the World...tym4 Celebration.. Coz..
#MSG2Crossed270 .....    3beantgill
```

Note that we have retrieved the value contained in the structure by specifying the full name `user.screen_name` of the element contained in the structure.

Creating the 360-degree view

In the previous sections, we have imported raw data in HDFS and created tables in Hive to query the data using SQL statements. Now we will first find the relevant information in the tables, and then join them to retrieve the information.

First, we want to find out which brands most users are visiting on the Cosmetica web shop. We will query the table `t_accesslogs` to fetch this information:

```
hive> select count(*) b, ip, regexp_extract(uri, '[a-zA-Z]+',0) from
t_accesslog a where uri not like '%prod%' group by ip, uri order by ip, b
desc limit 5;
```

In the SQL query, we have used a few new elements as follows:

```
regexp_extract(uri, '[a-zA-Z]+',0)
```

In our table, the `uri` column contains a / prefix. With the help of a regular expression, we remove the / from the output of the SQL query:

```
where uri not like '%prod%'
```

Using this expression, we exclude the URIs from the output of the select statement that refers to individual products. We are only interested in finding out which brand pages have been visited by users.

After the successful execution of the query, your output should look similar to the following:

```
98 129.205.99.233 Gucci
98 129.205.99.233 Revlon
97 129.205.99.233 Dior
95 129.205.99.233 YSL
91 129.205.99.233 Bvlgari
```

Here, the first column is the number of visits, the second column is the IP address of the visitor, and the third column is the brand name visited by the user.

Let's store the output of this query in another table using the following command:

```
hive> CREATE  TABLE t_brandvisits  as select count(*) cnt, ip,
regexp_extract(uri, '[a-zA-Z]+',0) brand from t_accesslog a where uri not
like '%prod%' group by ip, uri order by ip, cnt desc;
```

This command creates a new table named t_brandvisits, which contains the data that we need in our 360-degree view.

To build a customer 360-degree view, we should find ways to join various datasets on the basis of common keys. The selection of keys depends upon the problem we are trying to solve, and the joining patterns present in the data.

In this case, the customer master data contains an IP address that has been used by the customer when he/she registered for a loyalty program. We can use the IP address as the key to joining customer master data with the access logs. Keep in mind that in this case, while we have used an IP key to join the two tables, the same user can access the website from a different network. In this case, the IP address for the same user will be different. So, we will have to find another method to identify the user correctly.

The following query joins the tables t_customer and t_accesslog to create the first part of the 360-degree view:

```
select first_name, last_name, gender, email, userid, brand, cnt from
t_customer as c, t_brandvisits as b where c.ip_address = b.ip order by
userid, cnt desc;
```

We can store this view in the new table called t_custbrandvisits:

```
CREATE  TABLE t_custbrandvisits  as select first_name, last_name, gender,
email, userid, brand, cnt from t_customer as c, t_brandvisits as b where
c.ip_address = b.ip order by userid, cnt desc;
```

Using the following command, we will extract the tweet text and follower count for the customers of Cosmetica by joining the `screen_name` in the tweet with the `userid`:

```
create table t_usertweets as select distinct text as tweettext,
b.user.screen_name as userid, b.user.followers_count as followercnt from
tweets as b, t_custbrandvisits as a where b.user.screen_name=a.userid sort
by userid;
```

Note that we have assumed that the Twitter screen name of the user is same as his `userid` in our table `t_customers`. Connecting tweets with customers in some other situations will require you to find a suitable criterion to match the tweets with your customer records.

So far we have used Hadoop and Hive extensively to store and transform data. Our datasets are small. In real life, large datasets will require a multimode Hadoop cluster.

Exporting data from Hadoop

Once the customer 360-degree view has been created, it will be integrated into a web application used by the call center people. Hadoop is not a suitable platform for the type of fast interactive queries that web applications require.

We will export the tables containing the 360-degree view to a MySQL database, which is being used as the backend for the web application in use in the call center. We will use Sqoop to export the data from the Hive database to MySQL.

Note that Sqoop does not create the table definition in MySQL when data is exported from Hive to MySQL. Therefore, we will create the tables in MySQL before we can run Sqoop to export data from Hive to MySql.

We are interested in exporting two tables from Hive to MySQL. The first table is `t_custbrandvisits,` which contains the basic data about customers from the customer master data, and the number of visits on the brand pages. The second table is called `t_usertweets` and contains customer tweets that are relevant for Cosmetica.

Create a new database on the MySQL server called customer360. Note that in real life this database can reside in a different instance of the MySql server or in some other RDBMS. In this database, we will create the tables required to hold the customer 360-degree view information. Now use the newly created database and run the following SQL statements:

```
create table t_custbrandvisits(
first_name              varchar(30),
last_name               varchar(30),
gender                  varchar(1),
email                   varchar(40),
userid                  varchar(30),
brand                   varchar(30),
cnt                     bigint
)


create table t_usertweets(
tweettext               varchar(140),
userid                  varchar(30),
followercnt             int
);
```

The preceding two statements will create the tables required by Sqoop to store the data exported from Hive. Run the following commands to export the tables from Hive to MySQL. After the successful execution of the following commands, please run select queries on the tables to verify if they contain data exported from Hive:

```
sqoop export --connect jdbc:mysql://localhost/customer360  --username root
--table t_custbrandvisits --direct --export-dir
/apps/hive/warehouse/customer360.db/t_custbrandvisits --fields-terminated-
by  '\001'


sqoop export --connect jdbc:mysql://localhost/customer360  --username root
--table t_usertweets --direct --export-dir
/apps/hive/warehouse/customer360.db/t_usertweets --fields-terminated-by
'\001'
```

Let's examine the new command line arguments in the Sqoop export commands you have used just now:

```
--export-dir /apps/hive/warehouse/customer360.db/t_usertweets
```

Using the argument-export-dir, we specify where the directory containing the data of the exported table is located in the HDFS. You can use the SQL statement define formatted t_usertweets to find the location of the HDFS directory of a table stored in Hive:

```
--fields-terminated-by '\001'
```

Using the arguments --fields-terminated-by, we specify the field separator used in our table in Hive. In the Sqoop export commands shown earlier, we have used \001' as the separator, which is the default in Hive.

In this section, we have imported data into MySQL. In the next section, we will present this data using a web application in the browser.

Presenting the view

After extracting, loading, and transforming the data in the HDFS data warehouse, and loading it onto the customer360 database in MySQL, we will present it using a web interface.

MySQL is a popular database suitable for fast interactive queries. It can perfectly serve as the backend database for web applications. When you create a 360-degree view, you might have to integrate it into an existing web application, or build a new application to present your 360-degree to the users. In this section, we will cover building an elementary web application, which can display the 360-degree view.

In order to build the web application, we assume that we get the user ID as the input field that will be used to query the customer360 database. This user ID is the same as the user ID stored in t_customers. Using this user ID, we will present the brand names visited by the user and his latest tweets. Note that we do not have the web access log for all the users present in the customer master. Similarly, we do not have tweets from all the users in our tweet logs. So far, only those user IDs for which data is available will show up in our 360-degree customer view.

Building a web application

You can build a simple web application using many programming languages such as Java, PHP, Perl, JavaScript, and .NET. In this example, we will use Node.js, which is a server-side JavaScript engine.

As discussed earlier, the 360-degree view of the customer will contain the following information:

- Full name of customer and gender
- User ID and e-mail address
- Recently visited brands on the web shop
- Relevant tweets
- Circle of influence

> We have taken a simple Node.js program as an example to illustrate how the 360-degree web application might work. You can learn more about Node.js at `http://nodeschool.io/`.

Installing Node.js

We will first install Node.js in our Hadoop Sandbox. We will use the **EPEL** (**Extra Packages for Enterprise Linux**) repository, which is available for CentOS and related distributions.

Log on as `hduser` in Sandbox and run the following commands:

```
$ sudo yum install epel-release
```

You now have access to the EPEL repository. You will install Node.js now, using the regular `yum` commands:

```
$ sudo yum install nodejs
```

```
$ sudo yum install npm
```

Note that NPM is the package manager for NodeJS. Using `npm` you can download the Node packages from the NPM repository.

You can verify a successful installation of Node.js and NPM as follows:

```
$ node --version
v0.10.36

$ npm -version
1.3.6
```

Coding the web application in Node.js

The code of our web application is based upon Express, which is a web application
framework on the top of Node.js. We will also use the MySQL driver to connect from our
web server with MySQL:

```
var express = require("express");
var mysql = require('mysql');
var url = require('url');
var connection = mysql.createConnection({
    host: 'localhost',
    user: 'root',
    password: '',
    database: 'customer360'
});

var app = express();
```

We include the packages that are required in this program, create an instance of the connect
object, and create an instance of the Express application as shown in the preceding block.

```
connection.connect(function(err) {
    if (!err) {
        console.log("Database is connected ... \n\n");
    } else {
        console.log("Error connecting database ... \n\n");
    }
});
```

We make an attempt to connect with the MySQL database. We log on to the console
whether the connection is successful or has failed, as shown in the preceding block.

```
app.get("/", function(req, res) {
    res.setHeader('Content-Type', 'text/html');
    res.writeHead(200);
res.write("<h2>Get Customer 360 degree View</h2>")
    res.write("<form action="fetch" method="get">");
    res.write("Enter Customer Id  <input type="text" name="userid">");
    res.write("<input type="submit" value="Submit">");
    res.end("</form>");
});
```

Here, we define the first route of the web application (which displays a form, as shown in *Figure 8)* to input the user ID, and submit it to the server using the **Submit** button.

Get Customer 360 degree View

Enter Customer Id [   ] Submit

Figure 8 Get Customer 360 degree View Web Form

The following part of our code will be used when the form is submitted to fetch the customer 360-degree data from the MySQL database:

```
app.get("/fetch", function(req, res) {
    var url = require('url');
    var queryData = url.parse(req.url, true).query;

    var sqlQuery = "SELECT * from  t_custbrandvisits where userid='" +
                    queryData.userid.trim() + "'";
    console.log(sqlQuery);
```

The route /fetch is called when the form shown in *Figure 8* is submitted to the web server. We extract the userid from the URL submitted to the route /fetch:

```
connection.query(sqlQuery, function(err, results) {
    res.setHeader('Content-Type', 'text/html');
    res.writeHead(200);
    if (results.length > 0) {

        res.write("<table border="1" style="width:80%">");
        res.write("<tr><th colspan="2">Customer 360 Degree View
        </th></tr>");
        res.write("<tr><th colspan="2">");
        res.write("User ID: " + results[0].userid +
            " User Name: " + results[0].first_name + " "
            + results[0].last_name +
            " Gender: " + results[0].gender +
            " Email: " + results[0].email);
        res.write("</th></tr>");

        for (var i = 0; i < results.length; i++) {
```

```
            res.write("<tr><td>");
            res.write(results[i].brand);
            res.write("</td><td>");
            res.write("Visits: " + results[i].cnt);
            res.write("</td></tr>");
        }
        res.write("</table>");

    } else {
        res.write('No matching brand data for ' + queryData.custid.trim());
    }

    var sqlQuery = "SELECT * from  t_usertweets where userid='" +
        queryData.userid.trim() + "' order by followercnt desc";

    console.log(sqlQuery);

    connection.query(sqlQuery, function(err, results) {

        if (results.length > 0) {

            res.write("<table border=\"1\" style=\"width:80%\">");
            res.write("<tr><th>Latest Tweets from Customer</th></tr>");
            res.write("<tr><th>");
            res.write("Followers: " + results[0].followercnt);
```

The preceding code fragment runs two select statements. First, the select statement retrieves the customer data and the web shop visit data from the `t_custbrandvisits` table. The second select statement retrieves the tweets and followers count, for the selected customer, from the table `t_usertweets`. It presents the output in a tabular format on a web page.

The following code is an example of applying a business rule during the 360-degree view presentation. An example of such a rule is that, when a customer has more than 1,000 followers, he/she or should be treated as a VIP customer:

```
    if (results[0].followercnt > 1000) res.write("VIP Customer");
```

Here we will print the tweets for the user; if no tweets are found then we will output text to say that no matching tweets are present in the database:

```
    res.write("</th></tr>");

    for (var i = 0; i < results.length; i++) {

        res.write("<tr><td>");
        res.write(results[i].tweettext);
        res.write("</td></tr>");
```

```
    }
    res.write("</table>");

} else {
    res.write('No matching tweet data for ' + queryData.userid.trim()
    + '<BR>');
    }
res.end("");
});

    if (err) {
        console.log('Error while performing Query.');
    }
});

});
```

The route /end will be used to terminate the connection to the MySQL database before
exiting the web application. Note that in this application you will have to restart the web
application server because we have not implemented reconnection logic in the code:

```
app.get("/end", function(req, res) {
    res.setHeader('Content-Type', 'text/html');
    res.writeHead(200);
    res.end("Session Ended");
    connection.end();
});
```

The Express application will start listening on port 3000 for incoming HTTP connections:

```
app.listen(3000);
console.log("Started the web server on port 3000");
```

You should now understand how this program has been set up. We will now install two
node modules that this program depends upon:

```
$npm install mysql express
```

Let's run this program as follows:

```
$node cust360webapp.js
Started the web server on port 3000
Database is connected ...
```

Now open your browser. Type the IP address and port number in the address bar, and see this program in action. I am running this program on my local machine so the starting URL is `http://localhost:3000`.

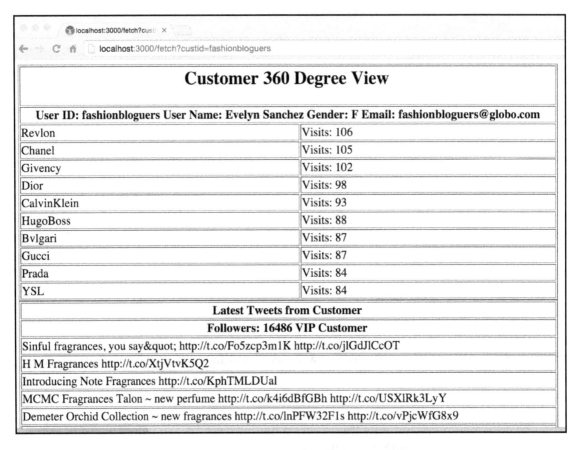

Figure 9 Customer 360-degree view

The web application covered in this section is a simple example we have used to clarify the concepts involved; it should not be used in a production environment. A well-designed web application should take care of security separately from concerns about its look and feel. These topics are beyond the scope of this book.

Summary

In this chapter, we started with basic understanding of a customer 360-degree view and how it can be useful. We explored tools such as Hive and Sqoop. We worked with MySQL and HDFS to extract, load, and transform data. We used structured data, web logs, and tweets to build our customer 360-degree view. We performed batch processing on various datasets that contribute to building the 360-degree view.

In this chapter, we carried out extract, load, and transform (ELT) tasks manually. This will not be practical in a real-life situation. With the help of schedulers and workflow tools, we can automate ELT tasks and build a data pipeline.

3

Building a Fraud Detection System

For fraud detection in financial systems, several commercial solutions are available on the market. However, Hadoop and its ecosystems of tools offer the opportunity to build a fraud detection system that can supplement existing fraud detection systems and lower their operational costs by downloading certain fraud detection tasks to Hadoop.

In this chapter, we have chosen Hadoop and Spark to build a simple fraud detection system. The following steps will be involved in building this solution:

1. Selecting and cleansing the dataset.
2. Designing the high-level architecture.
3. Creating the fraud detection model.
4. Putting the model to use.

You will learn how to build a machine learning model using Spark and Hadoop with the help of available datasets. You will use this model and Spark streaming to detect anomalies in real time that might be caused by fraudulent transactions.

In the upcoming sections of this chapter, we will cover how to build a basic fraud detection system by following the preceding steps.

Understanding the business problem

We will build a fraud detection system for a bank using Hadoop and Spark. The fraud detection system will predict whether a payment transaction is a suspect transaction. If such a suspicious transaction is detected, then the payment processing system can step up security and ask for more information from the account holder before the transaction can be processed. In our definition of a transaction, we will the cover payments made by a retail banking customer from his checking account to other parties. These payments can take place using a variety of modes, as follows:

- Using Internet banking to transfer money to another account
- Via swiping a card at a shop to pay for goods or services
- Payment for goods on an e-commerce site
- Direct debits for bill payment
- Cash withdrawal using an ATM card

Every mode of payment offers fraudsters the opportunity to indulge in fraudulent activities. These activities can take place by stealing the IDs, bank cards, and PINs to conduct unauthorized transactions without the knowledge of the legal user. For example, overall losses on UK cards from fraud totaled £479m in 2014, up 6% on 2013, according to Financial Fraud Action.

Therefore, fraud detection is always the highest priority in the financial sector to reduce financial losses and safeguard the credibility of institutions in the eyes of their customers.

Selecting and cleansing the dataset

We have selected the transaction history from a customer account as our dataset, which we will use to build the model for fraud detection. A large bank can have millions of customers. The historical transaction data of these customers can be used to build models that are unique for each customer, based upon his spending patterns.

We will start with the last 3 years of transaction history. Let's take a look at a single transaction to understand the information captured in it:

```
Datum;Naam / Omschrijving;Rekening;Tegenrekening;Code;AfBij;Bedrag
(EUR);MutatieSoort;Mededelingen

20151022;ZIGGO SERVICES
BV;NL54INGB07XXX32XXX;NL98INGB0000845745;IC;Af;52,5;Incasso;Europese
Incasso, doorlopend IBAN: NL98INGB0000845745 BIC: INGBNL2A Naam: ZIGGO
```

```
SERVICES BV ID begunstigde: NL30ZZZ333034790000 SEPA ID machtiging:
0007882554001011120090000000941 Kenmerk: 030176416129000 Omschrijving:
270934155
```

The preceding listing contains information about a single SEPA direct debit transaction. In this case, a TV company located in The Netherlands, Ziggo Services BV, has charged their customer EUR 52.50 using a direct debit. A line represents one complete transaction, in which the fields are separated by semicolons. This transaction data contains significant information about the transaction, which we can use to build our fraud detection system. However, not all the information is useful to build our model. The information contained in the transaction is not in the right format so it will require cleansing and transformation before we can use it to build our model.

Table 1 shows the meaning of various fields and their meanings in English. The last column in the table, **Relevance**, tells us whether this field is relevant from our perspective of building the model:

Field name	Contents	Relevance
Date (Datum)	20151022	Yes
Name/Description (Naam / Omschrijving)	ZIGGO SERVICES BV	No
From Account Number (Rekening)	NL54INGB07XXX32XXX	No
To Account Number (Tegenrekening)	NL98INGB0000845745	No
Code	IC	Yes
Debit Credit (AfBij)	Af	No
Amount (Bedrag) (EUR)	52,5	Yes
Type of Mutation (MutatieSoort)	Incasso	No
Comments (Mededelingen)	EuropeseIncasso, doorlopend IBAN: NL98INGB0000845745 BIC: INGBNL2A Naam: ZIGGO SERVICES BV ID begunstigde: NL30ZZZ333034790000 SEPA ID machtiging: 0007882554001011120090000000941 Kenmerk: 030176416129000 Omschrijving: 270934155	No

Table 1 Analyzing the fields in a banking transaction record

Finding relevant fields

We should understand why we have selected certain fields while excluding others. In real-life situations, too, you might encounter data that might not be directly relevant from the perspective of building a model.

We have considered date-relevant data because, generally, the expenses of individuals are cyclic in nature. These cycles repeat on a weekly, monthly, or yearly basis.

We are only interested in debits because they mean a loss to the customer if the transaction is fraudulent. We do not consider credits to customers' accounts as relevant data because they do not mean a loss to the customer. We exclude the comments field as it can contain long, unstructured text. We also exclude the name and account number of the party where the money has been sent as irrelevant. All the transactions in our dataset belong to a single account. We do not use this field for analysis.

After excluding various fields, the following list shows which fields we will use for building our model for fraud detection:

- Date
- Code
- Amount

In the following example, we have filtered out non-required data from the original transaction data. We have also filtered out the fields that do not change in our dataset:

Date	Code	Debit (Af)/Credit	Amount
20151030	BA	Af	9
20151030	BA	Af	54
20151029	IC	Af	188
20151029	IC	Af	135
20151028	BA	Af	12
20151026	BA	Af	7
20151026	BA	Af	27

Each transaction record contains a transaction code. The possible codes and what they indicate in the transaction record are as follows:

- **BA**: Payment at POS terminal
- **IC**: Direct debit
- **GM**: ATM cash withdrawal
- **DV**: Fee charged by the bank
- **OV**: Transfer from current account to own savings account
- **GT**: Transfer to third party using internet banking

Machine learning for fraud detection

Fraud detection is a machine learning problem wherein we use historical data to build a model, which we will use to predict the outcome for future situations.

With the help of our cleaned historical transaction data, we will build a fraud detection model. To build the fraud detection model, we will apply the concepts of machine learning. A definition of machine learning is as follows:

> *"A computer program is said to learn from experience E with respect to some task T and some performance measure P, if its performance on T, as measured by P, improves with experience E."*

> *–Tom Mitchell, Carnegie Mellon University*

Please note that the detailed explanation of machine learning is beyond the scope of this book.

If you are interested in learning more about machine learning, go to `http://www.r-bloggers.com/in-depth-introduction-to-machine-learn ing-in-15-hours-of-expert-videos/`, where you will find some excellent material on this topic.

We will briefly cover those machine learning topics that are essential to understanding our solution.

Machine learning methods work with historical data, which they learn from. The learning involves the detection of patterns that might be helpful in predicting future behavior. Machine learning methods can be classified into two distinct categories, known as **supervised learning methods** and **unsupervised learning methods**.

In supervised machine learning, we know the data and outcomes from the past. We use this information to "train" the model so that it can predict the outcome in the future. For example, in a large dataset containing bank customer profile data, we might know who has accepted an offer for a premium credit card product. We can use a supervised machine learning model built with this data to predict whether a new customer is likely to accept an offer for the same premium credit card product.

In unsupervised machine learning, we have the data but we do not know what we are looking for. This may happen when we just explore the data with experimental analytics to understand the patterns and relationship. For example, from a dataset, we might want to discover which two products are generally bought together on an e-commerce site. Unsupervised machine learning can also be used for customer segmentation when very few common attributes are known in a large customer dataset.

We will apply an unsupervised machine learning method to detect anomalies in our historical transaction data. These anomalies will give us a signal that a new transaction deviates from the regular transaction patterns of the user. This anomaly could be caused by a fraudulent transaction.

Once an anomaly has been detected, we can verify, with the help of the customer, whether the suspicious transaction has been authorized by them. If the customer has not authorized the transaction, then it is indeed a fraudulent transaction and the bank should take action to stop the transaction.

We have selected the unsupervised machine learning method because, in the historical transaction dataset, we do not have any fraudulent transactions. Unsupervised machine learning methods are used when we want to discover patterns in data when we do not know much about what we are looking for. Using unsupervised machine learning, we will detect anomalous transactions in the data, which will give us a hint that a transaction is suspicious. A suspicious transaction might still be a valid transaction but this can only be determined if we put additional questions to the customer.

For example, if a customer spends $25,000 on a single day to pay an individual, then this might be a suspicious transaction. But if we know that the customer has bought a car on that day, then we know that the transaction is not suspicious.

Clustering as an unsupervised machine learning method

Clustering is the most commonly used unsupervised machine learning method. It finds applications in the biomedical, insurance, and financial sectors when we want to discover patterns in large datasets. These datasets can contain millions of rows and hundreds of columns or dimensions. Clustering itself is not a single algorithm. We have several algorithms available to cluster our data.

The selection of an appropriate clustering algorithm falls in the domain of data science and may involve several iterations with different algorithms to create an appropriate model that works.

We will use the K-Means clustering algorithm for anomaly detection in our transactions. K-Means is a common algorithm implemented in the most popular programming languages, such as Java, Scala, Python, R, and JavaScript. In addition, other machine learning tools and frameworks, such as Spark, RapidMiner, BigML, and SAS, offer support for K-Means clustering. Refer to *A Tutorial on Clustering Algorithms, 2015* for a detailed introduction to K-means.

Designing the high-level architecture

The high-level architecture of the system that we are planning to build contains two parts. The first part is the model, which we will build using the historical transaction data. Once this model has been created, we will use it in the second part with new data to determine whether a particular transaction falls in a cluster of suspicious transactions.

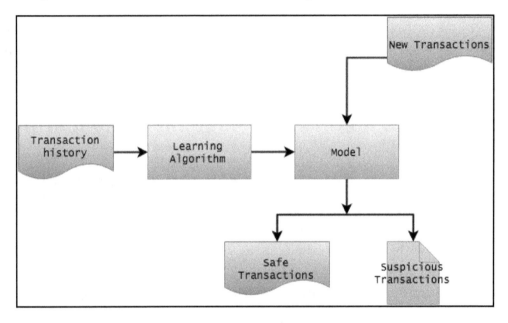

Figure 1 Design of a fraud detection system

In the previous section, we have already cleansed the transaction history file to make it suitable for the machine learning algorithm. For building the model, we will use Apache Spark.

Introducing Apache Spark

Apache Spark is an open source, big data processing framework, developed in 2009 in UC Berkeley's AMPLab. It has been developed around the goals of delivering speed, ease of use, and sophisticated analytics.

It was open sourced in 2010 as an Apache project and it has now become one of the most active projects among Apache Software Foundation projects. The Apache Spark framework is intended to perform large-scale data processing on a cluster of computers like MapReduce. MapReduce jobs on Hadoop are essentially batch processes that process data in multiple stages. Each stage involves disk I/O because the intermediate results have to be written on the disk.

Apache Spark does the data processing in memory. This means that, once data has been loaded in the memory, all the processing can be done in the memory and only when the processing is complete will the data be written on the disk. By limiting the disk I/O to the start and end stages, Apache Spark is able to deliver much better performance than Hadoop MapReduce:

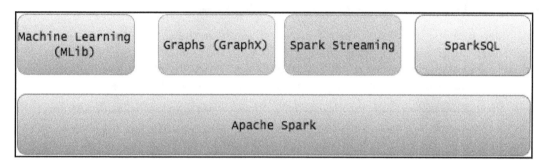

Figure 2 Apache Spark

Spark supports a variety of datasets, such as text datasets and graph datasets, and it supports both batch and real-time streaming data. We can write Spark applications in Java, Scala, R, or Python. MLib, included in Spark, offers support for several machine learning algorithms. MLib is also part of the Apache Spark project so it gets updated with each new release of Spark from Apache Software Foundation. The machine learning algorithms included in MLib support classification, regression, recommendations, and clustering. We will use K-means implementation in MLib to build our fraud detection model. Spark comes with a built-in set of over 80 high-level operators to perform transformations on the datasets.

Spark also offers an interactive query shell, which can be used to perform various operations on data without the need for program compilation before execution. *Figure 1* shows the components of Spark.

Apache Spark architecture

When an application is running on a Spark cluster, then the following three components are used for execution:

- Driver program
- Worker nodes—executor
- Worker nodes—executor Cluster manager

The driver program coordinates the execution on various nodes of the cluster. Worker nodes actually perform computations and run on the nodes of the Spark cluster with the help of executor tasks. They receive tasks from the driver program and execute them. The executor also handles the memory and cache for the worker.

The cluster manager handles all the resources available on the cluster. During the execution of the driver program, first a connection is made with the cluster manager and then it requests the available executors on the worker nodes. When the resources have been allocated by the cluster manager, the execution starts on the worker nodes:

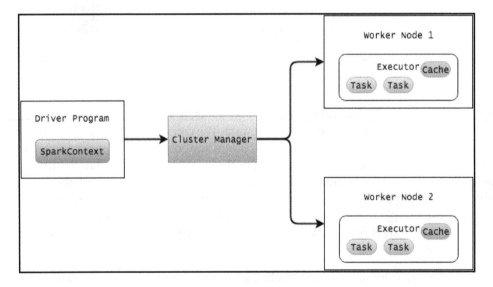

Figure 3 Apache Spark execution model

Spark acquires the executor process but it does not care about the underlying details of the cluster manager. Spark can make use of the cluster manager shipped with the Spark distribution but it can also make use of Hadoop YARN as the cluster manager.

Resilient Distributed Datasets

Spark is based upon in-memory data representation of datasets known as **Resilient Distributed Datasets (RDDs)**. RDDs are collections of data distributed across the cluster of computers. On RDDs, operations can be done in parallel. RDDs can hold any type of data. RDDs are immutable collections of data objects. This means RDDs, once created, cannot be changed or updated. When RDDs are transformed by carrying out some operation, such as a group by or average operation, then a new RDD is created while the original RDD remains unchanged.

The concept of immutability implies that Spark does not have any function that can alter the contents of an RDD. The benefit of immutability is that all the RDDs can always be evaluated for their original value with zero likelihood that, by a programming error or by intention, they will be overwritten.

RDDs are distributed data structures which support two kinds of operation on them using Spark functions. These operations are transformation and action. You will see later in this chapter that, using these operations, we can write useful programs to process data using Spark.

Transformation functions

A transformation function operates on an RDD and creates a new RDD as the result of it. A newly created transformed RDD will contain the new values. These new values may contain fewer values as a result of filtering out the values from the original RDD. It may also contain new values, which might be the result of the calculations applied to the original dataset.

Transformation functions in Spark are map, filter, flatMap, groupByKey, reduceByKey, aggregateByKey, repartition, pipe, and coalesce, (Spark, 2015) to name but a few.

Actions

Actions are functions that operate on RDDs. For example, an action on an RDD can count the number of rows contained and return it in a variable. Using an action, an RDD can be read from a file in the memory or persisted on a file from the memory. The key difference between an action and a transformation is that the former returns a single value when applied to an RDD while the latter returns a new RDD. Spark includes actions such as account, collect, take, saveAsTextFile, and first. (Spark, 2015).

Test driving Apache Spark

You can download Spark from `https://spark.apache.org/downloads.html`. Choose the prebuilt version for Hadoop 2.6 or later.

Untar and unzip the download file on a directory on your system. In this example, we will start the Python shell for Spark. We will use the Python language throughout the chapter to explain the solution. A basic Python knowledge should be sufficient to understand the solution:

```
[tdeshpande2@link-instance-1 bin]$ ./pyspark
Python 2.7.5 (default, Nov 20 2015, 02:00:19)
[GCC 4.8.5 20150623 (Red Hat 4.8.5-4)] on linux2
Type "help", "copyright", "credits" or "license" for more information.
Using Spark's default log4j profile: org/apache/spark/log4j-defaults.properties
Setting default log level to "WARN".
To adjust logging level use sc.setLogLevel(newLevel).
16/09/14 05:37:23 WARN NativeCodeLoader: Unable to load native-hadoop library for your platform... using builtin-java classes where applicable
Welcome to

      ____              __
     / __/__  ___ _____/ /__
    _\ \/ _ \/ _ `/ __/  '_/
   /__ / .__/\_,_/_/ /_/\_\   version 2.0.0
      /_/

Using Python version 2.7.5 (default, Nov 20 2015 02:00:19)
SparkSession available as 'spark'.
>>>
```

Figure 4 PySpark command line shell

As shown in *Figure 4*, we have started Spark using the PySpark script. The prompt >>> indicates that the interactive Spark shell is ready to accept commands from the user.

Calculating the yearly average stock prices using Spark

We will now use the dataset containing the daily stock price for IBM to calculate the yearly average using Spark. You have already used this dataset in Chapter 1, *Hadoop and Big Data,* and Chapter 2, *A 360-Degree View of the Customer*. You might recall that this dataset contains the daily stock price of IBM, starting from 1962. The file containing the dataset is called `ibm-stock.csv` and it is located in the directory where we started the Spark shell. The Spark shell is an interactive command interpreter that you can use to experiment with Spark.

You can enter each step described here in the Spark shell. The steps to calculate the average stock price are as follows:

```
>>>csvFile = "ibm-stock.csv"
```

First, we start the Spark interactive shell using the script `pyspark` and specify the name of the file containing the data:

```
>>>stockData = sc.textFile(csvFile)
```

In the statement above, `sc` stands for SparkContext. It is the main entry point for Spark functionality. SparkContext is used to invoke Spark functions. You can think of SparkContext somewhat like an object that has a connection reference to a Spark cluster. You can create initial RDDs from the files saved on disk using SparkContext and thereafter apply the transformations on them to create new RDDs.

We have used SparkContext to create an RDD, `stockdata`, for our file `ibm-stock.csv` using the above statement:

```
>>> pair = stockData.map(lambda x:(x.split("-")[0], x.split(",")[1]))
```

Now we use our RDD `stockdata` and transform it into another RDD using the `map` function. In the transformation process, we will extract the year and the first value after the comma as the stock price, which we will use to create the averages. The new RDD is called pair:

```
>>>sumCount = pair.combineByKey(lambda value: (value, 1), lambda x, value:
(float(x[0]) + float(value), x[1] + 1),lambda x, y: (x[0] + y[0], x[1] +
y[1]))
```

Using the preceding statement, we have created another RDD using the `combineByKey` function. This function uses the year as the key and then creates tuples that contain the sum of stock prices and their count for the particular key. This transformation creates a new RDD `sumCount`:

```
>>>averageByKey = sumCount.map(lambda (label, (value_sum, count)): (label,
value_sum / count))
```

Using the preceding statement, we calculate the average stock prices with the help of the map function, which creates another RDD known as `averageByKey`. Now that we have applied all the transformations to our data, we can print the final RDD to see the results using the following statement:

```
>>>averageByKey.sortByKey().collect();
```

You will notice that we are able to get the same results with Spark as we did using Hive and MapReduce in the previous chapters. In this example, we created an RDD using a text file stored on our local filesystem. However, Spark can also read files from HDFS and process them. In addition, Spark also supports other types of data source, such as Amazon S3, HBase, Hive, and MongoDB. Currently, Spark APIs are available in Scala, Java, and Python, while APIs in other languages are likely to be made available by the open source community or commercial software vendors. Spark can run on a standalone cluster of computers dedicated for Spark only but it can also run on Hadoop clusters, where YARN plays the key role in resource and job management.

Apache Spark is a large topic in itself. A detailed discussion of Spark is beyond the scope of this book. You can visit the Spark website `http://spark.apache.org/` to read about Spark or refer to the several books available on this topic.

Apache Spark 2.X

With the latest release of Spark 2.X, Spark has undergone significant changes in the way it computes and the way it operates. Spark introduced Structured Streaming, a declarative API that extends DataFrames and DataSet, to provide an easy programming model. With Spark 2.0, we will see the DataFrames and DataSet APIs being combined into one to make the developer's life easy.

Spark 2.X substantially improved SQL functionalities. Now it supports the SQL 2003 standard. It also has an improved parser, which parses ANSI SQL and Hive QL easily.

In terms of MLib, the RDD based API is entering maintenance mode and Data Frames API would be the primary one.

It is of course backward compatible with older versions of Spark.

Understanding MLib

MLlib is the scalable machine learning library available in the Spark toolset. It provides the implementation of machine learning algorithms and utilities. Algorithms such as classification, regression, clustering, collaborative filtering, and dimensionality reduction are included in MLib. MLlib can operate on local vectors and matrices stored on a single machine.

It also possible to process the distributed matrices residing on several machines backed by one or more RDDs using MLib. Local vectors and local matrices are simpler data models as compared to RDDs. MLlib is under active development. The solutions covered in this book have been developed on version 1.5.1 of MLib.

Spark is a comprehensive distributed data processing framework with good support for machine learning without the need for another external library. MLib makes machine learning algorithms scalable and easy to program. Spark works with immutable distributed datasets (RDDs), which can used as input to the common machine learning algorithms provided in MLib, such as classification, regression, clustering, and collaborative filtering. The solutions covered in this book have been developed on version 1.5.1 of MLib. MLib is rapidly evolving as a result of great interest in Spark by the open source community.

We will not cover all the features of MLib in this book but only those machine learning algorithms that are required to build our solution.

For our fraud detection system, we are planning to use the MLib implementation of the clustering algorithm K-means. Clustering is an unsupervised learning problem whereby we aim to group subsets of entities with one another based on some notion of similarity.

Test driving K-means using MLib

Clustering is the process of grouping several data points on the basis of some similarity. K-means algorithm is a widely used algorithm used for clustering data points. The input of the K-means algorithm should be an NxM dimensional array and the number of clusters we want to create. The K-means algorithm finds the centroids of these clusters. The nearest cluster centroid for a data point indicates which cluster that data point belongs to. Once we have found the cluster centroids, then for each new data point we can determine in which cluster it falls.

The process of clustering is hard to visualize for an NxM dimensional array, however it can be easily understood with a two dimensional dataset. For a two-dimensional array containing x,y coordinates, clustering using K-means is shown in *Figure 5*:

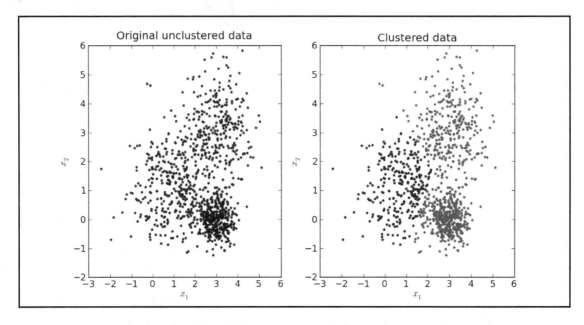

Figure 5 Clustering two-dimensional points in three clusters (Image source: http://pypr.sourceforge.net/_images/kmeans_2d.png)

MLlib comes with a parallel version of k-means++, known as k-means parallel. K-means is an iterative algorithm, therefore it is well suited for an in-memory framework such as Spark because the data from intermediate stages of iterations does not have to be written to the disk.

According to the Spark documentation available at `http://spark.apache.org/docs/latest/mllib-clustering.html`, the K-means implementation in MLlib accepts the following parameters:

- *k* is the number of desired clusters.
- *maxIterations* is the maximum number of iterations to run.
- *initializationMode* specifies either random initialization or initialization via k-means parallel.
- *runs* is the number of times to run the k-means algorithm (k-means is not guaranteed to find a globally optimal solution, and when run multiple times on a given dataset, the algorithm returns the best clustering result).
- *initializationSteps* determines the number of steps in the k-means|| algorithm.

- *epsilon* determines the distance threshold within which we consider k-means to have converged.
- *initialModel* is an optional set of cluster centers used for initialization. If this parameter is supplied, only one run is performed.

We will do clustering using K-means on a simple dataset contained in the file `stocks.csv` to test drive Spark. The structure of this dataset is as follows:

```
Microsoft, 91259, 60420, 54.19
IBM, 400000, 98787, 138.54
Skype, 700, 716, 28
SAP, 48000, 11567, 74.85
Yahoo!, 14000 , 6426 , 33.11
eBay, 15000, 8700, 29.06
```

In this CSV file, the first field is the name of company followed by the number of employees, revenue in million USD, and stock price in USD at some point in time. We will process this file using Spark and create clusters using K-means.

We start the Spark shell using the `pyspark` command. After we use the command line prompt >>> then run the following statements one by one:

```
>>> from pyspark.mllib.clustering import KMeans, KMeansModel
>>> from numpy import array
```

The preceding statement will import the required libraries for K-means.

```
>>> stocks = sc.textFile("stocks.csv")
```

We create a new RDD named stocks from the `stocks.csv` file using the preceding statement.

```
>>> data = stocks.map(lambda line: line.split(",", 1))
```

We transform stocks into a new RDD to split the company name because it cannot be used in the clustering.

```
>>>parsedData = data.map(lambda line: array([float(x) for x in
line[1].split(',')]))
```

We separate the number of employees, revenue, and stock price in an RDD array. Also, we convert the data from a Unicode string to float so that the K-Means algorithm can process it. Conversion from a string is essential because the K-Means algorithm can only process numbers.

```
>>> c = 2
```

We specify that we want to create two clusters and we will use this as a parameter in the train function in the next step.

```
>>> clusters = KMeans.train(parsedData, c)
```

We train the model using parsedData and specify the number of clusters we want to build.

```
>>>clusters.clusterCenters
[array([ 33791.8 , 17565.8 ,    43.842]), array([ 4.00000000e+05,
9.87870000e+04,   1.38540000e+02])]
```

The preceding statement shows that K-means has created two clusters and their centroids are shown in the two arrays returned.

You have now got an idea of how MLib works. Let us apply these principles in the next sections to build our fraud detection model.

Creating our fraud detection model

HDFS is a system designed for storing massive volumes of data. In our case, we start with the 3-year banking transaction history of a fictitious customer of a bank. Our dataset includes 2,191 transactions that have resulted in the transfer of money from the customer's account to other accounts. These transactions happened using a variety of methods, such as payments at a POS terminal, direct debits, transfers from internet banking, and so on. The result of these transactions is that money leaves the account of the customer and gets credited to another account. All the times, the customer's bank wants to ensure that the money only leaves the account of the customer when the customer has authorized it. Otherwise, a transaction is a fraudulent transaction and it must be stopped.

Storing and processing 2,191 records might seem a trivial task from the point of view of HDFS and Spark. However, if a bank has 10 million customers, then to build a fraud model for each customer, we will have to crunch 2,191 * 10,000,000 = 21,910,000,000 records. As the number of records to be crunched becomes huge, the cluster computing of Spark comes to our aid.

Spark comes with support to process streaming data. In our fraud detection system, we will be "listening" to a stream of incoming transactions and determining whether a transaction in the stream is a fraudulent transaction.

Building our K-means clustering model

Our fraud detection model will be based upon K-means clustering. We will take our historical transaction data and create two clusters. We expect that when we group data in two clusters then transactions that do not fit regular spending patterns will be segregated from the regular ones. We will consider these transactions to be anomalous transactions or suspicious transactions. Please keep in mind in this chapter that we are not attempting to build a perfect fraud detection model from the perspective of a data scientist but demonstrating how such a solution can be implemented using Hadoop and Spark.

Once our model is ready, we will check each new transaction against our model to determine in which cluster the new transaction falls. If a new transaction falls in the cluster where the majority of transactions are present, then we will consider it a normal transaction; otherwise, we will consider it as a suspicious transaction that requires further investigation.

In our approach, we will build our model once but we will not update it every time a new transaction is tested with our model. We expect that the model will be retrained at certain intervals but not in real time as we analyze the transactions.

Processing the data

Let's open the file containing the transaction history `INGB01.csv` and examine its contents:

```
$ head INGB01.csv
5,BA,Af,9
5,BA,Af,54
4,IC,Af,188
4,IC,Af,135
3,BA,Af,12
1,BA,Af,7
1,BA,Af,27
```

In order to hide privacy-sensitive information, we have already removed the fields that are not of direct importance to us. Also, we have calculated the day of the week of the transaction from the date of the transaction and converted it into a number, where 1 stands for Monday, 2 stands for Tuesday, and so on.

Let's load this transaction history file on HDFS:

```
$bin/hdfsdfs -put ~/INGB01.csv /hbp/chapt3/
$bin/hdfsdfs -ls /hbp/chapt3
Found 1 items
-rw-r--r--   1 hdusersupergroup    24084 2015-11-26 21:22
/hbp/chapt3/INGB01.csv
```

We have loaded this file on Hadoop. In the next step, we will use it to build the model using Spark.

Run the `transmodel.py` program on your computer using the `spark-submit` command:

```
$ spark-submit /Users/anurag/hdproject/eclipse/chapt3/transmodel.py

[array([  2.57129757,   1.83218707, 334.16827144]), array([  2.70000000e+00,
5.40000000e+00,   4.76395000e+04])]
```

If this program runs successfully, you will see a directory named `kmeansmodel01` in your local directory, which contains the model. The array shown in the output shows the centroids of two clusters created by K-means as follows:

- Cluster 0[2.57129757, 1.83218707, 334.16827144]
- Cluster 1 [2.70000000e+00, 5.40000000e+00, 4.76395000e+04] or [2.7, 5.4, 47639.5]

We will assume that if a transaction falls in cluster 0 then it is not a suspicious transaction and if it falls in cluster 1 then it is a suspicious transaction. A transaction falling in cluster 1 will require further investigation.

 You can also run the `transmodel.py` program using the Python command-line interpreter `pyspark`. In that case, you will execute each line separately. This will help you display the contents of RDDs using the `collect()` function and do some more experimentation.

Let's now examine the contents of the program `transmodel.py`:

```
from pyspark.mllib.clustering import KMeans, KMeansModel
from pyspark import SparkContext
from pyspark import SparkConf
```

We start by importing the required Python libraries. In this case, `KMeans` and `KMeansModel` are the MLib libraries that provide support for KMeans clustering.

```
defpaymentCode(code):
   if code == "BA":
     return 1
elif code == "IC":
     return 2
elif code == "GM":
     return 3
elif code == "DV":
     return 4
elif code == "OV":
     return 5
```

```
elif code == "GT":
    return 6
```

The payment Code function converts the two-letter transaction code into a numeric value. The KMeans algorithm requires numeric values to build the cluster.

```
conf = SparkConf().setAppName("model-kmeans")
```

Here, we create the Spark configuration and specify the name of the application.

```
conf = conf.setMaster("local[2]")
```

With this property, we set how many threads Spark is going to use in parallel to process our data.

```
sc = SparkContext(conf=conf)
```

We set the configuration in SparkContext.

```
f1 = sc.textFile("hdfs://192.168.2.103:9000/hbp/chapt3/INGB01.csv")
```

We now create our first f1 RDD by using the file ING01.csv, which is stored in HDFS. Note that, by adding hdfs://192.168.2.103/ in the file path, we have specified that our file is stored on HDFS.

```
f2 = f1.map(lambda line : [ x for x in line.split(",")])
```

We transform the f1 RDD using the map function and get the f2 RDD. We have used a comma (,) as the field delimiter.

```
f3 = f2.map(lambda line : [ line[0], paymentCode(line[1]),line[3]])
```

We transform the f2 RDD using the map function into a new f3 RDD. The lambda function extracts the following fields in the new f3 RDD:

- line[0] is the day of the week
- paymentCode(line[1]) converts the code into a numeric value
- line[3] is the amount debited

Note that we have ignored the field `line[2]`, which contains the same `Af` string in the entire dataset and therefore does not contribute to `KMeans` clustering.

```
#Create two clusters
clusters = KMeans.train(f3, 2)
print clusters.clusterCenters
```

We use the `f3` RDD to create two clusters using the `KMeans.train` function.

```
clusters.save(sc, "kmeansmodel01")
```

Using `clusters.save`, we save the clusters on the local filesystem, so that we can use our model later.

Spark properties should be configured for each application that runs on a Spark cluster. These properties define the application name and master URL in SparkConf but also other arbitrary properties with the key=value convention using the `set()` method. SparkConf is passed to SparkContext. When we set `local[2]` using the `setMaster` method then we configure two threads running in parallel. Using a minimum of two threads, we can run our program using the parallel processing features of Spark.

During the model building process, we have done several transformations on our original data as shown in *Figure 6*. But this time, instead of relying upon the batch processing model used by Hive or MapReduce, we have done all the transformations in the memory using Spark. This gives Spark a huge advantage over Hadoop. Machine learning algorithms are iterative in nature and therefore they are well suited for the in-memory computing model of Spark instead of the batch analytics paradigm used by Hadoop.

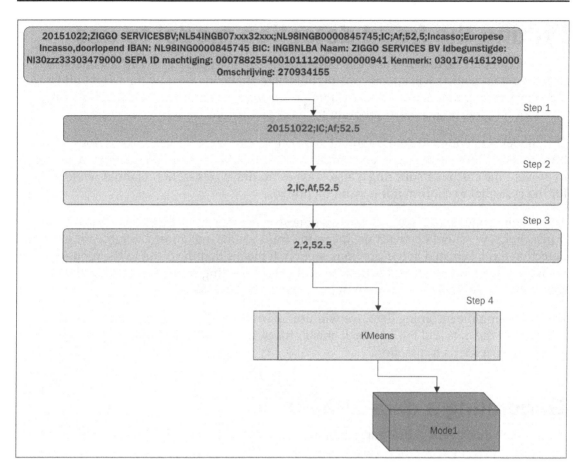

Figure 6 Transforming data to build the KMeans model

Now our model is ready and stored in the directory, we will use it to do real-time fraud detection.

Putting the fraud detection model to use

A model can only be useful when it is put into operation. Typically, a data scientist or a team of data scientists will spend considerable time analyzing the raw data and build a machine learning model from it. Once a model is ready, it can be used on a web portal, workflow engine, or in a batch program to make predictions.

Our model is intended to detect anomalies in transaction data signaling suspicious transactions. Once we detect an anomalous transaction then we can take several measures to prevent the customer suffering a loss, such as putting a transaction on hold while waiting for the customer to confirm if it is valid by phone.

To put this model to use, we will create a data stream that simulates incoming real-time transactions. We should convert the incoming transactions into a form suitable for our fraud detection model created in the previous section. It means that the input to the model should be in the form 1, 3, 75, where 1 is the day of the week starting from Monday, 3 is the transaction code, and 75 is the amount involved in the transaction.

For processing the incoming data, we will use Spark streaming. The streaming processor will receive the data and tell us which cluster it belongs to. Any data falling in cluster 1 will point to a suspicious transaction.

Generating a data stream

To simulate the stream of incoming data, we will use the nc (or netcat) utility. This utility can read data from stdin or a file and send it to a TCP port. We can run the nc command as follows:

```
$ nc -lk 9999
1,3,75
```

You can stop an nc session by pressing *Ctrl* + *Z*. In the preceding example, 1,3,75 is the transaction data that we want to test to see whether it is suspicious.

To generate a constant stream of data, we will use a simple shell script called
`transstream.sh`:

```
#!/bin/bash
while [ true ]
do
echo 1 2 $RANDOM
sleep 1
done
```

This script generates 1, 2, and a random number which is between 0 and 32,767 at intervals
of 1 second. We use the output of this script to pipe to our `nc` command as follows:

```
$./transstream.sh | nc -lk 8999
```

Our script is now generating a stream of data on port 8999. We will now run a program that
will read this data stream and detect a suspicious transactions based upon our model.

Processing the data stream using Spark streaming

To process our data stream (also known as data in motion or the v as in velocity of 3 V's of
big data), we will use Spark streaming. In the Hadoop ecosystem, several tools, such as
Apache Storm and Apache Flink, are available to process incoming streams of data to
perform analytics on them. We have chosen Spark streaming in this case because it offers
one consistent programming model for building the models and then using them in the
operational process.

The key difference between streaming and working with static data is that Spark uses a
discretized stream (DStream), which represents a continuous sequence of RDDs. You can
stream a never-ending flow of data points, processed by Spark as data is received (for
example, a second feed of stock prices that we can use to create a moving average of stock
prices over the last hour with the help of Spark streaming).

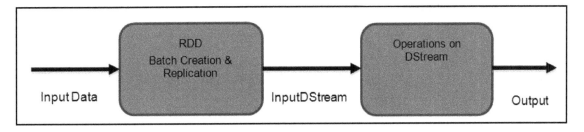

Figure 7 depicts the steps involved in Spark stream processing. When Spark receives a stream of data then it first creates a batch for a set of data points in an immutable RDD. This RDD is passed as a DStream input upon which the operations can be performed.

Run the following program using the `spark-submit` command:

```
$ spark-submit/Users/anurag/hdproject/eclipse/chapt3/transfrauddetect.py
(DenseVector([2.5713, 1.8322, 334.1683]), DenseVector([2.7, 5.4, 47639.5]))
************************* Loaded the model *********************
RDD -> 0
RDD -> 1
[[1.0, 2.0, 8900.0]]
Cluster -> 0 [1.0,2.0,8900.0]
RDD -> 1
[[2.0, 5.0, 76000.0]]
Cluster -> 1 [2.0,5.0,76000.0]
RDD -> 1
[[3.0, 4.0, 6788.0]]
Cluster -> 0 [3.0,4.0,6788.0]
```

The output of the program shows for each transaction whether it falls in cluster 1 or cluster 0. If a transaction falls in cluster 1 then it is a suspicious transaction. Note that our model is based upon the transaction history of one customer. If we build our K-means model with the transaction history of another customer with very different spending patterns, then cluster 0 and 1 will have different centroids. This means that a transaction could be suspicious for one customer but for another customer it may be just okay even if the day, code, and amount of the transactions are identical.

Let's now examine this program in detail.

```
from pyspark import SparkContext
from pyspark import SparkConf
from pyspark.mllib.clustering import KMeans, KMeansModel
from pyspark.streaming import StreamingContext
from pyspark.mllib.linalg import Vectors
```

Here, we import the libraries required for our program. Note that we have imported `StreamingContext` in this program to support streaming RDDs.

```
# Create a local StreamingContext with two working threads and batch
interval of 10 seconds

conf = SparkConf().setAppName("Fraud Detector")
conf = conf.setMaster("local[2]")
```

We create the configuration by setting the app name and specify that there will be two working threads for processing.

```
sc = SparkContext(conf=conf)
```

We set the configuration in SparkContext.

```
ssc = StreamingContext(sc, 1)
```

We create a Spark streaming context.

```
# Create a DStream that will connect to hostname:port, like localhost:8999

lines = ssc.socketTextStream("localhost", 8999)
```

We create a new socket to read the text stream (Dstream) from localhost port number 8999.

```
# Split each line into words

model = KMeansModel.load(sc, "kmeansmodel01")
print model.clusterCenters
```

We load our model from the directory kmeansmodel01, where we stored our KMeans model.

```
print "********* Loaded the model ***********"

def detect(rdd):
  count = rdd.count()
  print "RDD -> ", count
```

First, we count the number of elements in our RDD so that we can loop through them and check if any of the elements is a suspicious transaction.

```
if count > 0:
    arrays = rdd.map(lambda line: [float(x) for x in line.split(" ")])

print arrays.collect()
```

We create a new RDD that contains an array of three fields that we require as input to our model.

```
indx = 0
    while indx< count:
vec = Vectors.dense(arrays.collect()[indx])
```

We convert each element in RDD arrays into a dense vector to make it suitable for processing by our model.

```
clusternum = model.predict(vec)
indx += 1
```

We call the `predict` function using our model. The predict person return the index of cluster our transaction belongs to.

```
    print "Cluster ->", clusternum, vec
      return
lines.foreachRDD(detect)
```

For each RDD that we receive through the stream, we call the `detect` function, which detects whether a transaction is suspicious.

```
ssc.start()          # Start the computation
ssc.awaitTermination() # Wait for the computation to terminate
```

Note that we have built the model based upon the transaction history of one customer. In real situations, multiple models may be involved in detecting a suspicious transaction.

Putting the model to use

We have demonstrated how to build the core of a real-time fraud detection system with the help of Hadoop and Spark. A full-fledged real-time fraud detection system will have many more components, which need to be integrated to build a usable solution.

Figure 8 shows you an extended version of the fraud detection system. The parts shown in dashed lines indicate the components that should be the part of a full solution. For example, a customer can do a transaction using one of many channels available to him. As these transactions happen, the data will be received in real time. This data will be converted using the appropriate processing logic so that it is suitable for consumption by our fraud detection model. Once the data has been converted, it will be streamed to our model for further processing.

At the time of writing this book, Spark 1.5.2 streaming Python API supports several streaming sources. Spark can ingest data streams from many sources, such as Kafka, Flume, Twitter, ZeroMQ, Kinesis, or TCP sockets. After ingestion, the data stream can be processed using complex algorithms expressed with high-level functions such as map, reduce, join, and window and machine learning algorithms can be applied to it.

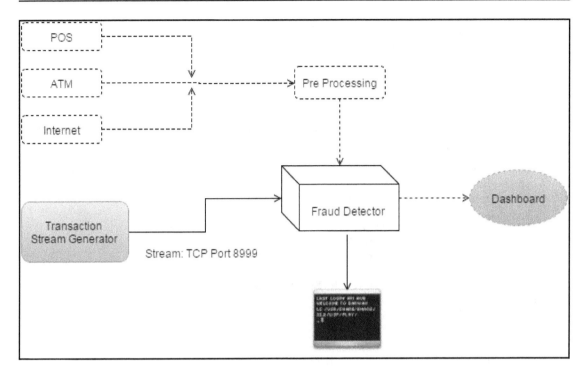

Figure 8 Putting the model to use

In our example, we have displayed the output of our fraud detector in the terminal window. However, in a fully-fledged fraud detection system, the processed data can be pushed out to file systems, databases, and live dashboards for the benefit of users.

Scaling the solution

In a production scenario, we expect that massive volumes of data will be processed to build the model. Real-time processing of transactions will require a Spark configuration that can cope with the demands of real-time processing.

Spark provides two deployment modes that can be used to run Spark jobs on YARN. In yarn-cluster mode, the Spark driver runs inside an application master process, which is managed by YARN on the cluster, and the client can terminate after initiating the application when the job is handed over to the Hadoop cluster.

In YARN-client mode, the driver runs in the client process. The application master is only used for negotiating resources from YARN.

The `spark-submit` script is used to launch applications on a cluster. We have used this script already when we built our model and ran our fraud detection script. It can use all of Spark's supported cluster managers through a uniform interface so you don't have to configure your application specially for each one.

In this chapter, we have run the programs in Spark local mode. However, these programs can also be run on YARN and on a Spark standalone cluster to take advantage of parallel computing. The following commands illustrate how it should be done:

```
# Run application locally on 8 cores
$ spark-submit --master local[8]
/Users/anurag/hdproject/eclipse/chapt3/transmodel.py

# Run on a Spark standalone cluster in client deploy mode
$ spark-submit --master spark://spar:7077
/Users/anurag/hdproject/eclipse/chapt3/transmodel.py

# Run on a YARN cluster in YARN client mode
export YARN_CONF_DIR=/Users/anurag/Java/hadoop-2.7.1/etc/hadoop
$ spark-submit --master yarn-client
/Users/anurag/hdproject/eclipse/chapt3/transmodel.py
```

Note that it is possible to run Spark programs in YARN-cluster mode but it is not supported for Python yet. You can find more information about submitting Spark jobs at `http://spark.apache.org/docs/latest/cluster-overview.html` and `http://spark.apache.org/docs/latest/submitting-applications.html`.

Summary

In this chapter, we started with the key concepts behind a machine learning-based fraud detection system. We learned about Spark and how it can be a complementary technology for Hadoop. Using historical transaction data, we created our fraud detection model. We simulated a transaction stream and then processed it to detect suspicious transactions. After exploring our clustering-based solution for fraud detection with Spark and Hadoop, we will build a marketing campaign management system using Hadoop in the next chapter.

4
Marketing Campaign Planning

In this chapter, we will cover batch analytics using Hadoop. Traditional marketing campaigns which involve direct mailing to the entire customer base are an expensive project for companies. A marketer does not know in advance who is going to respond to a marketing campaign. Generally, the response to a campaign is considered in the form of an action that we expect the recipient to take as the outcome of a campaign. If a campaign fails to evoke the expected or desired response then it is not considered a successful campaign.

In this chapter, we will use Hadoop to perform batch analytics on a customer database to increase the likelihood of customer response in a marketing campaign. We will follow the following steps towards building the solution:

- Understanding of classification as a supervised learning method
- Building a machine learning model using historical response data
- Using the machine learning model in a MapReduce job to generate a list of customers who are likely to respond to our offer

Let us consider a fictional furniture company known as Furnitica. Furnitica has large stores all over the country. Every month, they publish a furniture folder, which is sent to all of the customers in the country. A color furniture folder costs 4 USD a piece and the cost of delivery to the doorstep of each addressee is 1 USD. For a customer base of 5 million, the cost of folder-based marketing is 25 USD million.

The high costs of folder-based marketing has become a crucial talking point in the board meetings of the company and therefore the marketing team has to cut down the cost of folder based marketing while keeping the response the same. To cut down the cost, several options are being explored, such as reducing the printing and distribution cost, and applying predictive analytics to run a smart marketing campaign by targeting the right folder to the right customer.

The marketing team turns to the IT department of the company to find a smart solution to solve the problem of the high cost of marketing.

Creating the solution outline

Let us assume that at this moment we know nothing about who will respond to our marketing folders. In traditional marketing, we can provide discount coupons in the campaign folders with a barcode as a means to uniquely identify a customer. When a customer presents a discount coupon during the purchase then we know that the customer has responded to our marketing campaign. We can join the barcode on the discount coupon with the customer master data available in the company to find out who has responded to our campaign.

We will solve the problem of Furnitica using classification. Classification is a supervised learning method which uses historical data and past outcomes to predict future outcomes.

As an example, for a credit card company, the historical credit card approval data is shown in *Table 1*:

Gender	Age	Owns a House	Owns a Car	Annual Salary in EUR	Result
M	23	N	N	24000	Not Approved
F	35	Y	N	55000	Approved
M	40	Y	Y	52000	Approved
M	34	N	Y	59000	Approved
F	41	Y	Y	56000	Not Approved

Table 1 Sample credit card approval data

In the dataset shown in *Table 1*, we see five features or attributes of the people who have applied for a credit card. In the rightmost column, we see the credit car approval result. The column result itself is the outcome, which indicates whether an applicant was approved to own a credit card. The column, result, is also called the target variable in machine learning literature.

We will use binary classification in our solution. Given a dataset, the binary classification method can tell us if the outcome is 0 or 1. 0 and 1 can represent two mutually exclusive values, such as whether a credit card has been approved or not approved.

Supervised learning

In `Chapter 3`, *Building a Fraud Detection System*, we built a fraud detection model using clustering, which is an unsupervised learning method.

In this chapter, we can see a difference between supervised and unsupervised machine more clearly. In the case of credit card approval data, we have a clearly defined target variable, the result. We are only interested in the value of this target variable for new customers. The historical card approval data may be captured from a manual or automated card approval process.

You should keep in mind when a supervised learning method predicts the value of the target variable, it can never be 100% certain about the outcome. The process of building the model produces a model which provides a probabilistic estimate for the outcome for the data which has not been seen previously or the future data.

Supervised learning has two distinct steps. In the first step, we build the model by mining the historical data. Once the model is ready, it can be deployed in an operational process. The operational process feeds the model with new data for which we want to predict the outcome. The model predicts the outcome as well the probability estimate for the outcome.

Once a model has been put to use in the operational process, we can use the future outcomes to retrain the model.

Tree-structure models for classification

When we build our model, we have to find the informative attributes or the features contained in our data. A feature that never changes in our data set is not a very informative attribute. Some features will be more informative and they will influence the outcome more than the others. In other words, we can say that such features provide more information gain than the others. Once we have identified the features providing the information and sorted them in order of information gain, we can arrange them in the form of an inverted tree to create our model. The leaf nodes of the tree denote the outcome. Other nodes denote the features or attributes that provide information gain to reach the final outcome.

In the tree-based learning approach, we recursively divide the historical data. During the training of the model, various dividing criteria will be tried. If a feature has a non-numeric value then it is converted into binary. A classification tree can also be represented using if then else criteria as illustrated in *Figure 1*:

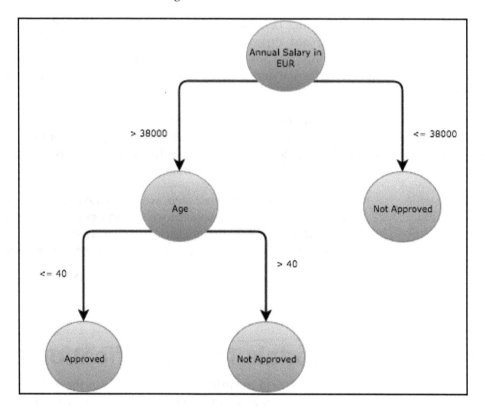

Figure 1 A classification tree

The preceding tree can be converted into a JavaScript-based function as follows:

```javascript
function predictResult(age, annualSalaryInEur) {

if (annualSalaryInEur > 38000) {
        if (age == null) {
            return "Approved";
        }
        else if (age > 40) {
            return "Not Approved";
        }
        else if (age <= 40) {
            return "Approved";
```

```
            }
        }

    else if (annualSalaryInEur <= 38000) {
            return "Not Approved";
        }

    }
```

We can pass the value of age and annual salary in EUR to our function to get the outcome predicted by our model.

In our folder-based marketing example, the outcome of the model is a binary value to indicate whether or not a person has responded to our catalog marketing offer.We will train the classifier using the historical data which will be used to predict the outcome of the campaign in the future.

Detailed discussion of tree-based classification is beyond the scope of this book. You can learn more about underlying theory and concepts of classification in Data Science for Business, Provost & Fawcett, 2013.

Finding the right dataset

We need a good historical dataset to build our model. We will mine this dataset to build our model. To continue with the example to our fictitious company, Furnitica, we will use historical campaign response data from a previous campaign run by Furnitica.

This is synthetic data, which means it has been synthesized using a random data generation algorithm. A few sample rows in our dataset are presented in *Table 2*:

Age	Income	Gender	Folder	Response
61	30974	0	1	0
42	38260	0	3	0
40	20135	0	4	0
88	30645	0	5	0
58	38078	1	3	0
73	20445	0	4	0
34	66198	0	3	0

65	48657	0	2	0
68	39309	0	1	0

Table 2 Sample credit card approval data

This dataset is generated from the response data of a campaign after joining it with the data in the customer relationship management system of the company. In the dataset preparation step, we have removed several features which are not directly useful in building our model. As a result, our dataset contains the following fields:

- **Age**: Age of the person to whom our folder has been mailed.
- **Income**: Annual income of the person based upon data available in the CRM system of Furnitica.
- **Gender**: 0 stands for male and 1 stands for female.
- **Folder**: 1 – 5, depending on the folder type received by a person. Furnitica has five types of folders with different colors and presentations. Each number represents a folder type.
- **Response**: This is the target variable. If a customer has responded to a specific folder by buying some stuff from Furnitica then this column is 1, otherwise it is 0.

We have provided this dataset, which is 15 MB in size, with this book. It contains a total of 1 million rows, which we will use to build our model.

Setting the up the solution architecture

The solution architecture for the marketing campaign system is essentially based on a batch process in which several enterprise information systems will participate. The solution has been described in Figure 2. The solution architecture can be divided into two major building blocks as follows:

- **Building the model**: Building the model involves preparing the historical data and using it to build the model. It rarely happens that the historical data is clean enough for consumption by our model-building algorithms. Therefore, building the model also involves the preparation of data beforehand.
- **Scoring**: The scoring process takes the new data for which we want to predict the outcome as input and predicts the value of the outcome. Scoring will tell us whether a person is likely to respond to a folder or not. Therefore, we can send the folders only to those who have a high likelihood of responding to our campaign. This will give us the opportunity to save the cost of folder printing and dispatching.

Let us examine the components of our solution architecture one by one as shown in *Figure 2*:

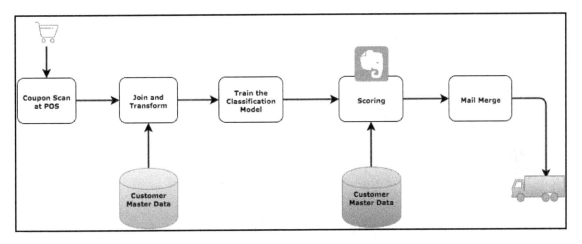

Figure 2 Solution architecture

Coupon scan at POS

A customer of Furnitica may present a coupon from the campaign folder during checkout at a payment counter in a Furnitica store. This coupon entitles the customer to get a discount. The coupon carries a barcode which is unique for each customer who received the campaign folder.

The cashier at the checkout counter scans the barcode. The resulting code is stored in a database which will be used later to prepare our historical dataset. Barcode scanning hardware and software are typically capable of handling this process.

Join and transform

The customer master data may contain much more information, such as address, past purchases, e-mail address, credit card numbers, and so on. In the join and transform step, we will filter out the fields which are not relevant to build the model. By joining the POS barcode presentation data with the customer master data where we have kept a record of all unique barcodes and the customers they have been sent to, we can find out who has responded to our campaign folder. We will calculate the age of the customer from his or her date of birth and extract other information such as income and gender. We will add the response column, where 0 will indicate that the customer has responded. 1 will indicate that the customer has not responded. Typically, the join and transform operations will be done using ETL tools. These tools can be Hadoop-based, such as Hive or Pig, or traditional RDBMS-based SQL tools.

Train the classification model

After the historical data has been prepared, we will use it to train our classification model. For training the classification model, we have several choices of tools available, such as Spark, Weka, R, BigML, and Mahout. In this chapter, we will introduce and use a tool called BigML to build our classification model.

Our classification model will be a decision tree similar to that discussed at the beginning of this chapter. However, the complexity of our model will be much more because a large dataset will be used to train it. Our tree will contain many more decision paths than we saw in our small dataset that contained the credit card approval history.

Scoring

The scoring process is responsible for generating the predictions for the input dataset. The output of the scoring process is the value of the target variable response. The response variable 1 implies that this customer is likely to respond to our campaign folder, which will result in sale of goods from a Furnitica store.

The scoring process is a compute-intensive activity. However, for a large number of records, the compute-intensive nature of scoring can also be time-consuming. We will apply MapReduce processing in Hadoop to perform scoring so that we can do scoring for a large number of records faster by taking advantage of the parallel processing offered by Hadoop.

Mail merge

After scoring has been completed, we will know which customer is going to receive our campaign folder. We will pass on this information to the printing department of Furnitica. They will print the campaign folders with barcoded coupons, and address and dispatch them to customers of Furnitica.

Once the campaign folders have been dispatched then we can expect that some customers will start presenting them in the Furnitica showrooms.

Building the machine learning model

We will start building a machine learning model with the help of historical data now with the help of BigML.

Introducing BigML

BigML is a web-based tool to build machine learning models from datasets. BigML has several advantages over other machine learning languages such as R and tools such as RapidMiner, such as:

- No local software installation is required. BigML is a web-based tool.
- Data processing is done in the cloud, which means you do not have to invest in expensive servers for building the models.
- No need to learn a new programming language to build models. BigML is a UI-driven tool.

Model building steps

We will go through six simple steps to build a machine learning model as follows:

1. Register as a user on the BigML site.
2. Upload the data file.
3. Create the dataset with the help of the data file.
4. Build the classification model using the dataset.
5. Download the classification model.
6. Run the model using MapReduce on Hadoop for scoring.

We will now explain these steps.

Sign up as a user on BigML site

You can sign up on the BigML website by visiting `https://bigml.com`. Once you have an account on BigML ready and you log in then you will see the page shown in *Figure 3*:

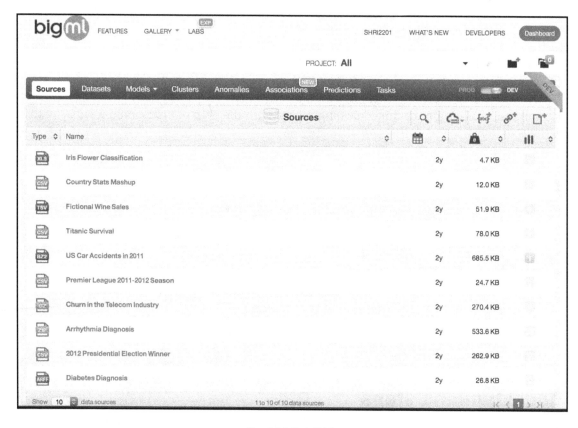

Figure 3 Data files in BigML

Most likely, your list of sources is going to be empty. In this list, we will upload our dataset.

Upload the data file

We will now upload the data file `responsedata.csv.gz` in BigML using the plus icon as shown in *Figure 3*. Note that BigML also allows you to upload compressed CSV files, which saves bandwidth and enables faster data upload for processing:

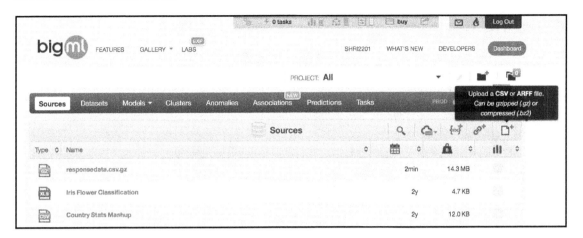

Figure 4 Upload a data file

Once you have uploaded the data file, it will show up in the list of data files as shown in *Figure 4*. You can examine the contents of the data file by clicking on the file as shown in *Figure 5*:

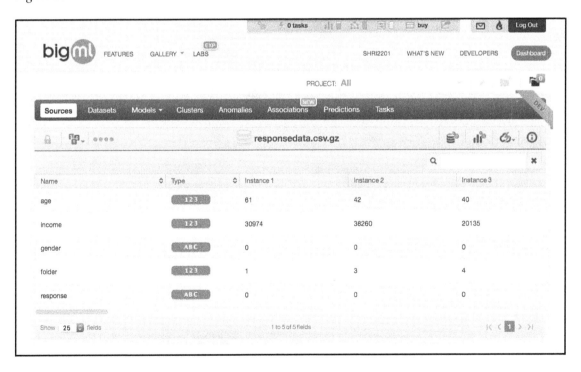

Figure 5 Examine the data file contents

Creating the dataset

In this step, we will create a new dataset with the help of the data file which we have just uploaded. For creating the dataset, we will click on 1-click dataset as shown in *Figure 6*:

Figure 6 Create the dataset

BigML will start creating the dataset. Because our data file has 1 million records, it will take some time. Once the dataset has been created, you will be able to see a summary of it:

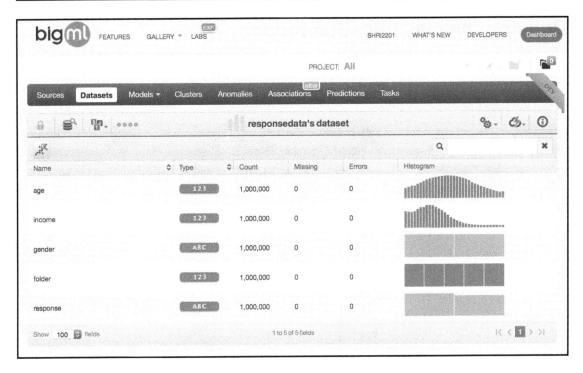

Figure 7 View the records in the dataset

In *Figure 7*, you can verify that BigML is able to use all the records contained in the dataset. You can also see the distribution of values in the histograms provided by BigML. You can see that almost half of the responses in our dataset have the value 0, which indicates no response. In our dataset, 20,293 records contain 1 in the response value, which indicates that the recipient of the campaign folder purchased a few items from the Furnitica store and presented the coupon contained in the campaign folder.

Building the classification model

The next step is building the classification model. The classification model will use the response as the target variable. The classification model contains a set of rules that predicts the target variable. You can build the classification model by using the create model button of BigML as shown in *Figure 8*:

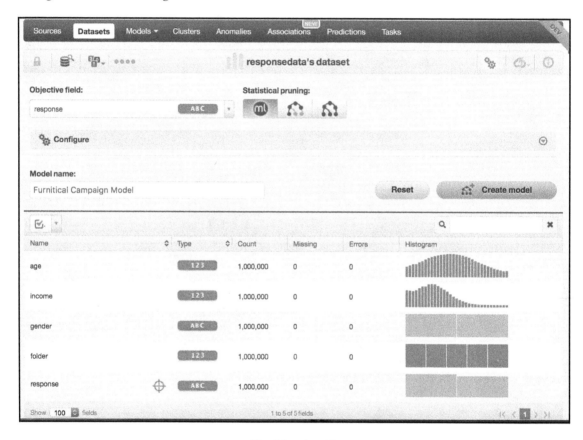

Figure 8 Create the model

After creating the model successfully, you can browse the decision tree created by BigML as shown in Figure 9. You can see various decision paths and the rules coupled with them:

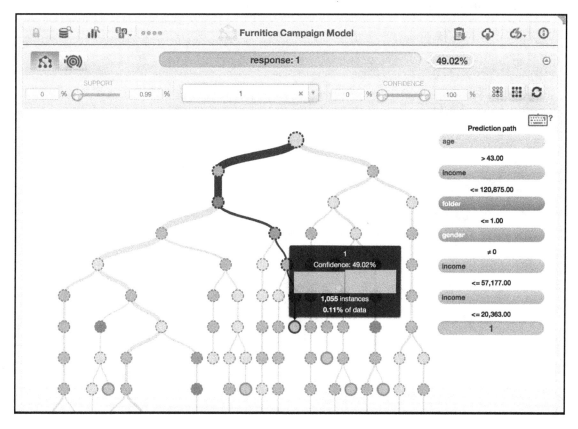

Figure 9 Browse the model

To better understand how the decision tree has been created, BigML provides you a model summary report as shown in *Figure 10*. The model summary report shows that income and age are the two most important factors to predict the target variable.

Data scientists rely on several such models to arrive at the predicted value. Detailed discussion about classification models is beyond the scope of this book so we will use just the one and only model created by BigML for our purpose:

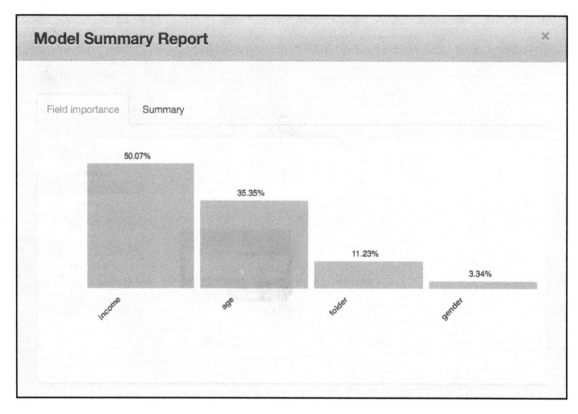

Figure 10 Model summary report

Downloading the classification model

Once we have created the classification model, we would like to use it predict the outcomes. When we want to run a new campaign, we will first make a selection of customers from the database. This selection can be based a geographical criterion such as people living in a city having an age greater than 18. We will use this selected list with our classification model to predict who is likely to respond to our campaign. This process is known as **scoring.** This process is explained in *Figure 11*:

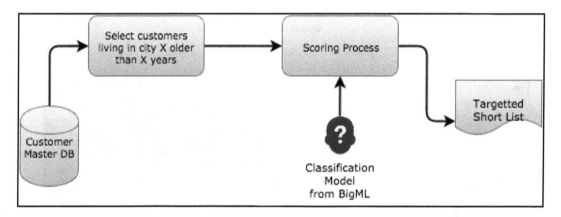

Figure 11 Selection and scoring

BigML provides us functionality to generate code from models in several high-level programming languages. Once the model has been converted into a high-level programming language, we can take advantage of that language to process the data.

We will download our model in Java as shown in *Figure 12*. This means when we run our program, it will be able take advantage of the parallel processing offered by Hadoop. The parallel processing offered by Hadoop will be able to score millions of records from the selected list of customers:

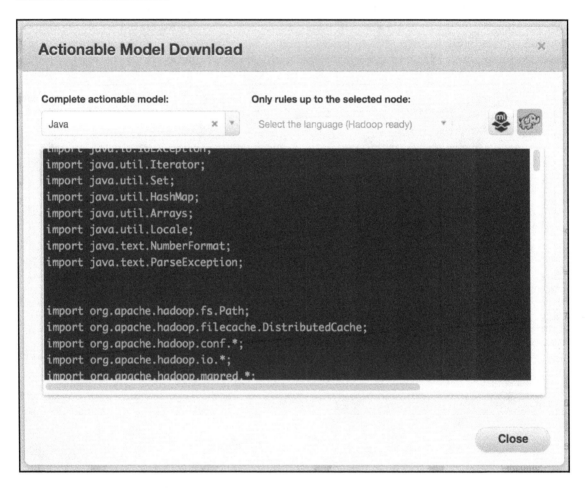

Figure 12 Actionable model download

You can cut and paste the model in your Java IDE. Before we run this model, we will examine its contents first.

We will show a few lines from the `predictResponse` method . It is the lengthiest method in the generated code:

```
/**
 *  Predictor for response from model/569245f21d55055c9f02418a
```

```
 *   Predictive model by BigML - Machine Learning Made Easy
 */
public class Response {

    public static String predictResponse(Double age, Double income, String
gender, Double folder) {
        if (age == null) {
            return "0";
        }
    }
```

If you examine the `predictResponse` method then you will find that BigML has coded the decision tree in the form of several if conditions.

Running the Model on Hadoop

We have used BigML for creating the classification tree with the help of historical campaign response data. This model is available in the form of Java code. We can now run this model on Hadoop by using it inside a MapReduce job.

We will need a MapReduce program, which you are already familiar with from the previous chapters of this book. This program is supplied with this book in the directory `/hbp/chapt4` as a file named `ResponsePrediction.java`. This file contains the code for a mapper, reducer, and driver in a single file. The following classes are included in this file:

```
public class ResponsePrediction {...}

public static void main(String[] args) throws Exception {
        JobConf conf = new JobConf(ResponsePrediction.class);
        conf.setJobName("responseprediction");
        conf.setOutputKeyClass(Text.class);
        conf.setOutputValueClass(IntWritable.class);
        conf.setMapOutputKeyClass(Text.class);
        conf.setMapOutputValueClass(Text.class);
        conf.setMapperClass(Map.class);
        conf.setReducerClass(Reduce.class);
        conf.setInputFormat(TextInputFormat.class);
        conf.setOutputFormat(TextOutputFormat.class);
        FileInputFormat.setInputPaths(conf, new Path(args[0]));
        FileOutputFormat.setOutputPath(conf, new Path(args[1]));
        JobClient.runJob(conf);
    }
```

This is the driver class which contains the main that serves as the entry point for the MapReduce job:

```
public static class Map extends MapReduceBase implements
Mapper<LongWritable, Text, Text, Text> {
        static enum Counters {
            INPUT_LINES
        }

public void map(LongWritable key, Text value, OutputCollector<Text, Text>
output, Reporter reporter)
            throws IOException {

        String line = value.toString();
        String[] data = line.split(",");
        output.collect(value, new Text(response(data)));
        reporter.incrCounter(Counters.INPUT_LINES, 1);


    }
  }
```

This is the mapper of our Hadoop job. It has been implemented as an inner class with the ResponsePrediction class:

```
public static class Reduce extends MapReduceBase implements Reducer<Text,
Text, Text, IntWritable> {

public void reduce(Text key, Iterator<Text> values, OutputCollector<Text,
IntWritable> output, Reporter reporter) throws IOException {
  int sum = 0;
  Text prediction = null;
    while (values.hasNext()) {
      sum += 1;
      prediction = values.next();
    }
    output.collect(new Text(key + "," + prediction), new
    IntWritable(sum));
  }
}
```

This is the reducer of our Hadoop job. It has been implemented as an inner class with the ResponsePrediction class.

In addition, the file `ResponsePrediction.java` contains two methods which are used by our MapReduce job as follows:

```
public static String predictResponse(HashMap<String, Object> inputData)
```

The method `predictResponse` is responsible for generating the prediction. The body of this method has been copied from the body of the Java method generated by BigML in the previous section. We have changed the signature of the method so that it can take inputs from the mapper.

```
public static String response(String[] data)
```

This method does key value conversion of data and stores the key value in a Hashmap.

In the directory `/hbp/chapt4`, you will also find `pom.xml`, which we will use to compile the source files into a jar which can run on Hadoop.

Let us create a maven project structure to hold our source code and pom file:

```
mvn archetype:generate -DgroupId=hbp -DartifactId=chapt4 -
DarchetypeArtifactId=maven-archetype-quickstart -DinteractiveMode=false
```

If this command has run successfully then you will find a new directory, chapt4, which contains a newly generated `pom.xml` and a directory tree under a directory where we will keep our source files.

We will now overwrite pom.xml with the version given with this book. When you have done this successfully, your `pom.xml` will look as follows:

```
<project xmlns="http://maven.apache.org/POM/4.0.0"
xmlns:xsi="http://www.w3.org/2001/XMLSchema-instance"
    xsi:schemaLocation="http://maven.apache.org/POM/4.0.0
http://maven.apache.org/xsd/maven-4.0.0.xsd">
    <modelVersion>4.0.0</modelVersion>

    <groupId>hbp</groupId>
    <artifactId>chapt4</artifactId>

    <version>0.0.1-SNAPSHOT</version>
    <packaging>jar</packaging>

    <name>chapt4</name>
    <url>http://maven.apache.org</url>

    <properties>
        <project.build.sourceEncoding>UTF-8</project.build.sourceEncoding>
    </properties>
```

```
         <dependencies>
            <dependency>
               <groupId>junit</groupId>
               <artifactId>junit</artifactId>
               <version>3.8.1</version>
               <scope>test</scope>
            </dependency>
            <dependency>
               <groupId>org.apache.hadoop</groupId>
               <artifactId>hadoop-client</artifactId>
               <version>2.7.1</version>
            </dependency>
         </dependencies>
      </project>
```

We have specified the dependency on Hadoop 2.7.1 for our project using the copied `pom.xml` file. Now copy `ResponsePrediction.java` to the directory `src/main/java/hbp/chapt4`.

You will notice that the directory `src/main/java/hbp/chapt4` also contains a file `App.java`. This file has been generated by maven during the project creation. You may remove this file because we will not use it. Now we have all the files at the right location, we will start build a process to compile the source code and build the JAR file using the following command:

```
$ mvn package
```

The last few lines from the output of the command are as follows:

```
[INFO] --- maven-jar-plugin:2.4:jar (default-jar) @ chapt4 ---
[INFO] Building jar: /Volumes/HD2/user/anurag/hdproject/
/playground/chapt4/target/chapt4-0.0.1-SNAPSHOT.jar
[INFO] --------------------------------------------------------------
----
[INFO] BUILD SUCCESS
[INFO] --------------------------------------------------------------
----
[INFO] Total time: 4.674 s
[INFO] Finished at: 2016-01-14T15:54:52+05:30
[INFO] Final Memory: 25M/227M
[INFO] --------------------------------------------------------------
----
```

You will find the file `target/chapt4-0.0.1-SNAPSHOT.jar` in your project directory, which is a compiled JAR file of our MapReduce job. You can run this file on Hadoop cluster by using the `hadoop jar` command by specifying the input and output directories and name of the job driver class, for example:

```
$ hadoop jar chapt4-0.0.1-SNAPSHOT.jar hbp.chapt4.ResponsePrediction
/hbp/chapt4/inputdata.csv /hbp/chapt4/output
```

In the preceding command line example, `inputdata.csv` is the input file while the output of the MapReduce job goes to the `/hbp/chapt4/output` directory.

Creating the target List

Now our MapReduce program is ready to run on the Hadoop cluster. We are now going to prepare the input data from the customer master database of Furnitica. The customer master data contains many details that might not be very relevant for our MapReduce job.

A subset of fields available in the master data is as follows:

- Customer ID
- Date of birth
- Income
- Gender

Let us assume here that we will now make a selection of customers living in the city where we are going to send the campaign folders. This city is the target of the campaign. A single row in our selection is shown in *Table 3*:

Customer ID	10023
Age (derived from date of birth)	55
Income	75000
Gender (derived from M/F, where 0 is male and 1 is female)	0

Table 3 A selection from the customer master data

We want to send the folder number 1 to our target customers so we will add this information in our `inputdata.csv` as well. The resulting input data file `inputdata.csv` is as follows:

```
10023,25,75000,1,1
10024,55,25000,0,1
10025,47,49000,1,1
10026,74,82000,0,1
10027,35,65000,1,1
10028,50,55000,0,1
10029,59,79000,1,1
10030,39,90252,1,1
10031,39,80224,1,1
```

We will run this program on Hadoop cluster:

```
$ hadoop jar chapt4-0.0.1-SNAPSHOT.jar hbp.chapt4.ResponsePrediction
/hbp/chapt4/inputdata.csv /hbp/chapt4/output
```

After running the MapReduce job on a Hadoop cluster, we examine the contents of the output directory as follows:

```
$ hadoop fs -ls /hbp/chapt4/output/
Found 2 items
-rw-r--r--   1 hduser supergroup          0 2016-01-14 17:22
/hbp/chapt4/output/_SUCCESS
-rw-r--r--   1 hduser supergroup        207 2016-01-14 17:22
/hbp/chapt4/output/part-00000
```

You will find that our job has run successfully and its output is stored in the file named `part-0000`. Let's copy this file and examine its contents:

```
$ hadoop fs -copyToLocal /hbp/chapt4/output/part-00000
$ cat part-00000
10023,25,75000,1,1,0 1
10024,55,25000,0,1,0 1
10025,47,49000,1,1,0 1
10026,74,82000,0,1,0 1
10027,35,65000,1,1,0 1
10028,50,55000,0,1,0 1
10029,59,79000,1,1,0 1
10030,39,90252,1,1,1 1
10031,39,80224,1,1,0 1
```

The `part-00000` file contains the results of our response predictor. The values contained in the file can be interpreted as shown in *Table 4*:

Customer ID	10023
Age (derived from date of birth)	25
Income	75000
Gender (derived from M/F, where 0 is male and 1 is female)	1
Folder	1
Response (0 means this customer will not respond to campaign folder 1)	0
Sum (output from the reduce stage which can be ignored)	1

Table 4 Understanding the output of the MapReduce job

Our input dataset has a tiny number of rows in it. In a real-life situation, this dataset would contain millions of rows. With the help of Hadoop, we can execute the task of scoring over multiple nodes in parallel. You will notice that the prediction takes place in this map phase of the MapReduce job, where the method `predictResponse` is called. The reduce phase in our job does not do much except counting the number of rows processed for a key.

The result of `predictResponse` shows who we can eliminate from the target customer list for the campaign for folder 1. This can be done by observing the output produced by the MapReduce job. In our sample dataset, we can see that the response predictor expects that the customer having `custid` 10030 will respond to folder 1 while other customers will not respond. We will now join the `custid` 10030 using regular SQL-based tools with customer name, address, and city data. The resulting data can be used to print the address stickers which can paste on our campaign folders. This process has been illustrated in *Figure 13*:

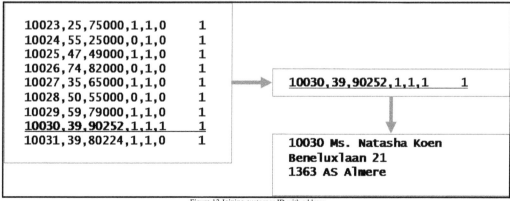

Figure 13 Joining customer ID with address

Post campaign activities

Once we have started the campaign by dispatching the folders to the customers then we should be ready to collect the actual response data. This will serve two purposes: we can measure how effective our model was and we can use the actual response data to build or improve the existing model. These topics are beyond the scope of this book.

Summary

In this chapter, we focused on the application of Hadoop in the marketing domain. We started by gaining a basic understanding of classification and supervised learning. We learned a machine learning tool known as BigML to build a classification model for Furnitica to predict the campaign response. We used this model in a MapReduce job to generate predictions of the response. You should be aware that building a good model is a highly specialized job performed by trained data scientists. In this chapter, we have demonstrated how such a model can be built and executed on Hadoop without going into the merits and quality of the predictions generated by the model itself.

In the next chapter of this book, we will cover the topic of churn prediction in the telecom domain.

5
Churn Detection

You have become familiar with some of the business applications of Hadoop presented in this book, such as fraud detection, 360-degree customer analytics, and increasing the response rate for campaigns. In this chapter, we will cover a common application of Hadoop known as churn detection. Churn refers to a customer leaving a subscription with company X to sign up for a subscription with company Y. The causes of churn can be manifold, such as company Y offering cheaper services or making a more attractive offer to the customer. Churn could also be an indicator of inferior services delivered by company X, leading to a dissatisfied customer who decides to move to company Y. No company in the world likes to see their customers leaving, but this problem is very acute in the mobile telephony business where the services offered by mobile service providers are not differentiated much, and the hurdle of switching over to another provider can be overcome with mobile number portability.

A business case for churn detection

Telecom companies lose more than 30% of customers annually as a result of customer churn in the US and Europe. The cost of acquiring a new customer is eight times than that of retaining an existing customer. This makes a strong business case for churn detection, a task which is ideal for Hadoop.

Analyzing telecom data with Hadoop to detect customer churn possess a unique set of challenges that stem from the massive datasets that need to be transformed and analyzed. The storage of this data is expensive due to its sheer volume, and the pre-processing of raw data before analysis is a time- and computing-intensive task. Hadoop offers low-cost storage for data processing, and it can efficiently deal with structured, semi-structured, and unstructured datasets, which makes Hadoop a useful technology for churn prediction.

In this chapter, we will use Hadoop MapReduce to analyze the data so that we can predict which customers are likely to churn. In order to do so, we will take the following steps:

1. Select the historical data suitable for analysis.
2. Select an appropriate algorithm for churn prediction.
3. Load data in Hadoop.
4. Run the analysis.
5. Analyze the results.

Creating the solution outline

A churn predictor or churn detector is a program that takes a dataset containing the customer records, one row per customer, as input. Each row is then fed to the churn prediction algorithm which predicts whether a customer will churn or not.

The churn predictor can simply be used in batch mode to generate outbound emails or calls, or it can be integrated with the inbound interactive channels, such as a website or call center. Once we know that the customer is likely to churn, then we can offer him or her an incentive, such as a special offer, to make him change his or her mind.

We can take a proactive or reactive approach to churn prevention. In the reactive approach, we offer special incentives to the customer when he or she informs us that he would like to terminate the service. This gives us a few weeks' time to retain the customer. The reactive approach is not very relevant for this chapter because, once the customer announces that he or she is planning to churn to another provider, the churn "prediction" becomes irrelevant because it is a fact.

Our solution will use the historical data on customer churn as an input to build a model to predict the future churners. We will load the historical customer churn data on HDFS and then, with the help of MapReduce programs, we will build the model. When the customer churn data runs to millions of rows, then the parallel processing offered by MapReduce can efficiently build the model in a short span of time.

Once our model has been created, then we will use it with future customer data to predict whether a customer is likely to churn or not. The models resulting from number crunching using MapReduce are essentially the aggregated totals. They are used to compute the probability by replacing the variables with the actual values from customer data that serves as the input.

Building a predictive model using Hadoop

You will notice that, for the first time in this book, we are building a predictive model using Hadoop. In the previous chapters, we used BigML and Spark to build our models and run those models on Hadoop.

In our solution, we assume that the model will find its applications in several business processes used by the company. For example, when a customer logs on to the self-service portal of the company, then we will use the customer profile to determine if he or she is likely to churn.

If our model predicts that the logged-in customer is likely to churn, then we can present a special offer to encourage him or her to continue to use the services of the company.

In a real-life scenario, my mobile service provider starts showing the special offers three months before the end date of my subscription so that I can continue to remain their customer for a longer period by accepting one of their offers. These offers are based upon my calling patterns in the past and my overall propensity to choose a new provider.

Before we start building our predictive model, let's understand the theory of building such models. In the next section, we will discuss Bayes' theorem, which is the foundation of the predictive model we will build in this chapter.

Bayes' Theorem

Bayes' Theorem, or Bayes' Rule, is a conditional probability model. It can be used to calculate the probability of a future event based on knowing the occurrence of events in the past. The Bayesian theorem finds its applications in many fields, such as data science. Bayes theorem can be expressed using the following formula:

$$P(A/B) = P(B/A)*P(A)/P(B)$$

$$P(A/B) = Probability\ of\ A\ given\ B$$

$$P(B/A) = Probability\ of\ B\ given\ A$$

$$P(A) = Probability\ of\ A$$

$$P(B) = Probability\ of\ B$$

We are all confronted with the problem of spam e-mails, which waste our time and computing resources. Bayes theorem has been successfully applied to detect spam mail using spam filters on mail servers and clients. A Bayes classifier can predict whether or not a mail message is likely to be a spam mail message with a degree of certainty.

Spam detectors scan the mail for certain keywords encountered in spam messages and then determine if the given mail message is a spam mail message.

For example, an email message containing the word Viagra can be a spam, but it can also be a genuine email message. If we have to determine the probability that a mail message containing the word Viagra is a spam mail message, then we can calculate it using the following formula:

$$P(Spam|Viagra) = P(Viagra/Spam)* P(Spam)/P(Viagra)$$

Let's say we received 100 e-mail messages. 10 of them are spam. 20 of them contain the word Viagra. 5 spam messages contain the word Viagra. Then we get the 101st message, which contains the word Viagra. The probability of the 101st message being spam when it contains the word Viagra can be calculated as follows:

$$P(Spam) = 10/100 = 0.1$$

$$P(Viagra) = 20/100 = 0.2$$

$$P(Viagra/Spam) = 5/10 = 0.5$$

$$P(Spam/Viagra) = 0.5*0.1/0.2 = 0.25$$

Therefore, the probability that an e-mail containing the word Viagra is a spam message is 0.25. In the Bayes formula, we first calculate the probabilities and conditional probabilities from the historical data. These calculated probability values from the historical data are used to draw an inference about the current event. If we do not have any historical event data, then we cannot use the Bayes' formula because the probability values will be zero. However, all machine learning models need historical data to train themselves, so this limitation is not unique to the Bayes formula.

The Bayesian theorem is a vast and fascinating topic. You can read more about the Bayesian theorem and its applications
at http://www.statisticshowto.com/bayes-theorem-problems/.

Playing with the Bayesian predictor

Before we start building the fully fledged churn predictor, let's try to build a simple churn predictor in JavaScript to understand how the Bayesian theorem can be put to use. Let's take a trivial example of customer churn data from a fictitious telecom company. The dataset is shown in *Table 1*:

Customer ID	Plan	Call Minutes	Age	Churn
0654 678890	gold	heavy	young	false
0655 678895	gold	medium	old	false
0657 678790	silver	heavy	young	true

Table 1 – Sample customer churn data

Let's understand what the sample customer churn data means:

- **Customer ID**: A unique subscription ID, which is the same as the mobile no. of the customer.
- **Plan**: The telecom company offers two calling plans called Gold and Silver. Gold and Silver plans give 90 and 45 free calling minutes respectively every month.
- **Call Minutes**: The calling minutes of users over the past year. Heavy users call twice their number of free minutes per month or more. Medium users call their free minutes as a minimum. Low users never use up their free minutes.
- **Age**: A subscriber younger than 45 years is considered young and all others are considered old.
- **Churn**: Indicates whether the customer has churned to another company at the end of the contract period.

You will notice that our table does not contain the actual numbers for uses, but categorical values. These categorical values are determined by some predefined categorization criteria. For example, instead of using the actual age of the customer, we categorize the age as old when the customer is older than 45 years. This categorization is necessary because the Bayesian algorithm only works with categorical values. When we have to deal with continuous values, several methods exist to convert them into categorical values. This is an advanced topic beyond the scope of this book. You can read more about this topic on `http://idiom.ucsd.edu/~rlevy/pmsl_textbook/chapters/pmsl_4.pdf`

For the purpose of creating a Bayesian model, we will ignore the field `CustomerId` as it is not a relevant set of data to build our model. The `Churn` field is our target variable, which predicts the outcome for the future customer data.

Running a Node.js-based Bayesian predictor

Using data similar to that shown in *Table 1*, we have built a Bayesian predictor in JavaScript. This predictor depends upon the npm package named prompt, which is used to accept the input from a standard input device such as a keyboard. You can find the program Bayesian.js in the code samples given with the code of this chapter in the folder named Chapter 5.

Let's run it after installing the npm package prompt:

```
$ npm install prompt
$ node Bayesian.js
```

Once you run the program, it will seek three customer data inputs from you, namely Plan, Calling Minutes, and Age, to predict whether this customer will churn or not.

The sample output of the program for the inputs Plan=gold, Calling Minutes=low, and Age=old is given in the following code. Note that we have inserted a few extra line spaces in the output for better readability.

```
$ node bayesian.js

****Calculating the frequencies and probabilities****

Total true=8 Total false=7

Ptrue=0.5333333333333333 Pfalse=0.4666666666666667

Pgoldtrue=0.5 Pgoldfalse=0.8571428571428571
Psilvertrue=0.5 Psilverfalse=0.14285714285714285
Plowtrue=0.125 Plowfalse=0.14285714285714285
Pheavytrue=0.375 Pheavyfalse=0.5714285714285714
Pmediumtrue=0.5 Pmediumfalse=0.2857142857142857
Pyoungtrue=0.375 Pyoungfalse=0.5714285714285714
Poldtrue=0.25 Poldfalse=0.2857142857142857
Pmiddletrue=0.375 Pmiddlefalse=0.14285714285714285

****Calculated the Data for Bayesian Model****


****Enter the input for predictor****
prompt: Plan [gold or silver]:  gold
prompt: Calling Minutes [heavy, medium, low]::  low
prompt: Age: [young, middle, old]:  old
**Input Received**
Plan: gold
```

```
Calling Minutes: low
Age: old
****Predicting Now****
Pchurntrue=0.008333333333333333   Pchurnfalse=0.03265306122448979
Churn=FALSE
```

Our program predicts that users with `Plan=gold`, `Calling Minutes=low`, and `Age=old` will not churn because the output churn is false.

This program does three tasks:

- Reading the input data and calculating the conditional probabilities
- Prompting for user input
- Calculating the result or the value of the target variable

Understanding the predictor code

Let's examine this program more closely.

- **Input Data**: We have provided input data in the form of a JavaScript array of arrays as follows:

```
var data = [
    ['gold', 'heavy', 'young', false],
    ['gold', 'medium', 'old', false],
    ['gold', 'medium', 'young', true],
    ..... many more elements....
    ['gold', 'medium', 'old', true]
];
```

- **Calculating the frequency**: The following code calculates the frequency or count of input values, first when the value of the target variable churn is true and then when it is false, for (i = 0; i<data.length; i++) {

```
if (data[i][3] === true)
{
    trueTot++;
    if (data[i][0] === 'gold') trueGold++;
    if (data[i][0] === 'silver') trueSilver++;
    if (data[i][1] === 'heavy') trueHeavy++;
    if (data[i][1] === 'low') trueLow++;
    if (data[i][1] === 'medium') trueMedium++;
    if (data[i][2] === 'young') trueYoung++;
    if (data[i][2] === 'middle') trueMiddle++;
    if (data[i][2] === 'old') trueOld++;
```

```
    } else
     if (data[i][3] === false)
   {
       falseTot++;
       if (data[i][0] === 'gold') falseGold++;
       if (data[i][0] === 'silver') falseSilver++;
       if (data[i][1] === 'heavy') falseHeavy++;
       if (data[i][1] === 'low') falseLow++;
       if (data[i][1] === 'medium') falseMedium++;
       if (data[i][2] === 'young') falseYoung++;
       if (data[i][2] === 'middle') falseMiddle++;
       if (data[i][2] === 'old') falseOld++;
   }
```

- **Calculating the probabilities**: In this step, we first calculate the probability of having Churn=true and Churn=false for the entire dataset. After that we will calculate the conditional probabilities for each categorical value. The first few lines from the program are shown here:

```
varPtrue = trueTot / total;
var Pfalse = falseTot / total;

varPgoldtrue = trueGold / trueTot;
varPsilvertrue = trueSilver / trueTot;
```

If we divide the total true frequency by the total number of true, then we get the conditional probability. For example, `Pgoldtrue` shows the probability of a customer having a Gold plan when he has churned.

- **Read user input**: In this step, we prompt a user for the inputs. We have used the npm library prompt to capture the user inputs. You can learn more about the prompt library at `https://www.npmjs.com/package/prompt`.
- **Predicting the churn**: We predict the churn with the help of a Naïve Bayesian classifier. The Naïve Bayesian classifier formula is based upon the Bayesian theorem. It assumes that the different variables or predictors used are independent from each other. Though the Naïve Bayesian classifier looks very simple, it works very well and delivers better results than more complex and sophisticated methods.

The Bayes theorem gives us a formula to calculate the probability of `Churn=Y` for a customer with data `[Plan=gold, CallingMinutes=low, Age=old]` as follows:

```
P(Churn=yes/[Plan=gold, CallingMinutes=low, Age=old]) = P(yes/X)
P(gold/yes)*P(low/yes)*P(old/yes)*P(yes)
```

Where X is [Plan=gold, CallingMinutes=low, Age=old].

Similarly, using the Bayes theorem we can calculate the probability of Churn=N for a customer with data [Plan=gold, CallingMinutes=low, Age=old] as follows:

```
P(Churn=no/[Plan=gold, CallingMinutes=low, Age=old]) = P(no/X)
P(gold/yes)*P(low/yes)*P(old/yes)*P(yes)
```

Where X is [Plan=gold, CallingMinutes=low, Age=old].

Now we can say whether the following is true:

```
P(yes/X) > P(no/X)
```

If this is the case, then the customer will churn; otherwise, he/she will not. This logic has been implemented in the following code:

```
if (plan == "silver") {
    P1true = Psilvertrue;
    P1false = Psilverfalse;
}
else if(plan == "gold") {
    P1true = Pgoldtrue;
    P1false = Pgoldfalse;
}

if (callingminutes == "medium") {
    P2true = Pmediumtrue;
    P2false = Pmediumfalse;
} else if (callingminutes == "low") {
    P2true = Plowtrue;
    P2false = Plowfalse;
} else if (callingminutes == "heavy") {
    P2true = Pheavytrue;
    P2false = Pheavyfalse;
}

if (age == "young") {
    P3true = Pyoungtrue;
    P3false = Pyoungfalse;
} else if (age == "middle") {
    P3true = Pmiddeltrue;
    P3false = Pmiddlefalse;
} else if (age == "old") {
    P3true = Poldtrue;
    P3false = Poldfalse;
}
```

```
Pchurntrue = P1true * P2true * P3true * Ptrue;
Pchurnfalse = P1false * P3false * P3false * Pfalse;

console.log("Pchurntrue=" + Pchurntrue + "  Pchurnfalse=" + Pchurnfalse);
  if (Pchurntrue>Pchurnfalse)
    console.log("Churn=TRUE");
  else
    console.log("Churn=FALSE");
```

You can read more about Naïve Baysian classifiers at `http://www.saedsayad.com/naive_b ayesian.htm`.

Limitations of our solution

You will have noticed by now that this program uses a very small dataset to build the model. While this is sufficient to demonstrate the concept, it is unlikely to scale when we have millions of rows (with columns in the orders of hundreds) to process and with which to build our model. In order to process large volumes of data to build our model, we will use Hadoop because it is an appropriate technology to crunch large datasets with.

Building a churn predictor using Hadoop

In this section, we will apply the knowledge gained in the previous section to build a churn predictor that can scale up for use with very large datasets. Hadoop is particularly suited to the processing of very large datasets.

Synthetic data generation tools

To build our churn prediction using Hadoop, we will work with a synthetic dataset. Synthetic datasets are good for testing and learning purposes because they do not carry the risk of personal information leakage, and they are simple to obtain or create. But they also carry the limitation that, unlike a real-life dataset, they never contain the truth. Synthetic data offers a good alternative to real life datasets if you want to get started quickly.

Some synthetic data generation techniques and tools are covered as follows:

Synthetic Data Generation

To generate synthetic datasets, you can use a site such as `http://www.generatedata.com/`, which offers the generation of 100 rows in a dataset for free.

If you want to try synthetic data generation using your own programs, then you can try many packages available in the Nodejs community, such as Chancejs.

Chancejs
`http://chancejs.com/`

Chance generates random strings, phone numbers, zipcodes, numbers, GUIDs, and so on.

Charlatan
Charlatan can generate dummy names, addresses, phones, IPs, and others.
`https://github.com/nodeca/charlatan` **Moniker**
Moniker is a random name generator for Nodejs.
`https://github.com/weaver/moniker`

Preparing a synthetic historical churn dataset

Let's start preparing a synthetic dataset that contains the historical churn data about a fictitious telecom company. Our synthetic data contains categorized data values from a customer call data record and CRM, as shown in the table.

Variable	Categorized Values	Remarks
Churn	Yes, No	Indicates if the customer has churned. This is our target variable
Call Minutes	Low, Medium, High	Calling minutes classified in three categories
Age Group	Young, Middle, Old	Age of the customer classified into three categories
Call Customer Support	More, Less	How often the customer has called customer support

Call Drops	Normal, Above Normal	How many weekly call drops have been experienced by the customer
Phone Type	IOS, Android	What type of phone the customer is using
Plan	Frequent, Regular, Basic	What kind of calling plan the customer has

Here are a few rows from the file `dataMar-5-2016.csv`, which contains our dataset:

Churn	Call Minutes	Age Group	Call Customer Support	Call Drops	Phone Type	Plan
Yes	Medium	Middle	More	Normal	IOS	Frequent
Yes	High	Young	Above	Normal	Android	Frequent
No	Medium	Old	Normal	Normal	IOS	Regular

You might have noticed that in our sample dataset real-life customer data coming from call data records and CRM systems has already undergone some transformation to get converted into categorical values. For example, an average of fewer than 2 call drops per week in the past three month has been considered normal and more than 2 above normal. Similarly, the number of call minutes has been categorized as Low when, in the last three months, the average is fewer than 60, Medium when it's 60-120, and High when it's more than 120. To bring in data in its present format, we can use Hive or some other transformation tools within the Hadoop ecosystem.

We have also taken care that the categorical values for one variable are not shared with other variables. Bayesian classification calculates the frequency of occurrence of a value. By not sharing the values among the variables, we do not mix two different concepts together, such as age and calling minutes.

The processing approach

Once we have our dataset ready, we can process it using MapReduce. The MapReduce program will calculate the count of each variable value when the value of the target variable Churn is Yes and No. This data will help us calculate the conditional probability required by the Naïve Bayesian classifier when we build our predictive model.

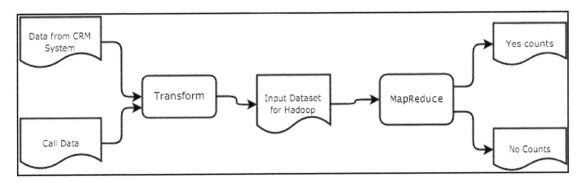

Figure 1 – Data processing flow

Figure 1 shows the full process flow; however, in our example, we have assumed that the dataset is ready to be processed by a MapReduce program.

Once we have calculated the counts, then we can feed the data to another program, which will build the model using the Bayesian formula presented earlier in this chapter. For building the model, we will use a POJO-based Java, which will not make use of Hadoop. Once the model has been built, it is stored in the program memory. Calculations for predictions can be performed pretty quickly once the input data is available because these calculations are not very computing-intensive tasks. *Figure 2* show this process:

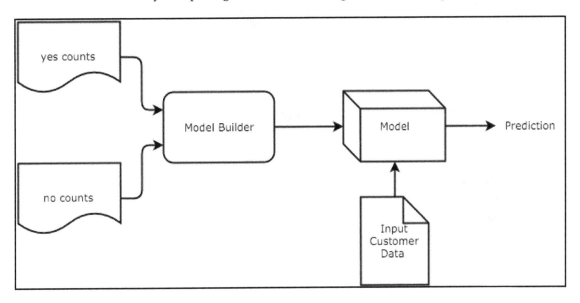

Figure 2 Building the predictive model

Let's run the MapRreduce program in the next section.

Running the MapReduce program

The next steps in this section assume that you already have a running Hadoop cluster in single node or multi-node configuration.

First, we create a directory structure in the Hadoop filesystem as follows:

```
$hadoop fs -ls /hbp/chapt5/
Found 2 items
drwxr-xr-x   - hduser supergroup          0 2016-03-13 21:09 /hbp/chapt5/in
```

We have created the `/hbp/chapt5/in` directory to hold the input data and `/hbp/chapt5/out` has been created to store the output from the MapReduce program.

Let's copy the input data file `p1.dat` to HDFS and examine the contents of the directory after the copy. Note that the input data file `p1.dat` is the same file as `dataMar-5-2016.csv` but with the header removed.

```
$ hadoop fs -put ~/p1.dat /hbp/chapt5/in
$ hadoop fs -ls  /hbp/chapt5/in/
-rw-r--r--   1 hduser supergroup       4557 2016-03-13 21:13
/hbp/chapt5/in/p1.dat
```

Before we can run our MapReduce program, we should compile and build it. In the code samples for this chapter, you will find the source code of the MapReduce program and `pom.xml`, which can be used to build it using Maven.

```
$ mvn package
```

This command will create a jar file named `chapt5-1.0-SNAPSHOT.jar` in the target directory. This JAR file contains our MapReduce program. The program takes the following command line arguments:

- Input directory, where input data is located
- Output directory for MapReduce out
- `yes` or `no` determines whether the program is going to calculate the count for the yes or no rows.

You will remember that our input data has the following format:

```
no  Medium  Middle  More  Normal  Android  Basic
yes Medium  Young   Less  High    IOS      Basic
```

Here, `yes` and `no` signify whether a customer has churned or not. We now run the MapReduce program using the following command:

```
$ hadoop jar chapt5-1.0-SNAPSHOT.jar hbp.chapt5.WordCount  /hbp/chapt5/in
/hbp/chapt5/output-yes yes
```

We will copy the output of the MapReduce job to the local filesystem and examine it:

```
$ hadoop fs -copyToLocal /hbp/chapt5/output-yes/*  ~/out-yes/

$ cat out-yes/part-r-00000
Android  14
Basic 17
Frequent 9
High   34
IOS    19
Less   23
Low    18
Medium    12
Middle    9
More   20
Normal    22
Old    15
Regular   17
Windows   10
Young 19
yes    43
```

The output of the MapReduce job contains the count or frequency of variables when the value of churn is `yes`. In addition, we can see in the last row that the rows containing the value `yes` for churn are 43 in total.

Likewise, we will now run the program to calculate the count for `no`.

```
$ hadoop jar chapt5-1.0-SNAPSHOT.jar hbp.chapt5.WordCount  /hbp/chapt5/in
/hbp/chapt5/output-nono
```

Make sure that the `/hbp/chapt5/output` directory does not exist, otherwise the program will throw an error and generate no output. Now copy the output of the MapReduce job to a local directory:

```
$ hadoop fs -copyToLocal/hbp/chapt5/output-no/* /out-no/
```

Let's examine the contents of the output directory:

```
$ cat out-no/part-r-00000
Android  25
Basic 20
```

```
Frequent 20
High    47
IOS     14
Less    32
Low     15
Medium      18
Middle      15
More    25
Normal      34
Old     21
Regular 17
Windows 18
Young 21
no 57
```

The output of our MapReduce job contains the count or frequency of variables when the value of churn is no. In addition, we can see in the last row that the rows containing the value no for churn are 57 in total.

Understanding the frequency counter code

Let's understand our frequency counter MapReduce program by looking at the following code fragments from the WordCount.java file:

```java
public class WordCount {

    static String filterString = "";
```

The filterstring variable stores the churn value for which we have to count the values of variables.

```java
public static classTokenizerMapper extends Mapper<Object, Text, Text,
IntWritable> {

    privatefinalstaticIntWritableone = newIntWritable(1);
    private Text word = newText();

    @Override
    publicvoid map(Object key, Text value, Context context)
    throwsIOException, InterruptedException {
        StringTokenizeritr = newStringTokenizer(value.toString());
        System.out.println(value.toString());
        if (value.toString().startsWith(filterString)) {
            while (itr.hasMoreTokens()) {
                word.set(itr.nextToken());
                context.write(word, one);
```

```
          }
        }
      }
    }
```

Our mapper is a slightly modified version of the mapper used by popular word counting MapReduce program samples. We are interested in word count only if the churn value is yes or no. In order to do so, we do not process those rows that do not start with a yes or no value, as may be the case when the mapper emits the data. This ensures that we only count the word when our condition is met.

```
public static class IntSumReducer extends Reducer<Text, IntWritable, Text,
IntWritable> {
      privateIntWritableresult = newIntWritable();

      @Override
      publicvoidreduce(Text key, Iterable<IntWritable>values,
      Context context)
            throwsIOException, InterruptedException {
        intsum = 0;
        for (IntWritableval :values) {
          sum += val.get();
        }
        result.set(sum);
        context.write(key, result);
      }
    }
```

Our reducer is a simple reducer that sums up the word count and writes the output in the HDFS.

```
public static void main(String[] args) throws Exception {
      Configuration conf = newConfiguration();
      Job job = Job.getInstance(conf, "Frequency count");
      job.setJarByClass(WordCount.class);
      job.setMapperClass(TokenizerMapper.class);
      job.setCombinerClass(IntSumReducer.class);
      job.setReducerClass(IntSumReducer.class);
      job.setOutputKeyClass(Text.class);
      job.setOutputValueClass(IntWritable.class);
      FileInputFormat.addInputPath(job, new Path(args[0]));
      FileOutputFormat.setOutputPath(job, new Path(args[1]));
      WordCount.filterString = args[2];
      System.exit(job.waitForCompletion(true) ? 0 : 1);
    }
  }
```

In the `static main` method, we have the usual boilerplate code as well as code to read the command line arguments.

Now we have calculated the count or frequency of variables when the value of churn is `yes` or `no`. With this data in hand, we can start building our Bayesian predictor to calculate the conditional probabilities.

Putting the model to use

We will run our model builder program and predict the churn for a customer as follows:

```
$ java -classpathtarget/chapt5-1.0-SNAPSHOT.jar  hbp.chapt5.ModelBuilder
```

This program produces the output of the model building process and the prediction as explained here:

```
{Medium=12, Low=18, Regular=17, Middle=9, Young=19, Less=23, yes=43,
Windows=10, Frequent=9, Basic=17, Android=14, IOS=19, More=20, Normal=22,
Old=15, High=34}
```

In the preceding step, we read in the file `out-yes/part-r-00000` and print its contents:

```
{Medium=18, Low=15, Regular=17, Middle=15, no=57, Young=21, Less=32,
Windows=18, Frequent=20, Basic=20, Android=25, IOS=14, More=25, Normal=34,
Old=21, High=47}
```

In the preceding step, we read in the file `out-no/part-r-00000` and print its contents:

```
Model==>{PnoWindows=0.3157894736842105, PnoFrequent=0.3508771929824561,
PnoMedium=0.3157894736842105, PnoOld=0.3684210526315789,
PnoNormal=0.5964912280701754, PnoMore=0.43859649122807015,
PnoBasic=0.3508771929824561, PnoYoung=0.3684210526315789,
PnoMiddle=0.2631578947368421, PnoAndroid=0.43859649122807015,
PnoLow=0.2631578947368421, PnoHigh=0.8245614035087719, Pno=0.57,
PnoLess=0.5614035087719298, PnoRegular=0.2982456140350877,
PnoIOS=0.24561403508771928}
```

In the preceding step, we calculate the conditional probabilities when the value of churn is no. We also calculate the overall probability of no, which is indicated by the variable `Pno=0.57`.

```
Model==>{PyesHigh=0.7906976744186046, PyesWindows=0.23255813953488372,
PyesBasic=0.3953488372093023, PyesLow=0.4186046511627907,
PyesMedium=0.27906976744186046, PyesMiddle=0.20930232558139536,
PyesYoung=0.4418604651162791, PyesIOS=0.4418604651162791,
PyesAndroid=0.32558139534883723, PyesFrequent=0.20930232558139536,
```

```
PyesRegular=0.3953488372093023, PyesNormal=0.5116279069767442,
PyesLess=0.5348837209302325, PyesMore=0.46511627906976744,
PyesOld=0.3488372093023256, Pyes=0.43}
```

In the preceding step, we calculate the conditional probabilities when the value of churn is yes. We also calculate the overall probability of no, which is indicated by the `Pyes=0.43` variable.

```
YesLikely=0.005669972302203077 NoLikely=0.004247650023407238
```

In the preceding step, we calculate the likelihood of `churn=yes` and the likelihood of churn=no for a given dataset, and predict the outcome based upon whichever likelihood is higher.

```
High  Old  Less  Normal  IOS  Regular CHURN
```

In the preceding step, we output the result of the prediction. The result implies that a customer having `High` calling minutes, whose age is `Old`, who calls customer service `Less`, has a `Normal` call drop rate, `IOS` user with `Regular` calling plan is likely to churn.

This brings us to the final step of our solution, in the course of which we started with raw data, transformed it to make it suitable for consumption by MapReduce, built the predictive model using the Naïve Bayesian classifier, and predicted the outcome.

Our model builder and predictor is a simple Java program, as listed here with explanations. We have omitted getters and setters in the listing to avoid clutter because their purpose should be pretty obvious to a Java programmer.

```java
package hbp.chapt5;

import java.io.BufferedReader;
import java.io.FileReader;
import java.util.HashMap;
import java.util.StringTokenizer;

public class ModelBuilder {
    private HashMap<String, Integer>freqYesHmp = null;
    private HashMap<String, Integer> freqNoHmp = null;
    private HashMap<String, Double>modelYesHmp = null;
    private HashMap<String, Double>modelNoHmp = null;
    private inttotalRows = 0;
```

First, we initialize all the hashmaps that contain the frequencies and our churn detection model.

```
public void buildModel() {
    totalRows = freqYesHmp.get("yes") + freqNoHmp.get("no");
    modelNoHmp = calculateProbabilities(freqNoHmp, "no");
    modelYesHmp = calculateProbabilities(freqYesHmp, "yes");
}
```

The `buildmodel()` method builds the churn detection model by using the frequencies of yes and no.

```
public HashMap<String, Double>calculateProbabilities(HashMap<String,
Integer> frequency, String target) {
    HashMap<String, Double> model = new HashMap<String, Double>();
    double targetCount = frequency.get(target);
    for (String feature :frequency.keySet()) {
        if (!target.equals(feature)) {
            String key = "P" + target + feature;
            double featureFrequency = frequency.get(feature);
            model.put(key, featureFrequency / targetCount);
        } else {
            String key = "P" + target;
            model.put(key, targetCount / totalRows);
        }
    }
    System.out.println("Model==>"+ model);
    return model;
}
```

In the preceding method, we calculate the various values of probabilities to build the churn model using the Bayesian formula.

```
public HashMap<String, Integer>initFrequencyHmp(String fileName) {
    BufferedReader in;
    HashMap<String, Integer>freqHmp = new HashMap<String, Integer>();
    try {
        in = new BufferedReader(new FileReader(fileName));
        String line = "";
        while ((line = in.readLine()) != null) {
            String parts[] = line.split("\t");
            freqHmp.put(parts[0], Integer.parseInt(parts[1]));
        }
        in.close();
    } catch (Exception e) {
        e.printStackTrace();
    }
    System.out.println(freqHmp.toString());
```

```
    return  freqHmp;
  }
```

In the preceding method, we read the output files from our MapReduce program, and store the values in a Hashmap.

```java
public void predict(String row) {

    StringTokenizerst = new StringTokenizer(row, " ");
    double yesLikelyhood = modelYesHmp.get("Pyes");
    double noLikelyhood = modelNoHmp.get("Pno");

    while (st.hasMoreTokens()) {
        String token = st.nextToken();
        String yesKey = "P" + "yes" + token;
        String noKey = "P" + "no" + token;
        yesLikelyhood = yesLikelyhood * modelYesHmp.get(yesKey);
        noLikelyhood = noLikelyhood * modelNoHmp.get(noKey);
    }

    System.out.println("YesLikely=" + yesLikelyhood +
    "NoLikely=" + noLikelyhood);
    if (yesLikelyhood>noLikelyhood )
    {
        System.out.println(row + " CHURN");
    }
    else
    {
        System.out.println(row + " NOCHURN");
    }
  }

}
```

The `predict()` method does its job. First, it will read input data row by row, which contains the attributes of the customer for which the churn should be predicted. For each row, we substitute the values to calculate the likelihood. The calculated likelihoods of yes (churn) and no (no churn) are compared to predict whether a customer will churn.

```java
public static void main(String[] args) {
    ModelBuildermb = new ModelBuilder();
    mb.setFreqYesHmp(mb.initFrequencyHmp("out-yes/part-r-00000"));
    mb.setFreqNoHmp(mb.initFrequencyHmp("out-no/part-r-00000"));
    mb.buildModel();
    mb.predict("High  Old  Less  Normal  IOS  Regular");
  }

}
```

In the preceding code, we specify the input data files that will be used to build the model. After that, we build the model and then do a single prediction.

Integrating the churn predictor

In our example, we showed how our churn predictor can be used. In real life, our churn predictor could be integrated in a web application, and special offers can be displayed on the personalized web page of the customer, when the churn is predicted, to retain the customer.

To understand how to integrate of the churn predictor in the business process of customer analysis, let's consider a simple case where the company has created a special offer for customers who are likely to churn. This offer is called "Get 5 GB Data Free" upon subscription renewal. This offer has to be presented to every customer who visits the self-service portal and who is likely to churn.

Typically, the offer will be presented as a banner ad on the customer's home page in the self-service portal. Banner ads in the graphic form are kept in a content management system. Content management systems give graphic designers the freedom to change the design without knowing the technical details of web programming.

The offer manager is a repository containing various kinds of offer for customers. It is generally managed by marketers or business people. Some of these offers will be valid for churning customers while the others may be used to meet other business goals such as increasing the revenue from the existing customers. In a trivial case, when we have just one offer in the system for churning customers, we will just fetch and display the same offer for all the customers who are likely to churn. Once we have obtained the offer ID from the offer manager, then we will call a service in the content management system to fetch the banner AD, which will be displayed on the website.

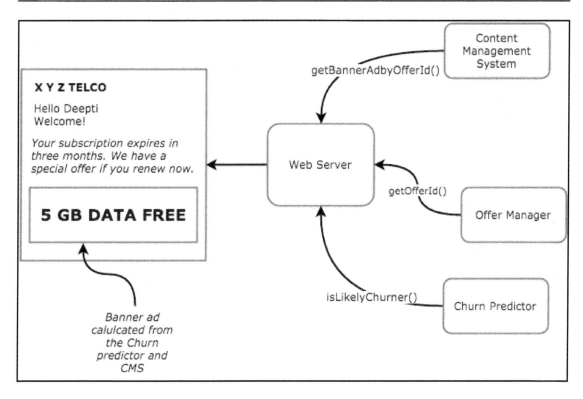

Figure 3 Integrating with a web portal

Figure 3 shows an example of the integration of a churn predictor with the self-service portal of the company. The left block depicts a web page the customer sees when he/she logs on to the self-service portal.

As the customer logs on, we fetch the customer's attributes from a database. Using these attributes, we call the service `isLikelyChurner()` of the churn predictor. If the answer is yes then we call the service `getOfferId()` of Offer Manager. After getting the offer ID, we call the `getBannerAdbyOfferId()` service of Content Management System, which returns the URL of the banner ad. The web server places this banner ad in the homepage of the user. Such a process demands good performance from various systems so that the customer does not experience slow page-load speeds.

While the system presented here explains the concept, the actual system is likely to be much more complex. The complexity will be introduced by other factors, such as the fact that we might not want to show the same banner ad twice by allowing the user to reject the displayed offer. Another complexity can be introduced by omni-channel marketing, which would require us to integrate the churn predictor across multiple channels. In that case, for example, the call center employees will need access to the offers that are likely to be given to the churning customers.

The integration of churn predictors with the Web and call centers goes beyond the scope of this book. The diversity of technologies and scalability aspects require good design before such a solution can go into production.

Summary

In this chapter, we learned about the concept of churn in telecom companies and why it is essential to minimize it. We covered Bayes' Theorem to understand how conditional probabilities can help us predict outcomes in the future. We used MapReduce to process a file to generate input for a model builder. We built the model in Java and then predicted an outcome with its help. The next chapter of this book will cover the application of Hadoop in the area of the Internet of Things.

6

Analyze Sensor Data Using Hadoop

In earlier chapters, we talked about various use cases that can be applied in the banking, retail, or telecom industry. In this chapter, we are going to learn how Hadoop and big data technologies can be helpful in the **Internet of Things (IoT)**. IoT is a network of connected devices that are useful in day-to-day life, such as physical devices, hand held items, wearable gadgets, electronic items, and so on. The concept of the IoT encourages such devices to be connected with each other all the time and to exchange data. Auto-driven cars, intelligent energy meters, and smart electronic gadgets are no longer a dream. Most companies now have their products built with integrated IoT smartness.

If you look at the cars around you, they already have sensors installed in them that constantly monitor the overall health and performance of the car. These sensors continually send the information to company servers, which collect, process, and analyze the data, and can predict and prescribe when a car needs servicing. Many companies have been designing and building driverless cars based on the IoT concept.

 The term IoT was coined by British entrepreneur **Kevin Ashton** in **1999** while working at the Auto-ID Center at MIT Labs. At the time, RFID was seen as a prerequisite for IoT in order to tag devices with unique identification.

In this chapter, we are going to talk about one such use case, and look at how we can use big data technologies to process the data and make more sense out of it.

A business case for sensor data analytics

Consider a factory that produces goods, with many people working under the same roof. Because of the activity of the machines in the factory, environmental conditions such as temperature, humidity, voltage, and light are always changing. In order to ensure that all the workers and machines stay healthy and in good condition, we need to constantly monitor these environmental conditions and make sure everything is under control. In order to achieve this, let's assume that the company has deployed sensors at various points, as shown in the following figure.

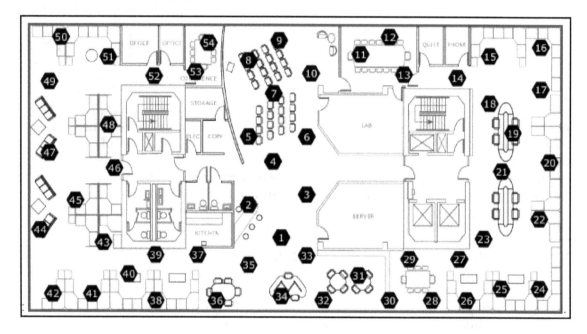

Image source – http://db.csail.mit.edu/labdata/labdata.html

The preceding image depicts the factory area, and the numbers in black indicate the places where sensors have been deployed.

Now we are going to implement a solution that collects and process this data in order to make sure that the conditions are under control.

Creating the solution outline

Let's start by diving straight into the solution right now. Our goal is to do the following things step by step:

1. Loading data into HDFS using batch mode: **Flume**.
2. Loading data into HDFS using streaming mode: **Kafka**.
3. Data analysis using **Hive**.
4. Data visualization using **Grafana** and **Open TSDB**.

The following is an architecture diagram for the solution:

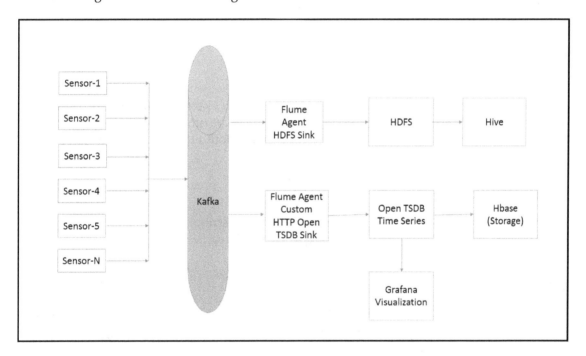

This architecture takes care of both real-time and batch analytics. We will be collecting data into Kafka topics. Then we will be using Flume agents to write this data to HDFS as well as to Open TSDB. Open TSDB is an open source time series database that uses HBase as its storage engine. We will also be using Grafana for the time series data visualization.

Now let's move on to the next step.

Technology stack

For the preceding solution, we would need to use various technologies. The details are as follows.

Kafka

Kafka is a publish-subscribe messaging service. It is distributed, reliable, durable, fast, and scalable by design. It gives us the ability to create topics and publish messages to them. We can then define the subscribers to these topics in order to start consuming these messages. More on Kafka at `http://kafka.apache.org/`.

Flume

Flume is a reliable, distributed system, designed to effectively collect and aggregate data from various systems. In our solution, we are going to use Flume to get data from Kafka and write it to HDFS and Open TSDB simultaneously. More on Flume at `http://flume.apache.org/`. We will be learning more about Flume in the next chapter.

HDFS

Hadoop Distributed File System (**HDFS**) is a reliable, distributed file storage system for effective data analytics. We have already explored this in earlier chapters.

Hive

Hive is an SQL dialect of Hadoop. The data stored on HDFS can be analyzed using SQL-like syntax via Hive. In this solution, we will be using Hive for batch data analytics. We have already explored Hive in earlier chapters.

Open TSDB

Open TSDB is a scalable time series database that uses Hbase as its storage engine. It provides APIs to write time series data in an effective manner. While storing the data, it converts it into Hex format for efficient storage and querying capabilities. For this solution, you need to install Open TSDB on your Hadoop cluster. More details at `http://opentsdb.net/`.

HBase

Hbase is a Hadoop database. It is a NoSQL database that stores the data in key-value pairs. Here we use HBase as a storage engine for Open TSDB. More information is available at `https://hbase.apache.org/`.

Grafana

Grafana provides powerful and efficient ways of querying and visualizing time series data from various sources such as Elastic Search, Open TSDB, Graphite, InfluxDB, and so on. In our solution, we are going to use Grafana for time series data visualization. More on Grafana at `http://grafana.org/`.

Before we start the implementation, make sure the services mentioned previously are installed and running well on your cluster.

Batch data analytics

Now let's start looking at the implementation of batch data analytics. Batch data analytics consists of two important elements:

1. Loading streams of sensor data from Kafka topics to HDFS.
2. Using Hive to perform analytics on inserted data.

Loading streams of sensor data from Kafka topics to HDFS

Let's assume that the sensors are enabled to write data to Kafka topics. Microcomputers such as the Raspberry Pi can be used to develop the interface between sensors and Kafka. In this section, we are going to see how we get the data from Kafka topics and write it to the HDFS folder.

To import the data from Kafka, first you need to have Kafka running on your machine. The following command starts Kafka and Zookeeper:

```
bin/zookeeper-server-start.sh config/zookeeper.properties
bin/kafka-server-start.sh config/server.properties
```

Next, we create a topic called `sensor`, which we will be listening to:

```
bin/kafka-topics.sh --create --zookeeper <ip>:2181
--replication-factor 1 --partitions 1 --topic sensor
```

Next, we will start a `producer`, which we will write to a weblogs topic:

```
bin/kafka-console-producer.sh --broker-list <ip>:9092 --topic sensor
```

Now that all Kafka-related infra is set up, we need to also create the Flume configuration, which will be listening to the weblogs topic and writing it to HDFS:

```
# Flume config to listen to Kakfa topic and write to HDFS.
flume1.sources = kafka-source-1
flume1.channels = hdfs-channel-1
flume1.sinks = hdfs-sink-1
# For each source, channel, and sink, set
# standard properties.
flume1.sources.kafka-source-1.type =
org.apache.flume.source.kafka.KafkaSource
flume1.sources.kafka-source-1.zookeeperConnect = localhost:2181
flume1.sources.kafka-source-1.topic = sensor
flume1.sources.kafka-source-1.batchSize = 100
flume1.sources.kafka-source-1.channels = hdfs-channel-1
flume1.channels.hdfs-channel-1.type = memory
flume1.sinks.hdfs-sink-1.channel = hdfs-channel-1
flume1.sinks.hdfs-sink-1.type = hdfs
flume1.sinks.hdfs-sink-1.hdfs.writeFormat = Text
flume1.sinks.hdfs-sink-1.hdfs.fileType = DataStream
flume1.sinks.hdfs-sink-1.hdfs.filePrefix = sensor
flume1.sinks.hdfs-sink-1.hdfs.useLocalTimeStamp = true
flume1.sinks.hdfs-sink-1.hdfs.path = /hdp/ch06/%{topic}-data/%y-%m-%d
flume1.sinks.hdfs-sink-1.hdfs.rollCount=100
flume1.sinks.hdfs-sink-1.hdfs.rollSize=0
# Other properties are specific to each type of
# source, channel, or sink. In this case, we
# specify the capacity of the memory channel.
flume1.channels.hdfs-channel-1.capacity = 10000
```

The preceding content needs to be put into one file; let's call it kafka.conf. Now we are all set to start fetching data from the Kafka topic and writing it to HDFS. The following command will start the flume agent:

```
bin/flume-ng agent -n flume1 -c /usr/hdp/current/flume-server/conf
-f /root/flume/kafka.conf -Dflume.root.logger=INFO,console
```

Now, as the sensors start publishing on the topic, they will start writing to HDFS by date.

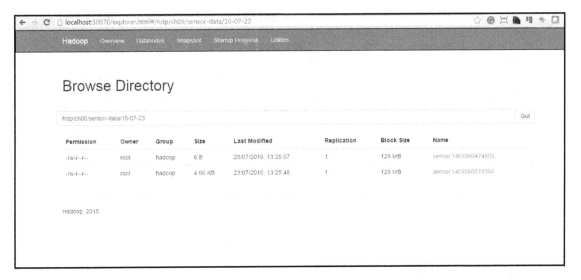

We can also see the sample data by executing the following command:

```
# hadoop fs -cat /hdp/ch06/sensor-data/16-07-23/sensor.1469260518566
2016-03-01 23:23:03.884838 8450 1 19.5376 40.7031 39.56 2.66332
2016-03-01 23:23:29.855559 8451 1 19.5572 40.7031 39.56 2.66332
2016-03-01 23:23:55.367961 8452 1 19.5572 40.6355 39.56 2.67532
2016-03-01 23:24:25.446765 8453 1 19.5572 40.6693 39.56 2.66332
2016-03-01 23:25:24.012614 8455 1 19.5572 40.6693 39.56 2.67532
2016-03-01 23:26:23.066751 8457 1 19.5768 40.568 39.56 2.66332
2016-03-01 23:26:55.520031 8458 1 19.6062 40.5004 39.56 2.66332
2016-03-01 23:27:33.251284 8459 1 19.5964 40.5004 39.56 2.67532
2016-03-01 23:29:38.957422 8463 1 19.567 40.5004 39.56 2.66332
2016-03-01 23:30:22.549366 8465 1 19.5376 40.5342 39.56 2.67532
2016-03-01 23:31:22.848775 8467 1 19.518 40.568 39.56 2.66332
```

Using Hive to perform analytics on inserted data

Now that we have the data on HDFS, we can create external HIVE tables to start analyzing it. The following steps will help us understand how do we this.

First of all, let's check the data available on HDFS:

```
#hadoop fs -ls /hdp/ch06/sensor-data/16-07-23
Found 14 items
-rw-r--r--   1 root hadoop       4774 2016-07-23 07:55 /hdp/ch06/sensor-
data/16-07-23/sensor.1469260518566
-rw-r--r--   1 root hadoop       6204 2016-07-23 08:56 /hdp/ch06/sensor-
data/16-07-23/sensor.1469264191959
-rw-r--r--   1 root hadoop       6276 2016-07-23 08:56 /hdp/ch06/sensor-
data/16-07-23/sensor.1469264191960
-rw-r--r--   1 root hadoop       6258 2016-07-23 08:56 /hdp/ch06/sensor-
data/16-07-23/sensor.1469264191961
-rw-r--r--   1 root hadoop       6330 2016-07-23 08:56 /hdp/ch06/sensor-
data/16-07-23/sensor.1469264191962
-rw-r--r--   1 root hadoop       6413 2016-07-23 08:56 /hdp/ch06/sensor-
data/16-07-23/sensor.1469264191963
-rw-r--r--   1 root hadoop       6424 2016-07-23 08:56 /hdp/ch06/sensor-
data/16-07-23/sensor.1469264191964
-rw-r--r--   1 root hadoop       6425 2016-07-23 08:56 /hdp/ch06/sensor-
data/16-07-23/sensor.1469264191965
-rw-r--r--   1 root hadoop       6360 2016-07-23 08:56 /hdp/ch06/sensor-
data/16-07-23/sensor.1469264191966
-rw-r--r--   1 root hadoop       6317 2016-07-23 08:56 /hdp/ch06/sensor-
data/16-07-23/sensor.1469264191967
-rw-r--r--   1 root hadoop       6349 2016-07-23 08:56 /hdp/ch06/sensor-
data/16-07-23/sensor.1469264191968
-rw-r--r--   1 root hadoop       6361 2016-07-23 08:56 /hdp/ch06/sensor-
data/16-07-23/sensor.1469264191969
-rw-r--r--   1 root hadoop       6359 2016-07-23 08:56 /hdp/ch06/sensor-
data/16-07-23/sensor.1469264191970
-rw-r--r--   1 root hadoop       1338 2016-07-23 08:57 /hdp/ch06/sensor-
data/16-07-23/sensor.1469264191971
```

Now start the Hive prompt and write the following create table statement. You can alternately use beeline for creating the table:

```
hive> CREATE EXTERNAL TABLE sensordata
    > (datecol date,
    > timecol string,
    > epoch int,
    > sensorid int,
    > temperature double,
    > humidity double,
```

```
> light double,
> voltage double)
> ROW FORMAT DELIMITED
> FIELDS TERMINATED BY ' '
> LOCATION '/hdp/ch06/sensor-data/';
OK
```

As we already have data stored on HDFS, we are creating an external hive table. Now let's check if the data is properly loaded in the Hive table by executing the following command:

```
hive> select * from sensordata limit 20;
OK
2016-03-01      23:23:03.884838 8450    1       19.5376 40.7031 39.56
2.66332
2016-03-01      23:23:29.855559 8451    1       19.5572 40.7031 39.56
2.66332
2016-03-01      23:23:55.367961 8452    1       19.5572 40.6355 39.56
2.67532
2016-03-01      23:24:25.446765 8453    1       19.5572 40.6693 39.56
2.66332
2016-03-01      23:25:24.012614 8455    1       19.5572 40.6693 39.56
2.67532
2016-03-01      23:26:23.066751 8457    1       19.5768 40.568  39.56
2.66332
2016-03-01      23:26:55.520031 8458    1       19.6062 40.5004 39.56
2.66332
2016-03-01      23:27:33.251284 8459    1       19.5964 40.5004 39.56
2.67532
2016-03-01      23:29:38.957422 8463    1       19.567  40.5004 39.56
2.66332
2016-03-01      23:30:22.549366 8465    1       19.5376 40.5342 39.56
2.67532
2016-03-01      23:31:22.848775 8467    1       19.518  40.568  39.56
2.66332
2016-03-01      23:32:03.023943 8468    1       19.518  40.6018 39.56
2.66332
2016-03-01      23:32:23.437163 8469    1       19.4984 40.6355 39.56
2.66332
2016-03-01      23:32:53.46926  8470    1       19.5082 40.6018 39.56
2.67532
2016-03-01      23:33:52.556486 8472    1       19.4886 40.7706 39.56
2.66332
2016-03-01      23:34:24.021879 8473    1       19.4984 40.7706 39.56
2.66332
2016-03-01      23:35:02.183562 8474    1       19.4886 40.8043 39.56
2.67532
2016-03-01      23:35:27.226975 8475    1       19.4886 40.7031 39.56
2.66332
```

```
2016-03-01       23:35:55.722915 8476     1        19.4886 40.7031 39.56
2.67532
2016-03-01       23:37:09.852995 8478     1        19.4788 40.7706 39.56
2.66332
Time taken: 0.222 seconds, Fetched: 20 row(s)
```

Now we can start analyzing this data. First, let's see how many records we have date-wise.

```
hive> select datecol, count(*) from sensordata group by datecol;
Query ID = root_20160723091014_09699950-17e8-4fec-a476-2236123a401e
Total jobs = 1
Launching Job 1 out of 1


Status: Running (Executing on YARN cluster with App id
application_1469246444682_0002)


--------------------------------------------------------------------------
-----
        VERTICES      STATUS  TOTAL  COMPLETED  RUNNING  PENDING  FAILED
KILLED
--------------------------------------------------------------------------
-----
Map 1 ..........     SUCCEEDED    1        1         0        0       0
0
Reducer 2 ......     SUCCEEDED    1        1         0        0       0
0
--------------------------------------------------------------------------
-----
VERTICES: 02/02  [==============================>>] 100%  ELAPSED TIME: 9.64 s
--------------------------------------------------------------------------
-----
OK
2016-02-28       12221
2016-03-01       12366
2016-03-02       12221
Time taken: 11.46 seconds, Fetched: 3 row(s)
```

Next, we can find out the maximum temperature per day:

```
hive> select datecol, max(temperature) from sensordata group by datecol;
Query ID = root_20160723091359_307d48b7-1124-48ce-9aef-5ec67f8b3036
Total jobs = 1
Launching Job 1 out of 1
Status: Running (Executing on YARN cluster with App id
application_1469246444682_0002)
--------------------------------------------------------------------------
-----
```

```
VERTICES        STATUS  TOTAL  COMPLETED  RUNNING  PENDING  FAILED  KILLED
--------------------------------------------------------------------------------
-----
Map 1 ....      SUCCEEDED    1        1        0        0        0        0
Reducer 2.      SUCCEEDED    1        1        0        0        0        0
--------------------------------------------------------------------------------
-----
VERTICES: 02/02 [============================>>] 100% ELAPSED TIME: 8.93 s
--------------------------------------------------------------------------------
-----
OK
2016-02-28      24.9864
2016-03-01      19.6062
2016-03-02      19.3514
Time taken: 10.317 seconds, Fetched: 3 row(s)
```

Next, we find out minimum temperature per day:

```
hive> select datecol, min(temperature) from sensordata group by datecol;
Query ID = root_20160723091550_d819f116-8846-4949-91f8-c9522a40b6a1
Total jobs = 1
Launching Job 1 out of 1
Status: Running (Executing on YARN cluster with App id
application_1469246444682_0002)
--------------------------------------------------------------------------------
-----
VERTICES        STATUS  TOTAL  COMPLETED  RUNNING  PENDING  FAILED  KILLED
--------------------------------------------------------------------------------
-----
Map 1 ....      SUCCEEDED    1        1        0        0        0        0
Reducer 2       SUCCEEDED    1        1        0        0        0        0
--------------------------------------------------------------------------------
-----
VERTICES: 02/02 [============================>>] 100% ELAPSED TIME: 7.88 s
--------------------------------------------------------------------------------
-----
OK
2016-02-28      17.509
2016-03-01      19.3318
2016-03-02      19.2044
Time taken: 9.977 seconds, Fetched: 3 row(s)
```

Similarly, we can find out the average temperature per day:

```
hive> select datecol, avg(temperature) from sensordata group by datecol;
Query ID = root_20160723091733_6a909d2e-2e67-47e2-ad19-7cb6834c893f
Total jobs = 1
Launching Job 1 out of 1
```

```
Status: Running (Executing on YARN cluster with App id
application_1469246444682_0002)
-------------------------------------------------------------------------
-----
          VERTICES       STATUS  TOTAL  COMPLETED  RUNNING  PENDING
FAILED  KILLED
          -------------------------------------------------------------------------
---------
     Map 1 ..........    SUCCEEDED     1          1        0        0
0        0
     Reducer 2 ......    SUCCEEDED     1          1        0        0
0        0
          -------------------------------------------------------------------------
---------
     VERTICES: 02/02  [============================>>]  100%   ELAPSED TIME:
12.14 s
          -------------------------------------------------------------------------
---------
     OK
     2016-02-28      21.13268845208841
     2016-03-01      19.473312
     2016-03-02      19.273784000000006
     Time taken: 14.134 seconds, Fetched: 3 row(s)
```

The same set of queries can be fired for humidity:

Maximum humidity per day:

```
hive> select datecol, max(humidity) from sensordata group by datecol;
   OK
   2016-02-28      39.4502
   2016-03-01      40.9055
   2016-03-02      40.9055
```

Minimum humidity per day:

```
hive> select datecol, max(humidity) from sensordata group by datecol;
   OK
   2016-02-28      29.8981
   2016-03-01      40.5004
   2016-03-02      40.6018
```

Average humidity per day:

```
hive> select datecol, avg(humidity) from sensordata group by datecol;
   OK
   2016-02-28      35.653489762489706
   2016-03-01      40.68684599999999
   2016-03-02      40.744935999999996
```

The same set of queries can be fired for light levels:

Maximum light per day:

```
hive> select datecol, max(light) from sensordata group by datecol;
OK
2016-02-28      507.84
2016-03-01      39.56
2016-03-02      39.56
```

Minimum light per day:

```
hive> select datecol, min(light) from sensordata group by datecol;
2016-02-28      43.24
2016-03-01      37.72
2016-03-02      39.56
```

Average light per day:

```
hive> select datecol, avg(light) from sensordata group by datecol;
2016-02-28      185.95377559377226
2016-03-01      39.37599999999997
2016-03-02      39.559999999999974
```

Let's get similar numbers for voltage as well:

Maximum voltage per day:

```
hive> select datecol, max(voltage) from sensordata group by datecol;
2016-02-28      2.76242
2016-03-01      2.67532
2016-03-02      2.67532
```

Minimum voltage per day:

```
hive> select datecol, min(voltage) from sensordata group by datecol;
2016-02-28      2.66332
2016-03-01      2.65143
2016-03-02      2.65143
```

Average voltage per day:

```
hive> select datecol, avg(voltage) from sensordata group by datecol;
2016-02-28      2.7116914414414204
2016-03-01      2.667406599999999
2016-03-02      2.664768799999999
```

We can also query for all these metrics in one go as follows:

```
hive> select datecol, avg(temperature), avg(light), avg(humidity),
avg(voltage) from sensordata group by datecol;
    2016-02-28      21.13268845208841       185.95377559377226
35.653489762489706      2.7116914414414204
    2016-03-01      19.473312       39.37599999999997
40.68684599999999       2.667406599999999
    2016-03-02      19.273784000000006      39.55999999999974
40.744935999999996      2.664768799999999
```

Data visualization in MS Excel

We can also visualize these numbers in MS Excel. Simply export the data into CSV files and import them into an Excel sheet, and you can easily create state-of-the-art visualizations in MS Excel.

For data export, you can use the following command:

```
hadoop fs –copyFromLocal <path-to-hive-table><local-unix-path>
```

The following screenshot shows a sample dashboard of reports from MS Excel.

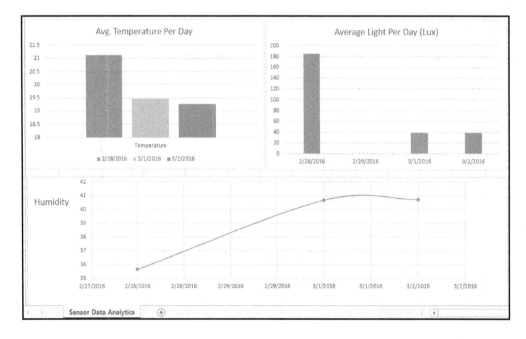

The following screenshot shows the Average Temperature Per Day report on the average temperature per day; we can see that February 28 was the hottest day.

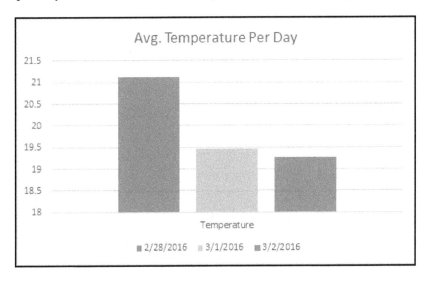

The following screenshot shows the Average Humidity Per Day report; we can see that February 28 was the brightest day.

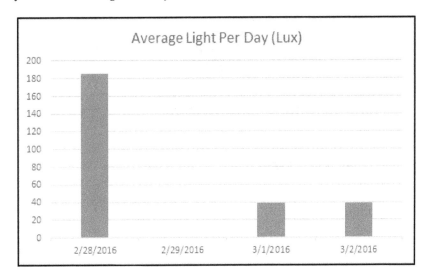

The following screenshot shows the Average Voltage Per Day report; we can see that March 1 was the most humid day.

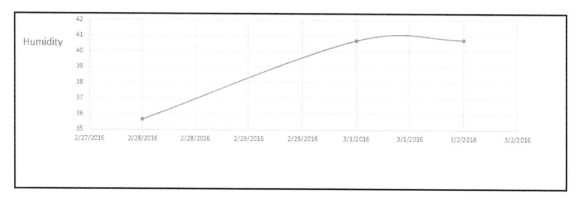

The following screenshot shows the report on the average voltage per day.

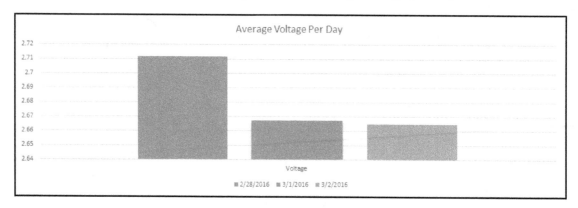

Stream data analytics

Now let's start looking at the implementation of stream data analytics. Stream data analytics consists of two important elements:

- Loading streams of sensor data
- Data visualization using Grafana

Loading streams of sensor data

For batch data analytics we loaded data from Kafka to HDFS, but we will load streaming data into Open TSDB. To do this, first of all please make sure the following services are installed and tested successfully:

- Kafka
- Open TSDB
- Grafana

To extract the data from Kafka topics, we will be using Flume Kafka source and memory channel. But to load the data into Open TSDB, Flume does not provide a suitable sink by default, so I have written this simple sink. The code for the sink is available at `https://git hub.com/deshpandetanmay/flink-opentsdb-sink`.

In order to get this sink, first of all you will need to download the source code from GitHub and build it using Maven.

The following command will help:

```
mvn clean install
```

This will create a JAR file, which needs to be copied to `FLUME_HOME/lib`.

You can also use a pre-built JAR, which can be download from `https://github.com/deshpandetanmay/flink-opentsdb-sink/releases/download/v1.0/original-flume-opentsdb-sink-1.0.jar`.

Now we need to write a configuration file that will be used by the Flume agent. The following is a sample file. Let's call it as `opentsdb.conf`.

```
# Flume config to listen to Kakfa topic and write to OpenTSDB.
flume1.sources = kafka-source-1
flume1.channels = opentsdb-channel-1
flume1.sinks = opentsdb-sink-1
# For each source, channel, and sink, set
# standard properties.
flume1.sources.kafka-source-1.type =
org.apache.flume.source.kafka.KafkaSource
flume1.sources.kafka-source-1.zookeeperConnect = localhost:2181
flume1.sources.kafka-source-1.topic = sensor
flume1.sources.kafka-source-1.batchSize = 100
flume1.sources.kafka-source-1.channels = opentsdb-channel-1
flume1.channels.opentsdb-channel-1.type = memory
flume1.sinks.opentsdb-sink-1.channel = opentsdb-channel-1
```

```
flume1.sinks.opentsdb-sink-1.type =
in.co.hadooptutorials.flume.opentsdb.sink.HttpSink
flume1.sinks.opentsdb-sink-1.protocol  = http
flume1.sinks.opentsdb-sink-1.host  = some-ip
flume1.sinks.opentsdb-sink-1.port  = 4242
flume1.sinks.opentsdb-sink-1.path  = /api/put
flume1.sinks.opentsdb-sink-1.contentTypeHeader  = application/json
flume1.sinks.opentsdb-sink-1.acceptHeader  = application/json
# Other properties are specific to each type of
# source, channel, or sink. In this case, we
# specify the capacity of the memory channel.
flume1.channels.opentsdb-channel-1.capacity = 10000
```

In the preceding configuration file, we are using Kafka as the source memory channel and Open TSDB as the sink. The custom sink fetches data from the Kafka topic, parses it into a JSON message acceptable to Open TSDB, and then executes its POST API.

For example, say we get the following message:

```
Date~Time~Epoch~SensorId~Temperature~Humidity~Light~Voltage
2016-02-29 02:27:49.297161 3060 1 18.4106 40.2299 43.24 2.67532
2016-02-29 02:28:21.136379 3061 1 18.4106 40.2299 43.24 2.67532
2016-02-29 02:28:49.412238 3062 1 18.4106 40.2299 43.24 2.67532
2016-02-29 02:29:21.742951 3063 1 18.4106 40.2299 43.24 2.67532
```

The sink will transform this message as shown:

```
{
    "metric": "temperature",
    "timestamp": 1456712288491,
    "value": 18.4792,
    "tags": {
        "sensor": "1"
    }
}
```

We will call this message API HTTP POST, `http://opentsdb-ip:4242/api/put`.

To start this Flume agent, execute the following command:

```
bin/flume-ng agent -n flume1 -c /usr/hdp/current/flume-server/conf -f
/root/flume/opentsdb.conf -Dflume.root.logger=INFO,console
```

Now, as and when the sensors will start publishing the message to the Kakfa topic, the Flume agent will fetch the message, transform it, and send it to Open TSDB.

Here is a snapshot of the logs from the Flume agent:

```
2016-07-24 09:44:18,890 (SinkRunner-PollingRunner-DefaultSinkProcessor)
[INFO -
in.co.hadooptutorials.flume.opentsdb.sink.HttpSink.process(HttpSink.java:12
3)] Recieved Message:2016-02-29 02:12:48.338627 3030 1 18.4694 40.0607
43.24 2.67532
2016-07-24 09:44:18,891 (SinkRunner-PollingRunner-DefaultSinkProcessor)
[INFO -
in.co.hadooptutorials.flume.opentsdb.sink.HttpSink.process(HttpSink.java:13
7)] Final Message:{"metric": "temperature", "timestamp": 1456712306627,
"value": 18.4694, "tags": {"sensor" : "1" }}
2016-07-24 09:44:19,324 (SinkRunner-PollingRunner-DefaultSinkProcessor)
[INFO -
in.co.hadooptutorials.flume.opentsdb.sink.HttpSink.process(HttpSink.java:14
3)] Response :HTTP/1.1 204 No Content
2016-07-24 09:44:19,325 (SinkRunner-PollingRunner-DefaultSinkProcessor)
[INFO -
in.co.hadooptutorials.flume.opentsdb.sink.HttpSink.process(HttpSink.java:12
3)] Recieved Message:2016-02-29 02:13:21.287491 3031 1 18.4792 40.0945
43.24 2.68742
2016-07-24 09:44:19,326 (SinkRunner-PollingRunner-DefaultSinkProcessor)
[INFO -
in.co.hadooptutorials.flume.opentsdb.sink.HttpSink.process(HttpSink.java:13
7)] Final Message:{"metric": "temperature", "timestamp": 1456712288491,
"value": 18.4792, "tags": {"sensor" : "1" }}
2016-07-24 09:44:19,763 (SinkRunner-PollingRunner-DefaultSinkProcessor)
[INFO -
in.co.hadooptutorials.flume.opentsdb.sink.HttpSink.process(HttpSink.java:14
3)] Response :HTTP/1.1 204 No Content
2016-07-24 09:44:19,764 (SinkRunner-PollingRunner-DefaultSinkProcessor)
[INFO -
in.co.hadooptutorials.flume.opentsdb.sink.HttpSink.process(HttpSink.java:12
3)] Recieved Message:2016-02-29 02:13:53.109369 3032 1 18.4596 40.0268
43.24 2.67532
2016-07-24 09:44:19,765 (SinkRunner-PollingRunner-DefaultSinkProcessor)
[INFO -
in.co.hadooptutorials.flume.opentsdb.sink.HttpSink.process(HttpSink.java:13
7)] Final Message:{"metric": "temperature", "timestamp": 1456712142369,
"value": 18.4596, "tags": {"sensor" : "1" }}
2016-07-24 09:44:20,157 (SinkRunner-PollingRunner-DefaultSinkProcessor)
[INFO -
in.co.hadooptutorials.flume.opentsdb.sink.HttpSink.process(HttpSink.java:14
3)] Response :HTTP/1.1 204 No Content
2016-07-24 09:44:20,157 (SinkRunner-PollingRunner-DefaultSinkProcessor)
[INFO -
in.co.hadooptutorials.flume.opentsdb.sink.HttpSink.process(HttpSink.java:12
3)] Recieved Message:2016-02-29 02:14:50.011619 3034 1 18.44 40.1284 43.24
```

```
2.67532
2016-07-24 09:44:20,159 (SinkRunner-PollingRunner-DefaultSinkProcessor)
[INFO -
in.co.hadooptutorials.flume.opentsdb.sink.HttpSink.process(HttpSink.java:13
7)] Final Message:{"metric": "temperature", "timestamp": 1456712101619,
"value": 18.44, "tags": {"sensor" : "1" }}
2016-07-24 09:44:20,553 (SinkRunner-PollingRunner-DefaultSinkProcessor)
[INFO -
in.co.hadooptutorials.flume.opentsdb.sink.HttpSink.process(HttpSink.java:14
3)] Response :HTTP/1.1 204 No Content
```

We can also look at the Open TSDB GUI and query it with exact parameters:

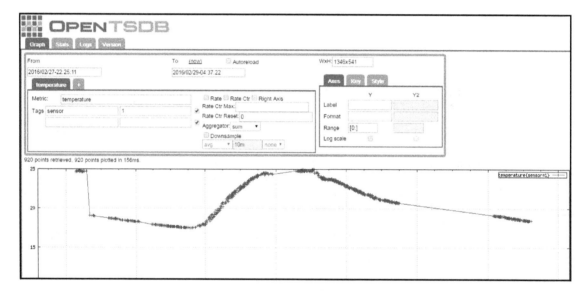

In the preceding screenshot, you can see the temperature variations over time. We can similarly see the variations for humidity, light, and voltage.

Now let's look at how to visualize the same events using Grafana.

Data visualization using Grafana

To perform the next steps, please make sure Grafana is installed. Grafana supports querying data from various sources such as Open TSDB, Elasticsearch, Graphite, and others. For us to start using Grafana, we need to add a source as Open TSDB and provide its details.

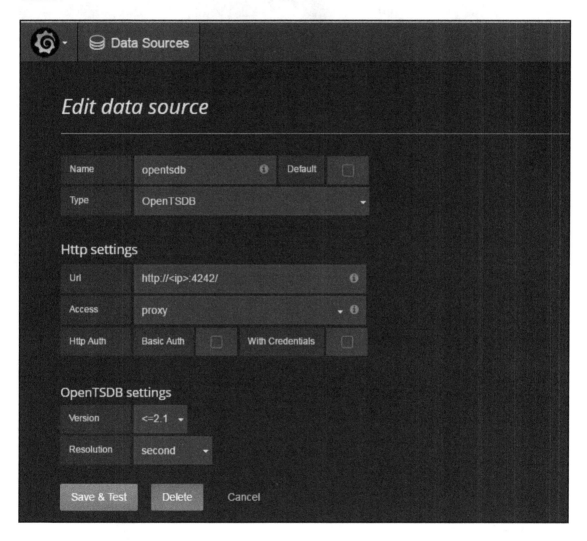

Next, we create a new dashboard named **Temperature Sensor Monitoring** and start adding new visualizations to it.

For example, if we want to get a line graph of temperature over time, then we can create the following settings:

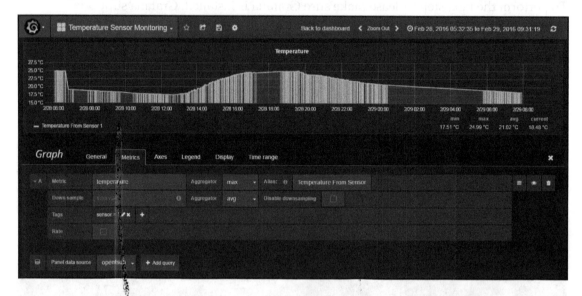

Similarly, we can add some more visualizations and present our dashboard as follows:

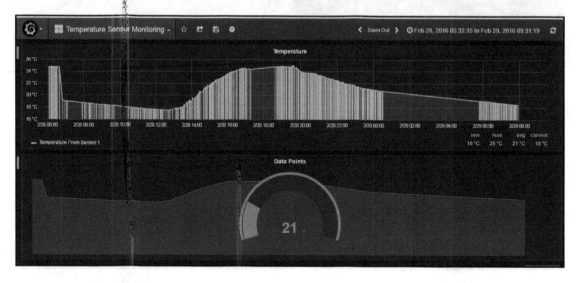

Summary

In this chapter, we learned the basic concept of the Internet of Things (IoT) and how big data can be used in this way to perform data processing. Then we tried to solve a business case for sensor data analytics, and we implemented software solutions as part of the use case. For any sensor data analytics use case, it is very important to focus on both batch and stream analytics. Both ways have their own meaning and importance. It is not mandatory to solve all such use cases using the aforementioned technologies; in fact, there are various similar options available. Based on your need, you can choose the preferred one.

In the next chapter, we will look at how to build a Hadoop-based Data Lake for large enterprises. We will learn how to set up the data pipeline and governance.

7
Building a Data Lake

In this chapter, we will cover building a Data Lake with the help of Hadoop. As we have learned in previous chapters, Hadoop offers low storage costs per terabyte of data compared to traditional data warehouse management systems, which makes it an alternative technology or a complementary technology for traditional data warehouse systems. Data Lake and data warehouse are both designed to store data, but a data lake can store a much larger volume of data than a data warehouse.

Data warehouses typically store clean data in pre-defined and structured relational tables. The tables are designed to hold the data in response to specific questions that the stakeholders ask of the data. In this process, the information contained in the data that has no direct value for the question that is being asked is purged when the data is loaded in the data warehouse. Once the information has been purged, there is no way to answer new questions that require the purged information to formulate the answer. In the past, when the cost of computing and storage was high, it made sense to think carefully about which information should be stored in data warehouse to keep the cost of data storage under control.

Hadoop has emerged as a preferred alternative to building data warehouses because of lower storage costs, as well as its ability to query data using multiple tools and programming languages. The Hadoop ecosystem also provides many options to import the data in Hadoop and run a variety of workloads. Hadoop can store structured, unstructured, and semi-structured data in HDFS without requiring any kind of schema definition at the time of data import. This makes Hadoop a very flexible system for storing previously discarded data.

A Data Lake is a single source of all kinds of data relevant for the enterprise. For example, it can contain data from structured data sources, such as CRM systems, and inventory management systems; semi-structured data from the sources such as web logs; and unstructured data from emails or call center transcripts.

The storage of a massive amount of data in the data lake is a serious challenge from the data engineering perspective where you have to think about the SLAs, backup policies, capacity management, and disaster recovery. When all the enterprise data is located in a single data repository, secure access to the data becomes a paramount concern. In the early releases of Hadoop, not much attention was paid to building the tools to deliver the fine-grained security a data lake would require. For example, when a data lake will store all the data of a company, then you might want to restrict the access to a certain dataset to certain groups.

In this chapter, we will focus on building a data lake with a fine-grained security arrangement using the tools available in the Hadoop ecosystem. In this chapter, you will learn the following:

- Data lake building blocks
- Hadoop Security Model
- Introduction to Apache Ranger
- Introduction to Apache Flume
- Introduction to Apache Zeppelin
- Setting up a data lake with Hadoop

The scope of our discussion will be Hadoop-centric, but in a data lake it is also possible to have other storage systems, such as In-Memory databases, NoSQLdatabases, and data warehouse appliances. In-Memory and NoSQL database have been explained in the `Chapter 8`, *Future Directions*, of this book. All these systems might come with their proprietary vendors' specific tooling.

Data lake building blocks

A data lake is an abstract concept which requires technological tools and systems to implement. Since there is no standard definition of what a data lake must consist of, it is not uncommon to see slightly differing names of the constituent building blocks of data lakes in the definitions proposed by vendors and industry analysts. The building blocks of a data lake will fall into three tiers:

- Ingestion tier
- Storage tier
- Insights tier

Ingestion tier

In general, a data lake should be able to take data feeds from multiple sources. This data feed can come in real time, micro batches, or in large batch files. A data lake should be able to ingest the data from difference sources. For each type of data source, the data ingestion tools may be identified. The ingestion tier can also provide scheduling tools to import the data at predefined intervals.

Storage tier

Data lakes will have a data storage system, such as HDFS, where the data resides in its raw form. Though this data is in its raw form, it may still contain confidential information. To protect the information, the data lake will have some kind of data security system in place, which will provide the means to set up the data security policies and auditing facilities. The data storage system might also have In-Memory data and a **Massively Parallel Processing (MPP)** database appliance. After the refinement and transformation of raw data, data can be stored in the in-memory databases or MPP database appliance. The storage tier can also contain a metadata management system and enterprise data dictionary.

Insights tier

Data lakes will also have a variety of tools available to query the data stored in the data lake and create actionable insights. Thqe query tools can be SQL-based or based upon 3 GL, such as Java. In addition, a data lake might have spreadsheet-like data analysis tools and visualization tools.

Ops facilities

An operational data lake will be equipped with system monitoring and management tools so that we can deliver service as per **Service Level Agreement (SLA)** and carry out system maintenance at regular intervals. A data lake will have a security layer where we can grant and revoke the access to the data resources in the data lake as per the data governance policies of the organization.

The ecosystem of Hadoop provides several tools which can be used to the implement the building blocks of a data lake. We will use the tools such as Ranger, Flume, and Zeppelin to build our data lake.

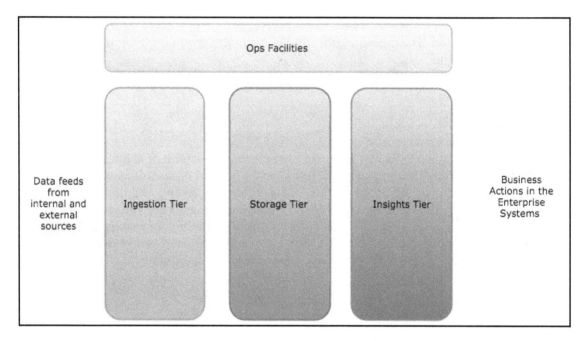

Figure 1 Data lake tiers

Limitation of open source Hadoop ecosystem tools

In Chapter 1, *Hadoop and Big Data*, we covered several tools in the Hadoop ecosystem. Despite our ever growing list of tools, the configuration of these tools to build a data lake requires considerable expertise. The Hadoop ecosystem has grown as a result of contributions from the community, which has resulted in rapid innovations. However, the downside of the community process is that the tool ecosystem remains fragmented and lacks good documentation. Building a solution using Hadoop requires considerable coding expertise in programming languages, such as Java.

Hadoop security

When it was first created, Hadoop was not designed to work as the repository of an enterprise's entire store of data, as the data lake concept proposes. It was assumed that Hadoop will be operated in the trusted environment by the trusted users. Moreover, the early versions of Hadoop were used to store the data from public web logs, the confidentiality of which was not an issue. As Hadoop started getting positioned as the platform for enterprises, the Hadoop security concerns came to the forefront. To address these concerns, open source and proprietary solutions came on the market. These solutions focused upon a single security aspect such as data encryption and perimeter security, however they did not offer the fine-grained authorization on the data stored in Hadoop. A detailed discussion on Hadoop security is available at `http://www.infoq.com/articles/HadoopSecurityModel`.

HDFS permissions model

In our data lake use case, HDFS is the storage system for raw data. HDFS organizes the data in directories and files, which is similar to the POSIX model used in the Unix-based systems; however, unlike Unix systems distributes the data contained in a file on a cluster of computers. A file or a directory on the file system has three levels of permissions associated with the user, group, and world.

In the file permissions, the r flag is required to read the file, and the w flag is required to modify or write a new file. In the directories, the r flag is required to list the contents of the directory, the w flag is required to create or delete files or directories in the directory, and the x flag is required to access a child directory.

Let us consider a company which has sales operating in two regions—Europe and Asia. Jim works in the European region and Tim works in the Asian region. They receive a daily feed of sales data from their region which is stored in the HDFS for further analysis. The data owned by Jim can be viewed by Tim, but Tim cannot modify it or create new data. The same restrictions apply to Jim when it comes to accessing the data owned by Tim.

Using the HDFS file permissions model, we can create two directories, `europe` and `asia`, with sales as a parent directory. The directory named `europe` is readable and writable by Jim and readable by everyone else. The `asia` directory is readable and writable by Tim and readable by everyone else, as shown in the following code:

```
tim@ell-Aspire-5750G:~$ hadoop fs -ls /sales
16/05/11 02:59:37 WARN util.NativeCodeLoader: Unable to load native-hadoop
library for your platform... using builtin-java classes where applicable
```

```
Found 2 items
drwxr-xr-x - tim asia 0 2016-05-11 02:38 /sales/asia
drwxr-xr-x - jim europe 0 2016-05-11 02:31 /sales/europe
```

As you can see, both directories have the permission mask 755. This permission mask can also be composed using a web-based tool such as http://chmod-calculator.com/. If Tim tries to store a file in /sales/europe, the operation will fail because Hadoop will deny the permission.

```
tim@ell-Aspire-5750G:~$ hadoop fs -put salesasia.txt /sales/europe
put: Permission denied: user=tim, access=WRITE,
inode="/sales/europe/salesasia.txt._COPYING_":jim:europe:drwxr-xr-x
```

Because of the read permission, Tim will be able to read a file in the /sales/europe directory as follows:

```
tim@ell-Aspire-5750G:~$ hadoop fs -cat /sales/europe/sales.txt
Sales Data
USD 15m
```

The basic HDFS permission model allows us to restrict the access to a file or directory to a user and group. However, in some cases this model may have limitations. For example, we might want that the users belonging to two different groups to have read access to a file. In the basic permission model, it is only possible to specify the access permissions for the group that is the owner of the file. In the basic HDFS permission model, we can have only one user and one group for which we can specify the access rights. In the large organizations, with hundreds of groups and thousands of users, this model may not be sufficient. Fortunately, HDFS also supports **access control lists** (**ACL**) which offer a fine-grained permission control on the HDFS files.

Fine-grained permissions with HDFS ACLs

Hadoop has support for ACLs from Apache Hadoop version 2.4.0 onwards. An ACL feature has been developed by the Apache community to address the number of large scale Hadoop adoption concerns in the enterprises. The security of data stored in data lakes is a key issue in the wake of ever increasing data security breaches and resulting financial losses suffered by the enterprises.

The basis for Hadoop Access Control Lists is POSIX ACLs, available on the Linux filesystem. These ACLs allow you to link a set of permissions to a file or directory that is not limited to just one user and group who owns the file. The HDFS ACLs give you a fine-grained file permissions model that is suitable for a large enterprise where the data stored on the Hadoop cluster should be accessible to some groups and inaccessible to many others.

The ACLs on Hadoop are configured on NameNode. The configuration setting for ACLs is stored in the file `hdfs-site.xml` in the property named `dfs.namenode.acls.enabled`. This property is disabled by default. To start using the ACLs, first we enable the ACLs by setting the value of this property to true in the configuration, and then restarting NameNode in order for the settings to take effect.

```
<property> <name>dfs.namenode.acls.enabled</name> <value>true</value>
</property>
```

Once you have started the NameNode again, you can read the ACLs using getfacl command as follows:

```
hduser@el1-Aspire-5750G:~$ hadoop fs -getfacl /sales/europe/q.txt
# file: /sales/europe/q.txt
# owner: jim
# group: europe
user::rwx
group::---
other::---
```

So far we, have not associated an ACL with the file `q.txt`, so we just se the file permission for a single owner and group. Let's give user `tim` the full access to the file `q.txt` using the `setacl` command:

```
hduser@el1-Aspire-5750G:~$ hadoop fs -setfacl -m user:tim:rwx
/sales/europe/q.txt
    hduser@el1-Aspire-5750G:~$ hadoop fs -getfacl  /sales/europe/q.txt
    # file: /sales/europe/q.txt
    # owner: jim
    # group: europe
    user::rwx
    user:tim:rwx
    group::---
    mask::rwx
    other::---
```

By running the setacl command, we have given `rwx` access in file `q.txt` to the user tim. Likewise, we can specify the ACLs for multiple users and groups for the files stored in HDFS.

The command ls shows us if ACLs are associated with a file by appending a plus (+) sign to the file permissions column in the output of `ls` command, as shown here:

```
hduser@el1-Aspire-5750G:~$ hadoop fs -ls /sales/europe/q.txt
-rwxrwx---+  1jimeurope        1024 2016-05-12 03:03 /sales/europe/q.txt
```

HDFS file permissions and ACLs enable fine-grained access control to the files stored on HDFS. However, with data lakes, users would access the data using a number of tools. Similarly, data lakes will get data feeds from a number of tools. HDFS file-based security is limited to files alone, and does not cover the tools accessing the data stored on the Hadoop cluster such as Hive. Apache Ranger offers much better centralized control of the Hadoop security that is required in a data lake.

Apache Ranger

Apache Ranger is a security framework which lets you define the policies to control the data access in Hadoop. It provides a web-based console that can be used by the system administrators of the Hadoop cluster to define and activate the access policies. Apache Ranger understands how different tools interact with Hadoop and lets you define permissions accordingly. For example, for Hive data, you can define whether a user is allowed to create or drop a table or read a column using Apache Ranger.

Apache Ranger also maintains an audit log and analytics data, which is useful information for risk and compliance personnel to access from a web-based console.

These features of Apache Ranger make it an important technology to use while building a data lake.

The examples of Apache Ranger in this chapter use the version 0.5.0, which can be downloaded from the website of the Apache organization.

Installing Apache Ranger

Before the installation of Apache Ranger, you need to make sure that you have Hadoop installation on your system. Apache Ranger sources should be downloaded from the Apache website and built on the machine that you will be running it from. Detailed installation instructions for Ranger are available at `https://cwiki.apache.org/confluence/display/RANGER/Apache+Ranger+0.5.0+Installa tion`

Test driving Apache Ranger

The default http port for the Apache Ranger web console is 6080. For example, I access the web console on `http://192.168.2.102:6080`. If your Ranger server is running, then you will see the login screen as shown in Figure 2.

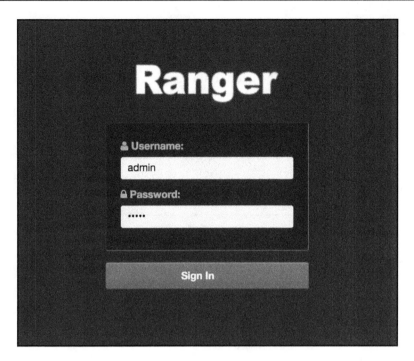

Figure 2 Ranger login dialog

You can now login using the default username admin and password admin. In my Ranger installation, I have used Unix as the authentication method, which allows me to log on using a valid Unix user id and password on the Ranger console. Ranger can also use LDAP and Active Directory as the user authentication system which is better suited to large enterprises.

> You should always change the admin password in the production installations.

After logging in, we see the Ranger console. In the Ranger console, we can carry out the following activities:

- Define services and access policies
- Examine the audit logs
- Users and groups

Define services and access policies

Let's explore these activities from the Ranger console. The Service Manager of the Ranger console, shown in *Figure 3*, shows the list of data access tools supported by Ranger. Before we can start defining the services in the Service Manager, we need to set up the Ranger plugins for the tools where we will enforce the access control policies defined by Ranger.

The steps to set up various plugins are available on the Apache website at `https://cwiki.apache.org/confluence/display/RANGER/Apache+Ranger+0.5.0+Installation`. Please note that Ranger does not require you to configure all the plug-ins, but only those tools for which you want to enforce the Ranger policies.

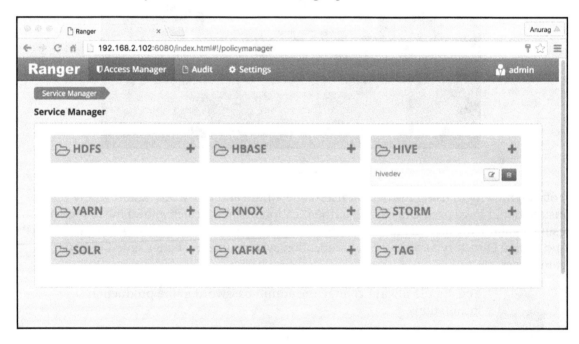

Figure 3 Ranger Service Manager

In my Ranger installation, I have set up the plugins for HDFS and HIVE. Let's set up the service for HDFS. By clicking on the + sign in the HDFS cell, you will see the service setup screen. In this screen, you can specify the username and password for the user who will make the connection to HDFS, as well as the URL of NameNode. In my Hadoop cluster, I have not enabled Kerberos, so I have chosen the authentication type Simple.

Once you have entered the parameters, you can test the connection to the Hadoop cluster by clicking on the **Test Connection** button. You will receive the message, **Connected Successfully**, if your Hadoop cluster is running and Ranger is able to connect with it. Now click on the **Add** button to add the service:

Figure 4 Creating a Service in the Service Manager

The newly defined service named **hadoopdev** appears in the main panel of Service Manager, as shown in the following screenshot. For this service, we will create the policies by clicking the hyperlink on the service named **hadoopdev**.

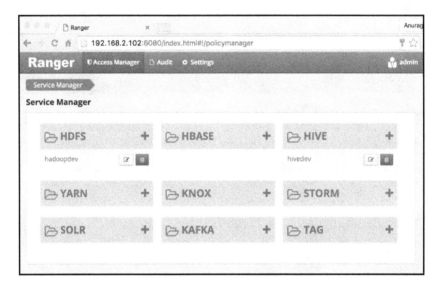

Figure 5 Services in the Service Manager

In the next screen, we see the list of policies. For now, there is only one policy that has been defined during the service creation.

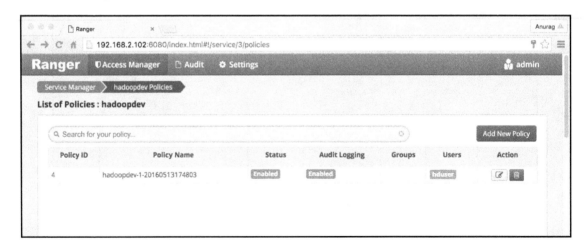

Figure 6 Setting policies in the Service Manager

Let's now define a new policy for a department called legal. The user mike works in this department.

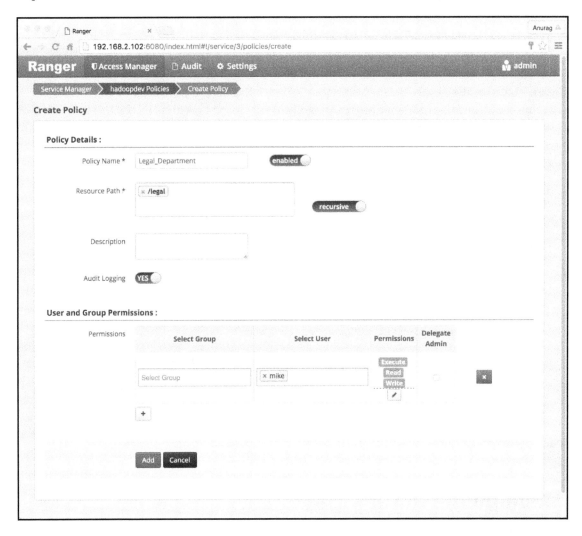

Figure 7 Setting the policy details in the Service Manager

Now, save the policy by clicking on the **Add** button. To understand the effect of policies in Ranger, let's create a directory in HDFS by logging on as the `hduser` user.

```
hduser@el1-Aspire-5750G:~$ hadoop fs -mkdir /legal
hduser@el1-Aspire-5750G:~$ hadoop fs -ls /
Found 1 items
drwxr-xr-x    - hdusersupergroup          0 2016-05-13 21:49 /legal
```

Please note that the newly created directory /legal has all the permissions for the owner legal and read and execute for the group and others. Please note that HDFS has no notion of executable files, so we can ignore the x flag which denotes an executable file on the Unix filesystem.

Next, we will change the permissions on the /legal directory to the most restrictive settings so that nobody is able to read or write in the directory using HDFS commands.

```
hduser@el1-Aspire-5750G:~$ hadoop fs -chmod 000 /legal
hduser@el1-Aspire-5750G:~$ hadoop fs -ls /
Found 1 items
d---------    - hduser supergroup          0 2016-05-13 21:58 /legal
```

Let's now log on as the user mike and try to create a sub directory in the /legal directory.

```
mike@el1-Aspire-5750G:~$ hadoop fs -mkdir /legal/africa
mike@el1-Aspire-5750G:~$ hadoop fs -ls /legal
Found 1 items
drwxr-xr-x    - mike supergroup          0 2016-05-13 21:59 /legal/africa
```

Let's now log on as the user `tim` and try to create a sub directory in the directory /legal.

```
tim@el1-Aspire-5750G:~$ hadoop fs -mkdir /legal/asia
mkdir: Permission denied: user=tim, access=EXECUTE,
inode="/legal/asia":hduser:supergroup:d---------
```

Examine the audit logs

Ranger offers an audit log where we can see how the different resources on HDFS were accessed. To check the audit log, go to Audit and then click the tab Access. You can see that the user mike attempted to create a sub directory in /legal which was permitted by the ranger-acl. This ranger-acl-based permission is the result of the access policy that we defined in Ranger.

You will also see a log entry with the result denied in red color. This entry indicates that the user `tim` was not allowed to create a subdirectory under the directory `/legal`. However, this action was prevented by Hadoop ACLs on directory `/legal` because we did not have any policy for the user `tim` in Ranger.

Ranger will fall back to Hadoop ACLs if no matching policy is found in its database.

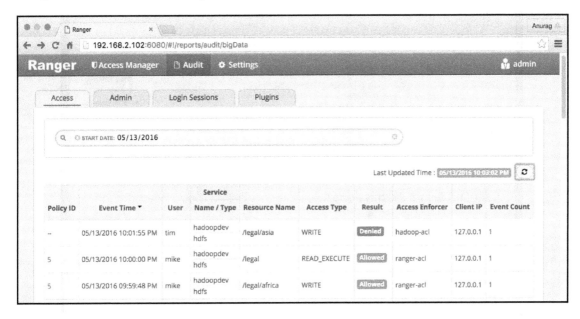

Figure 8 Access Audit Log in Ranger

To verify the name of the policy that **ranger-acl** has enforced to allow the creation of the subdirectory, please click on the green **Allowed** label.

A dialog as shown in the following screenshot pops up where you can see the policy name.

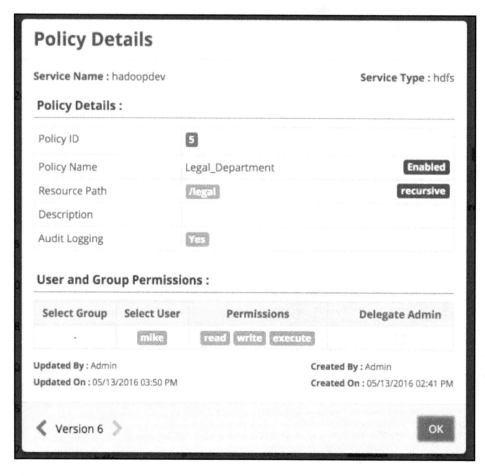

Figure 9 Policy details and versioning in Ranger

The policies created in Ranger are versioned, and any modifications to them can be audited. We can test this by modifying the policy named **Legal_Department** to include `tim` as a user having rwx permissions in the `/legal` directory.

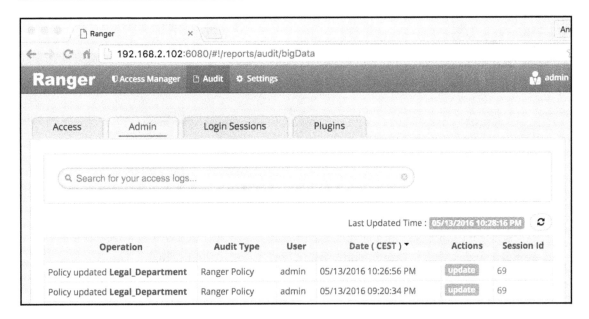

Figure 10 Policy update log in Ranger

If you click on the orange **update** button, then you can see the full details about what has changed in the policy and who performed the change, as shown in the following screenshot:

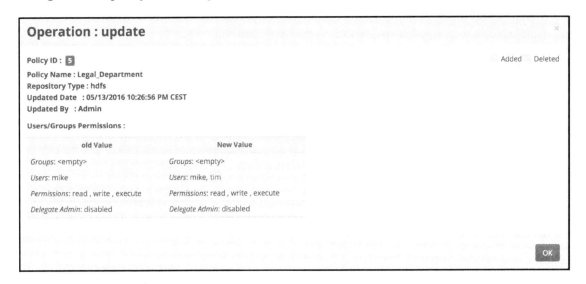

Figure 11 Policy update details in Ranger

Viewing users and groups in Ranger

You can view the list of users and groups who can access the Ranger portal or its repositories. Click the menu button User/Groups under the drop-down menu settings. Ranger supports three kinds of users:

- **Internal users**: These users can log on to Ranger's web console. They are defined by the admin users of the web console.

- **External users**: These users can access services controlled by the Ranger portal. In our previous examples, mike and tim are the external users. Generally, these user accounts reside on another system, such as Unix, LDAP, or Active Directory server. With the help of a user-sync plugin, Ranger periodically syncs the user information in its database.

- **Admins**: Admins are the only users with permission to create users, create services, run reports, and perform other administrative tasks. Admins can also create child policies derived from the parent policy.

Data Lake security with Apache Ranger

The fine-grained permissions model of Apache Ranger is a powerful tool to secure the data resources stored in the Hadoop-based data lake. It provides a web-based console that offers a centralized toolbox to perform various security related operations on HDFS and in its ecosystem of tools. In our data lake design, HDFS and Apache Ranger will be the two important technologies in our storage tier and ops facilities.

Now that we have covered the tools that ensure the security of data in the data lake, we will examine Apache Flume, which will be used to load data on HDFS in the ingestion tier.

Apache Flume

Data Lakes can be filled with data coming from multiple sources at different speeds. The tools in the ingestion tier, such as Apache Flume, can handle the massive volume of incoming data and store it on HDFS.

Apache Flume is a distributed and scalable tool that can reliably collect the data from different sources and move it to a centralized data store on HDFS. Massive volumes of data can be generated in the form of weblogs or sensor data and stored on HDFS for analysis and distribution. Though the typical use cases of Apache Flume involve collection and storage of log data, it can be used to ingest any kind of data in HDFS.

Understanding the Design of Flume

Flume is an agent-based system. It contains three components:

- **Source**: The source receives the events from an external system or from the sink of another Flume agent.
- **Channel**: This offers the means to let events flow from a source to a sink. A channel is a transient store that holds the event coming from a source until it is removed by a sink. A persistent channel backed by storage in a database gives the flows durability.
- **Sink**: The sink sends the events to the destination system, or to the source of another Flume agent.

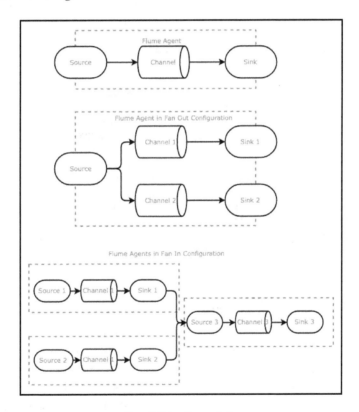

Figure 12 Various Flume topologies

The Flume components can be arranged in various combinations to create a topology for data ingestion as shown in *Figure 12*.

Events in Flume are byte payloads with optional string headers. The events contain the data, which Flume receives at the source and transports to a sink and beyond. The Flume agent is executed as an independent process on a JVM instance. This process executes source, sink, and channel as its runtime components. The several sinks of agents can deliver events to a common source to aggregate the data. In exactly the opposite fashion, a source can fan out an event to multiple sinks.

Installing Apache Flume

You can download Apache Flume from the apache.org website. The examples in this book are based upon Apache Flume version 1.6.0. You can install Flume by unpacking the downloaded binary file in a directory. The following listing shows the directory structure of Flume after unpacking the downloaded zipped TAR file.

```
$ tar xvzf apache-flume-1.6.0-bin.tar.gz
$~/apache-flume-1.6.0-bin$ ls -lcp
total 144
drwxr-xr-x  2hduserhduser   4096 May 25 20:26 bin/
-rw-r--r--  1hduserhduser  69856 May 25 20:26 CHANGELOG
drwxr-xr-x  2hduserhduser   4096 May 25 22:17 conf/
-rw-r--r--  1hduserhduser   6172 May 25 20:26 DEVNOTES
drwxr-xr-x 10 hduserhduser   4096 May 25 20:26 docs/
drwxrwxr-x  2hduserhduser   4096 May 25 20:26 lib/
-rw-r--r--  1hduserhduser  25903 May 25 20:26 LICENSE
drwxrwxr-x  2hduserhduser   4096 May 25 22:09 logs/
-rw-r--r--  1hduserhduser    249 May 25 20:26 NOTICE
-rw-r--r--  1hduserhduser   1779 May 25 20:26 README
-rw-r--r--  1hduserhduser   1585 May 25 20:26 RELEASE-NOTES
drwxrwxr-x  2hduserhduser   4096 May 25 20:26 tools/
```

Running Apache Flume

You can start a Flume agent by running `flume-ng`, which is located in the bin directory of Flume installation. `flume-ng` is a shell script that sets up the environment variable before running the JVM to start the Flume agent. The script `flume-ng` also requires the name of agent, name, and location of a Flume configuration file as input. The Flume configuration file contains the definition of Flume runtime topology in the form of source, sink, and channel definitions.

Let's say that we are interested in logging the stock prices of a few companies at regular intervals with the help of Flume. To read the latest stock prices in the comma-separated value format, we will need to write a script. This script will execute every two seconds to fetch the stock quotes from a service, such as Yahoo! Finance.

The script is as follows:

```
$ cat stock.sh
#!/bin/bash
while true;
do
curl
"http://download.finance.yahoo.com/d/quotes.csv?s=RHT,MSFT,GOOG,INFY&f=sb2b
3jk";
sleep 2;
done
```

The output of this endlessly looping script is as follows:

```
"RHT",N/A,N/A,59.59,84.44
"MSFT",N/A,N/A,39.72,56.85
"GOOG",N/A,N/A,515.18,789.87
"INFY",N/A,N/A,15.30,20.47
```

We are interested in ingesting the output of this script using Flume. The stock.sh script is located in the root directory of Flume, and it has execute permission on Linux.

Next, we will copy the Flume configuration file named stockloader.conf in the conf directory of your Flume installation. This file is supplied with the code samples of this chapter in this book. This file contains the Flume configuration necessary for reading data from the shell script in the Flume source, putting it in the channel and then writing it into a file using a Flume sink. The Flume sink, in this case, is a file appender, which writes data in the file located in the directory httpsink located in the Flume root directory. Create this directory under your Flume root directory.

Let's run the Flume agent now:

```
$ bin/flume-ng agent --conf conf --conf-file conf/stockloader.conf --name
a1 -Dflume.root.logger=INFO,console
```

The Flume agent will generate several log messages during the startup. In the end, you will see a log message similar to the following:

```
2016-05-28 19:04:16,138 (lifecycleSupervisor-1-0) [INFO -
org.apache.flume.instrumentation.MonitoredCounterGroup.start(MonitoredCount
erGroup.java:96)] Component type: SOURCE, name: r1 started
```

This message indicates that the Flume has successfully started, and has set up a flow to ingest the output of the `stock.sh` file. Now we will go to the directory `httpsink`, where we can see the output from the sink is being collected in a file.

```
$ cd httpsink
$ ls -l
total 4
-rw-rw-r-- 1 hduserhduser 327 mei 28 19:07 1464455261754-1
$ cat 1464455261754-1
"RHT",N/A,N/A,59.59,84.44
"MSFT",N/A,N/A,39.72,56.85
"GOOG",N/A,N/A,515.18,789.87
"INFY",N/A,N/A,15.30,20.47
"RHT",N/A,N/A,59.59,84.44
"MSFT",N/A,N/A,39.72,56.85
"GOOG",N/A,N/A,515.18,789.87
"INFY",N/A,N/A,15.30,20.47
```

In this example, Flume is writing to a single file using a sink type `file_roll`, which allows you to roll the log files over a configurable time interval and specify the batch size which will be used to write the events in the file.

Let's examine the configuration file `stockloader.conf` used in this example, which is the most crucial part of setting up Flume:

```
# A single-node Flume configuration to read the output of a shell script
# Name the components on this agent
a1.sources = r1
a1.sinks = k1
a1.channels = c1
```

In the preceding lines, we create a new Flume agent `a1` and defined a source `r1`, which has a sink k1 and a channel c1 in it.

```
# Describe/configure the source
a1.sources.r1.type = exec
a1.sources.r1.command = ./stock.sh
```

In the preceding lines, we configured the source. Flume supports several types of sources. In this example, we used source type exec, which can execute a shell script and ingest the stdout of the shell script in the Flume agent. Here, we specified the type of source, which command to execute, and the channel where the event will be put.

```
# Describe the sink
a1.sinks.k1.type = file_roll
a1.sinks.k1.sink.directory = ./httpsink
a1.sinks.k1.sink.rollInterval = 600
a1.sinks.k1.sink.serializer = TEXT
a1.sinks.k1.batchSize = 1
```

The preceding lines in the configuration file define the sink as being of type file_roll, which lets us write the events in a file. Flume supports several types of syncs, such as an HDFS Sink, Hive Sink, and Logger Sink. We defined the directory name, where the file_roll will write the files, and the batch size. We set the roll interval to 600 seconds, which allows the output file to grow to rollover every 10 minutes.

```
# Use a channel which buffers events in memory
a1.channels.c1.type = memory
a1.channels.c1.capacity = 1000
a1.channels.c1.transactionCapacity = 100
```

In the preceding lines, we defined a memory-based channel and its capacity. Because we are using a memory-based channel here, the events received by the agent will not be durable. For example, if the flume agent crashes then the events in the channel that are waiting to be flushed in the sink will be permanently lost. To overcome this problem, we can use persistent channels where the events in the channel are kept in a persistent store, such as database or file.

```
# Bind the source and sink to the channel
a1.sources.r1.channels = c1
a1.sinks.k1.channel = c1
```

Finally, we tie all the components together, establishing a simple Flume topology. For example, this configuration file is passed as input to our Flume agent startup script.

Apache Flume is the data ingestion tool of choice in our data lake design. We will use Apache Flume to read data in an HDFS cluster. So far, we have determined the tools that we will use to build the ingestion and storage tier in the data lake. The next step is to choose a tool to fulfill the needs of the insight tier.

To build the insights tier, we will use a tool called Apache Zeppelin. At the time of writing this book, Apache Zeppelin is an Apache incubator project. We have several tool options to create the insights depending upon the problem we are trying to solve and the available budget to build the solution. These insights tools can be focused upon machine learning, such as R, or reporting-based, such as QlikView, and so on. Let's explore Apache Zeppelin to understand how it can be useful to build the insights tier of data lake.

Apache Zeppelin

Apache Zeppelin is web-based tool which supports data analytics and visualization. Unlike other tools, it does not require any separate programming environment to design the queries and reports. Apache Zeppelin has the concept of web-based notebooks. In the notebooks, you can perform a wide variety of programing and query tasks. It also offers you a few ready-to-use charts that let you visualize the data quickly with the help of simple graphs and pie charts.

Apache Zeppelin can read data from many data backends, such as Hive, Postgress, and Cassandra. To connect with a data processing back end, you need a Zeppelin interpreter. Zeppelin comes with several interpreters that can be used to create web-based notebooks. In this section, we will test drive Zeppelin.

Installation of Apache Zeppelin

You can download Apache Zeppelin from the website of Apache Software Foundation. The download URL is https://zeppelin.apache.org/download.html. At this URL, you will find both Zeppelin's source code and binaries. We have used Apache Zeppelin v. 0.5.5. for the examples covered in this book.

To install Zeppelin, download the binary package and unpack it in your local directory. I installed Zeppelin on a machine running Ubuntu 14.04.4. After successful installation, the top level directory contents look as follows:

```
hduser@el1-Aspire-5750G:~/zeppelin-0.5.5-incubating-bin-all$ ls -la
total 1380
drwxr-xr-x 10 hduserhduser     4096 Jun  9 19:37 .
drwxr-xr-x 53 hduserhduser     4096 Jun 20 18:36 ..
-rw-r--r--  1hduserhduser      542 Nov 11  2015 DISCLAIMER
-rw-r--r--  1hduserhduser    27489 Nov 11  2015 LICENSE
-rw-r--r--  1hduserhduser     5627 Nov 11  2015 NOTICE
-rw-r--r--  1hduserhduser     6242 Nov 11  2015 README.md
drwxr-xr-x  2hduserhduser     4096 Jun  9 19:11 bin
```

```
drwxr-xr-x   2hduserhduser    4096 Jun  9 19:12 conf
drwxr-xr-x  15 hduserhduser    4096 Jun  9 19:11 interpreter
drwxr-xr-x   2hduserhduser    4096 Jun  9 19:11 lib
drwxr-xr-x   2hduserhduser    4096 Jun  9 19:11 licenses
drwxrwxr-x   2hduserhduser    4096 Jun  9 19:38 logs
drwxr-xr-x  15 hduserhduser    4096 Jun  9 19:47 notebook
drwxrwxr-x   2hduserhduser    4096 Jun  9 19:49 run
-rw-r--r--   1hduserhduser   49960 Nov 11  2015 zeppelin-server-0.5.5-
incubating.jar
-rw-r--r--   1hduserhduser 1267959 Nov 11  2015 zeppelin-web-0.5.5-
incubating.war
```

After the successful unpacking of the Zeppelin binaries, you should configure Zeppelin. The configuration files for Zeppelin can be found under the /conf directory. The `zeppelin-site.xml.templatecontents` file contains several configurable parameters. In order to configure Zeppelin, we will copy this file to a file named `zeppelin-site.xml`. Open this file. Notice that it contains several configurable parameters. For now, we will not alter this file and use its default values.

Though Zeppelin supports several different data sources, we will only use it to query data stores in Hive tables. For this purpose, you should copy a valid `hive-site.xml` file to the /conf directory. This will allow Zeppelin to connect with Hive to run the queries. This file allows us to connect with Hiveserver 2. A copy of this file is enclosed in the data for this chapter. Before copying the `hive-site.xml` file, you need to ensure that this is the correct file. You can verify this by running hiveserver2, connecting to it using beeline, and running a few queries after making the connection.

The binaries of Hive interpreter and other interpreters are located in the /interpreter directory. Each sub directory under the /interpreter directory contains the binaries for one interpreter.

After configuration, we will start the Zeppelin server daemon as follows:

```
$ cd  ~/zeppelin-0.5.5-incubating-bin-all/bin
$ ./zeppelin-daemon.sh start
Zeppelin start                                      [  OK  ]
```

Now that the Zeppelin server has started, we can open the home page of Zeppelin using a web browser. If you have not changed the default port configuration, then you can access Zeppelin on port number `http://<host_ip>:5001`. The following screenshot shows the Welcome screen of Zeppelin:

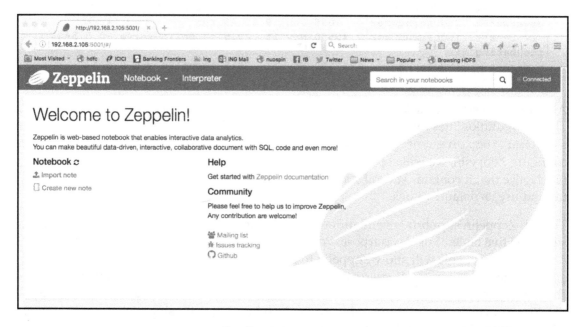

Figure 13 Apache Zeppelin Welcome Screen

Test driving Zeppelin

We are now all set to test drive Zeppelin by creating our first note in the notebook. A note in Zeppelin is a workspace where we can write and execute programs or commands. Our first note will run a few basic shell commands.

First, we will create a note using the menu **Notebook | Create new note**. The dialog shown in the following screenshot will pop up:

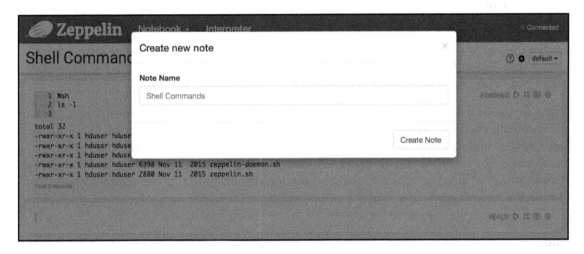

Figure 14 Creating a new note in Zeppelin

Let's call our new note Shell Commands and click on the **Create Note** button. Now you will see the empty note and workspace, where you can create and execute your notes as shown in *Figure 15*.

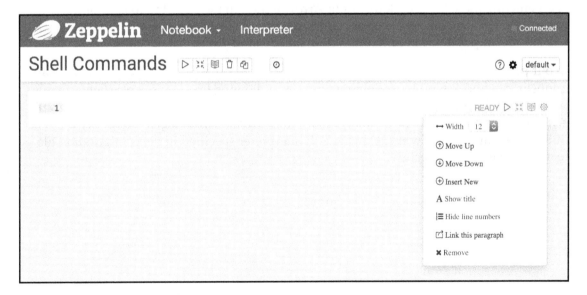

Figure 15 Zeppelin Note Workspace

You will notice two toolbars in the workspace. By hovering your mouse over these buttons, you will see the tool tips that explain the purpose of each button. A note in Zeppelin can contain one or more paragraphs. Each paragraph can be written in a different programming language if it is desired.

Each paragraph has its own toolbar in the top right that lets you execute only that paragraph. The setting menu in the paragraph provides you with buttons to toggle the line number display, show the output, and remove the paragraph.

Zeppelin needs interpreters to connect with various data sources. Some interpreters, such as the shell interpreter, which we will use first, do not require any configuration. But other interpreters might require the configuration of database connection strings, username, password and port numbers, or others in order to function. You can browse and change the configuration of interpreters by clicking on the Interpreter button in the configuration page shown in *Figure 5*.

In our newly created note, we will create a paragraph to invoke a shell command. If you find it convenient, then you can choose to show the line numbers. Now we enter three lines in the paragraph as follows:

```
1 %sh
2 echo "Hello, Zeppelin"
3 ls -la
```

After entering these lines, click the Right Arrow button in the right top toolbar of the paragraph. This will initiate the execution of paragraph. Once the execution finishes, you will see the output in the paragraph as shown in *Figure 3*.

In our paragraph, first we specified which interpreter to use by the `%sh` command so that Zeppelin can understand the following lines. The following lines are simple shell commands which echo a string and then list a directory. The line number 1 in a paragraph always specifies the name of the interpreter with `%` prefix. If you neglect to specify the interpreter name, then it will use the default interpreter specified in the configuration file located in the `/conf` directory.

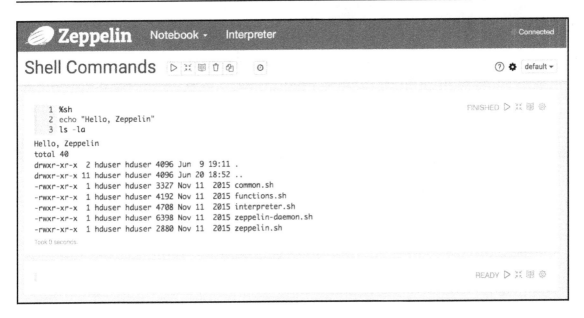

Figure 16 Running the first note on Zeppelin

While we have shown a very trivial example, it opens up a host of possibilities because you can invoke any shell command you wish in your browser, including HDFS commands. *Figure 4* illustrates an HDFS `ls` command executed inside a paragraph. It is also noteworthy here that we can keep adding the paragraphs in a note. These paragraphs can also use different interpreters within the same note. This allows us to generate output using one interpreter and then use it as input by another interpreter. We have executed a single paragraph, but it is also possible to execute all the paragraphs in the note at once by clicking the Run all paragraphs button in the top-level menu. You can also let your note run automatically using a scheduler. This scheduler is accessible by clicking the button with the little clock icon as shown by an arrow in *Figure 4*.

Exploring data visualization features of Zeppelin

Often the real needs of users of a data visualization tool such as Zeppelin are going to be well beyond running few basic shell commands on a web browser. Zeppelin provides very useful common data visualization tools, such as bar chart and pie charts, which we will explore here by solving a small problem.

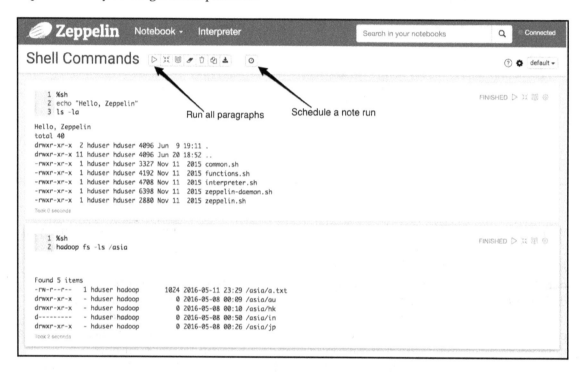

Figure 17 Running HDFS commands from Zeppelin

In this problem, we would like to generate a graph of gold prices. For this purpose, we have provided you a sample data set that contains the price of gold from the period 01-05-1996 to 01-04-2016. The following are a few lines from this dataset:

```
1-2-2016;1,199.50
1-3-2016;1,245.14
1-4-2016;1,242.26
```

This dataset contains two semi-colon-separated columns. The first column is the date, which is the first day of month, and the second column is the price of gold per troy ounce in US dollars on the first day of month. This dataset is clean, and free from any missing values, and ready to be imported in HDFS.

First, we create a new note in Zeppelin and name it Gold Price Movement Plotter. This note contains four paragraphs which we will now examine in detail.

Define the gold price movement table in Hive

This paragraph creates a table in Hive called `T_GOLDMONTHPRICE`. This table shall store the gold price movement data. The code for this paragraph is as follows:

```
%hive
CREATE TABLE `t_goldmonthprice` (
`yearmonth` date comment 'year and month',
`price` double comment 'price in usd per troy ounce'
)
ROW FORMAT DELIMITED FIELDS TERMINATED BY ';' STORED AS TextFile
```

You already know that the first line informs Zeppelin of the name of the interpreter we intend to use in the paragraph. In this, `%hive` informs Zeppelin that we will be running the Hive command here.

Once you have defined the paragraph, you can immediately run it. However, if you have not configured the Hive interpreter correctly, then the execution of paragraph will result in an error. Let us hold the running of this paragraph and first understand what the other paragraphs in this note do. We will configure Hive later in this section.

Load gold price history in the Table

This paragraph loads the data contained in the semi-colon-delimited file in the Hive table`T_GOLDMONTHPRICE`. This file is located in my home directory.

```
%hive
load data local inpath '~/gold-240-01.csv' into table T_GOLDMONTHPRICE
```

Run a select query

In this paragraph, we define a simple select query to see the how Zeppelin can render the output using various kinds of tools.

```
%hive
select * from T_GOLDMONTHPRICE
```

Plot price change per month

This paragraph runs a slightly complex query which calculates and plots the percentage price change per month. This query creates a new temporary table with the change in it, then joins that new table to the original.

```
%hive
SELECT t1.yearmonth, t1.price as rate, (t2.price – t1.price)*(100/t1.price)
as change
FROM T_GOLDMONTHPRICE t1
INNER JOIN T_GOLDMONTHPRICE t2
ON add_months( t1.yearmonth,1)  = t2.yearmonth
```

You can see the complete note in *Figure 19*.

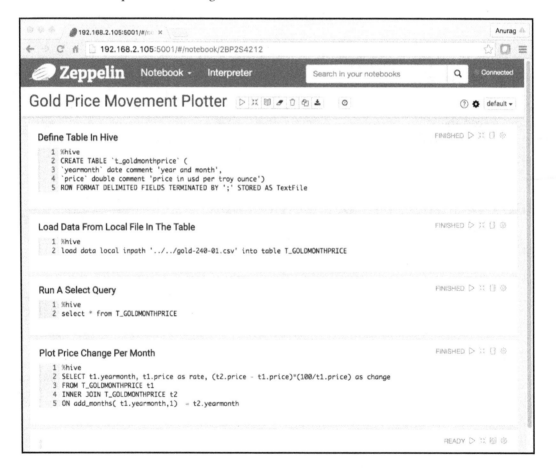

Figure 19 Zeppelin Note to Plot Gold Price Movement

Running the paragraph

Before we can run our paragraph, we need to configure the Hive interpreter in Zeppelin by using the Interpreter menu button and scrolling down until we find the Hive settings as shown in *Figure 20*.

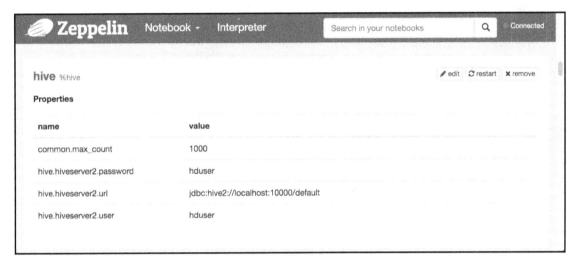

Figure 20 Hive Interpreter Settings in Zeppelin

The Hive interpreter requires the configuration of the following parameters:

- `common.max_count`: The maximum number of rows a single query is allowed to return.
- `hive.hiveserver2.password`: The password of the Hive user.
- `hive.hiveserver2.url`: The connection string to the Hive server. This connection string should be the same string that you use with beeline to connect with Hiveserver2.
- `hive.hiveserver2.user`: The username of the Hive user.

Click on restart after changing the settings so that the new settings can take effect. It is imperative that you have a valid user name and password for Hiveserver2 if you are to run your note inside Zeppelin.

We have defined our note and finished the Hive configuration in Zeppelin. Now it is time to see our note in action.

Note that the first two paragraphs—to create the table and to load the data—do not generate any output and, therefore, Zeppelin reports the message, "The query did not generate a result set!". This result cannot be rendered.

The third paragraph is a simple select query that returns the output in the tabular format, which should be familiar to any SQL user. If you click the toolbar then you can see the selection results presented in various graphs. The pie-chart will not make much sense in this case because we have not grouped the data in the select query by a criterion. Other graphs, one of which is shown in *Figure 21*, show a beautiful rendering of the query results. The results shown in the screenshot depict the time-series graph of the price of gold from 1996 to 2016.

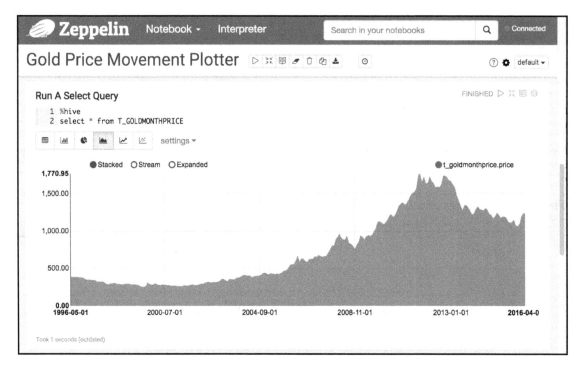

Figure 21 Zeppelin graph plot

The Settings drop down button gives you more control over the plot. Because our table only contains two columns, there is not much we can change with this option in this paragraph.

The next paragraph, which plots the month-to-month change in gold prices, is shown in *Figure 22*.

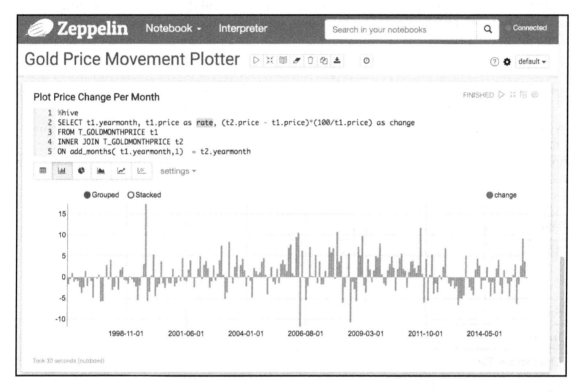

Figure 22 Price change plot

In this paragraph, we execute a query which inner joins the yearmonth column table `t_goldprice` with the yearmonth column in the next row and calculates the percentage price change.

Zeppelin in Data Lake

Zeppelin is a web-based tool which can be used by a wide group of Data Lake users who are interested in data analysis and creating data visualizations. Its web-based interface provides a low hurdle access to tools such as Hive or Spark. Since the web browser is the most common tool available on every desktop, Zeppelin can be accessed by the users without the need for the installation of any special software, as is the case with many other tools. In the large organizations where hundreds of users would need access to data stored in a data lake, zero footprint of Zeppelin on the users' desktop is a great advantage. Therefore, it is a good technology to build the insights tier of Data Lakes.

We still have to understand the Zeppelin security. Giving access to every user to run shell commands creates security risks. Because Zeppelin is still in the incubation stage, we expect that the community will provide more security features in this tool so that it can be adopted in the enterprises. In the forthcoming sections, we will examine how we can secure Zeppelin in Data Lakes.

Technology stack for Data Lake

We have covered a lot of ground so far. We discussed a conceptual, high level architecture of a data lake in *Figure 1*. After understanding some of the technologies available, we can now fill the conceptual data lake with real technologies which we will use to implement our data lake as shown in *Table 1*. Please note that we have already covered some of these technologies in the previous chapters of this book.

Data Lake Tier Name	Technology Used
Ingestion Tier	Apache Flume HDFS Copy Apache Sqoop
Storage Tier	HDFS
Insights Tier	Apache Zeppelin, Hive QL
Operations Tier	Apache Ranger HDFS Permissions

Table 1 Our technology choices to build Data Lake

Data Lake business requirements

Data lakes are supposed to provide access to structured, unstructured, and semi-structured data to users. The business requirements of data lakes drive what kind of data will be stored in a data lake and who will have access to it. In the next section, we will understand the business requirements of a company that wants to build a data lake.

Origins of the word Data Lake

James Dixon, the founder and CTO of Pentaho, coined the term data lake in his blog. He has defined the concept of a Data Lake as follows:*"If you think of a datamart as a store of bottled water – cleansed and packaged and structured for easy consumption – the data lake is a large body of water in a more natural state. The contents of the data lake stream in from a source to fill the lake, and various users of the lake can come to examine, dive in, or take samples."* (Dixon, 2010)

Understanding the business requirements

Let's look at a fictional financial services company called Big Gains Inc. This company does stock portfolio management for its customers and advises them as to which stocks to keep and which ones to sell. The company has a relatively small workforce, with each of its employees in one of the two roles. These roles are the analysts and account managers.

The employees in analyst roles perform the analysis of stock holding patterns, but they are not allowed to access personal information about the customers. They can have access to aggregated data, but never the customer-specific information, such as the customer names, date of birth, and their income.

The employees in account manager roles have access to all the information about the customers because they manage the relationship with the customers and advise them about which investment decisions to make.

These roles are strictly segregated to comply with the company policy about data protection, so it is unlikely that the same employee might be assigned the roles of Analyst and Account Manager at the same time.

Big Gains management wants to build a data lake to offload the data from the internal transactional systems, systems of records, and the data feeds from external sources in Hadoop. This data lake should allow the employees having analyst and account manager roles to analyze the data using various query tools and visualize it using graphs. While data lake should fulfil the information requirements of various employees, it should do so without compromising the data security. Any solution which Big Gains ultimately chooses must comply with the role segregation policies of the company.

Understanding the IT systems and security

The client master data is stored in a **Customer Relationship Management** (**CRM**) system. For the sake of simplicity, we have assumed that, for the customer master data, the following five fields shown in *Table 2* are useful for data lake users:

Table Name: T_CUSTMASTER	
Field Name	**Purpose**
ID	Unique 4 digit client ID
NAME	Name of the client
DOB	Date of birth
INCOME	Annual income of client
ACCTMNGR	User ID of account manager
CITY	City of client's home address

Table 2 Client Master Data Table

This data is updated daily and so we will allow a daily feed to copy the databases in HDFS from the source system. The source system is a relational database management system. We have read-only access to the relevant data in the RDBMS system which we will use to read the data using Sqoop and transfer it to HDFS.

The company manages the roles of account manager and Analyst using the Unix group and users. Each employee gets a Unix user ID, which is the same as his first name, and a group ID, which is same as his role in the company. The current user and role assignment is shown in *Table 3*:

User and Group Assignment	
Group	**User**
analyst	ryan
acctmngr	lynda, tom, roger, freddy, amy

Table 3 Mapping of business roles and users with Unix group and user IDs

To secure the access to data stored in Hive tables, we will use Ranger. Ranger comes with a plugin named User Sync plugin. Using this plugin, Ranger can synchronize the Unix users and groups with the Ranger database. The Ranger configuration guide covers how to configure the User Sync here: `https://cwiki.apache.org/confluence/display/RANGER/Ranger+Installation+Guide#RangerInstallationGuide-Install/ConfigureRangerUserSync`.

We have now understood the present IT landscape of the company. Let's create the first design of our Data Lake for the company in the next section.

Designing the data pipeline

Our data pipeline pulls the data from RDBMS of the CRM system once a day and stores it in a Hive table. We will use Sqoop and run it using a CRON job once per night to refresh the data in the data lake.

Using Ranger, we will restrict the table permissions to Hive as per the business requirements. We will use Zeppelin to give the users access to the data stored in the data lake. Although we will use Zeppelin to build the insights tier of our data lake, the Ranger table permissions offer us access control irrespective of which tool we use. Zeppelin uses Hiveserver2 to run Hive queries. If users try to access the Hive using the command line tool beeline then they will be subjected to the same access control rules as Zeppelin users. The first version of our data pipeline and the design of the data lake is shown in *Figure 23*.

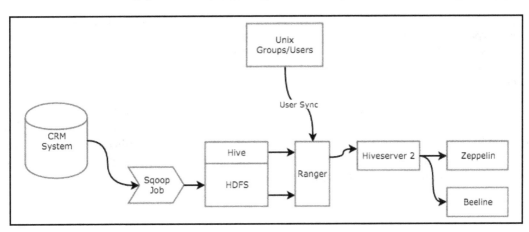

Figure 23 Data lake and data pipeline at Big Gains Inc.

Building the data pipeline

We have provided you with a script to create client master data in the `Chapter 7` sample. This script is called `clientmasterdata.sql`. Remember that this script will create synthetic data, so the data will be realistic but not real. The following listing shows a few lines from the script:

```
CREATE TABLE `T_CUSTMASTER` (
  `ID` mediumint,
  `NAME` varchar(255) ,
  `DOB` varchar(255),
  `INCOME` int,
  `ACCTMNGR` varchar(255),
  `CITY` varchar(255)
);

INSERT INTO `T_CUSTMASTER` (`ID`,`NAME`,`DOB`,`INCOME`,`ACCTMNGR`,`CITY`)
VALUES (1067,"Elton Mayo","1971-01-24","101698.07226354","tim","Wick");
```

We have a used a MySQL database to simulate the RDBMS of CRM system. If you are already running MySQL, you can execute the script file using the source command or `\.` command. The link `https://dev.mysql.com/doc/refman/5.7/en/mysql.html` gives you more information about the MySQL command-line tool.

After creating our client master database in MySQL, we move on to Sqoop to fetch and load information in Hive tables using the following command:

```
$ sqoop import --connect jdbc:mysql://localhost/customer --table
T_CUSTMASTER --username sqoop -P --split-by ID --hive-import --hive-
database default --create-hive-table --verbose --hive-overwrite --hive-
drop-import-delims--hive-table t_custmaster--warehouse-dir
/user/hive/warehouse
```

We have covered Sqoop already in `Chapter 2`, *A 360-Degree View of the Customer*. The preceding command is slightly different because it requires the username and password for the MySQL user, and it writes in the table `t_custmaster` in Hive. This command will be refreshing the client master data from a CRM system to the Data Lake. You can learn about how to create new users in MySQL databases in this article: `https://www.digitalocean.com/community/tutorials/how-to-create-a-new-user-and-grant-permissions-in-mysql`.

Once you have run the Sqoop command then you will be able to see the data in the Hive table.

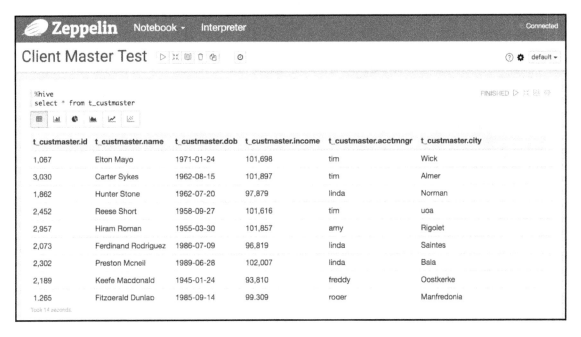

Figure 24 Viewing client master data in Zeppelin after Sqoop import

You should be able to verify the results by running a query using a Zeppelin note as shown in *Figure 24*.

Setting up the access control

After successfully loading data in HDFS, we will set up the permission settings for the data. In the following sections, we will cover the following:

- Synchronizing the users and groups in the Ranger database
- Setting up data access policies in Ranger
- Restricting the access in Zeppelin

Synchronizing the users and groups in Ranger

In order to set up the access control, we need to ensure that the users and groups are available in the Unix system. We will use these users and groups in Ranger by syncing them in the user and group database of Ranger using the User Sync plugin. For creating the groups and users, you can use the GUI-based tools on your Unix desktop or run the following commands and provide the inputs if asked for:

```
$sudo groupadd analyst
$sudo adduser ryan
$sudo usermod -g analyst ryan
```

The preceding commands will:

- Create a group called analyst
- Create a new user ryan and assign a password for the user
- Make the analyst group the primary group of ryan

I have created all the users and groups as shown in the *Table 3* on my Linux server where I am running Ranger and HDFS.

With the help of Ranger, we can verify whether our User Sync plugin has synced the users and groups in the Ranger database as shown in *Figure 25*.

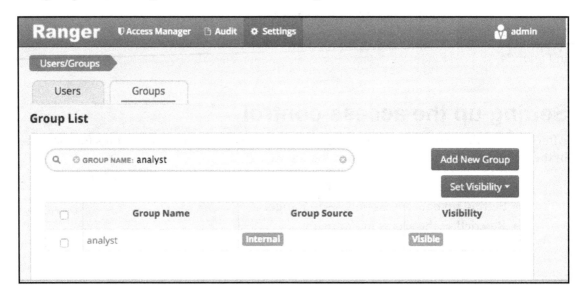

Figure 25 User Sync has synchronized the group "analyst"

You can access the **Users/Groups** screen by clicking on **Settings | Users/Groups**. In *Figure 25*, we have filtered the list by group name. If you click on the link **analyst** in the column **Group Name** then you will see the **Group Detail** screen. The field **Description** in this form informs you that this group has been copied from the Unix box as shown in *Figure 26:*

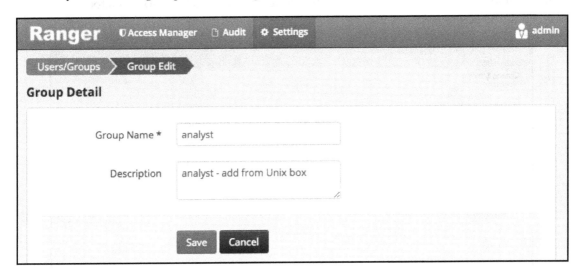

Figure 26 Group detail screen

After successfully syncing the users and groups, your Users tab in Ranger should have at least the entries as shown in *Figure 27*.

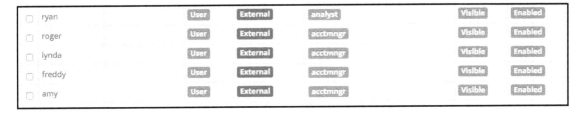

Figure 27 Users and Groups of Big Gains Inc. synced in Ranger

Setting up data access policies in Ranger

With the help of Ranger data access policies, we will restrict the access to two kinds of resource in Hadoop : Hive Tables and HDFS Directories. At this moment, we have only one table in Hive called t_custmaster, which belongs to our data lake, so let us focus upon protecting the access to it.

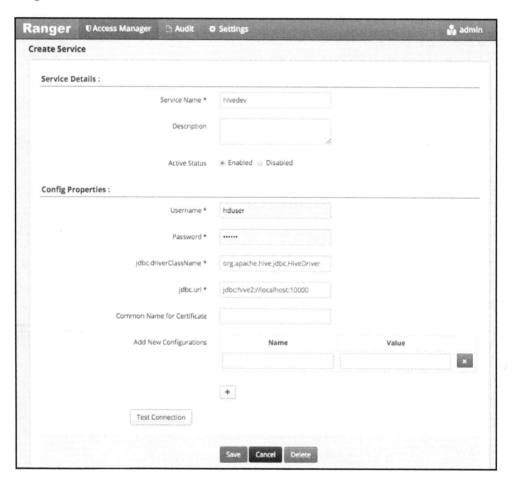

Figure 28 Creating services in the Access Manager

Without proper access policies, all the data lake users in Big Gains will be able to query all the columns in the table t_custmaster and run MapReduce jobs to perform additional operations on this data, such as calculating the averages. Before you set up the policies, check, by running different queries using Beeline or Zeppelin, that all the table columns are accessible to all the users.

First, we will define two new services in the Service Manager of Ranger which is accessible by clicking the menu button **Access Manager | Resource Based Policies**. In this service, we will define the various policies. *Figure 28* shows the **Create Service** screen and the values of various fields. After entering the values as shown in the figure, you can click test connection. If Ranger is able to successfully make a connection with Hive, then you will get a **Connected successfully** message. Click on the **Save** button to save the service. The creation of the HDFS service called**hadoopdev** has already been covered in this chapter already.

Figure 29 Policy definition screen in Ranger

In the service, **hivedev**, we have defined the following two policies:

- **Data Lake Analyst Users**: This policy grants access to the role analyst to the three columns of the hive table `t_custmaster` as per the business requirements. These columns are `income`, `city`, and `dob`. We have only given **select** permission to the role Analyst because this permission is sufficient for analysts to perform their work. You can look at the settings for this policy in *Figure 29*.

- **Data Lake Account Manager Users**: This policy grants access to the role `acctmngr` (Account Manager) to all the columns of the table `t_custmaster` as per the business requirements.

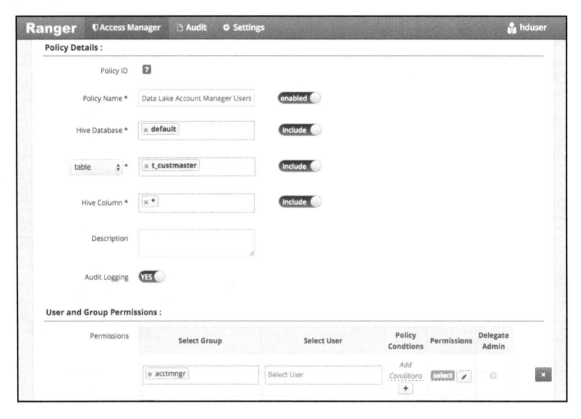

Figure 30 Policy settings for Account Managers

We have only given **select** permission to the role `acctmngr` because this permission is sufficient for the users. You can look at the settings for this policy in *Figure 30*.

After granting access to the Hive tables, we will grant access to the `/tmp` directory of HDFS to both roles. This will allow MapReduce jobs to use this directory to write temporary files when MapReduce jobs are executed. We can do this by adding two policies in the HDFS service **hadoopdev**. These policies are called Analyst-HDFS-Access and Manager-HDFS-Access.

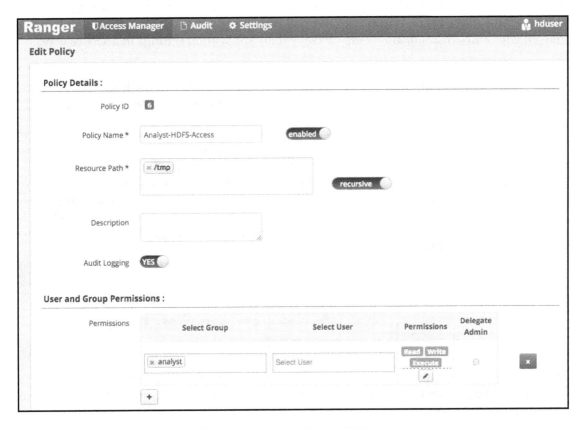

Figure 31 Adding policy for access to the /tmp directory in HDFS for the group Analyst

The Manager-HDFS-Access policy is identical to the Analyst-HDFS-Access policy, except that the group name should be `acctmngr`.

Restricting the access in Zeppelin

Zeppelin is a new tool which is under incubation stage. It provides you with a number of interpreters to run a variety of programs and commands from the web page. Like many other tools in the less mature state in the Hadoop ecosystem, the Zeppelin lacks the ability to run in a multi-user environment. It lacks user management and session management for the users. We expect that the community will contribute the features that will allow it to be used in the multi-user environments. There is an ongoing project that integrates the Apache Shiro security framework with Zeppelin, and provides basic authentication in Zeppelin. However, in a multi-user environment, we will need a system in which notes can only be viewed with authorization, and users can save their application settings in a secure way.

In the absence of comprehensive security features in Zeppelin, at Big Gain Inc., we can either choose commercial tools such as Datameer or Tableau to build the insight tier or live with the limitations of Zeppelin and use workaround as discussed in the next paragraph.

To make our Zeppelin installation secure, we will remove all the interpreters that our users do not need. Our users will access Hive tables using Zeppelin to run SQL queries so the rest of the interpreters can be removed. In the Interpreters page of Zeppelin, you will find a Remove button which lets you remove an interpreter from Zeppelin's user interface. If you remove an interpreter in this way, it can still be reconfigured, unless you also remove the interpreter from the Zeppelin site configuration file `zeppelin-site.xml`, located in the conf directory of your Zeppelin installation. The following XML fragment shows the settings when only a Hive interpreter is enabled:

```
<property>
<name>zeppelin.interpreters</name>
<value>org.apache.zeppelin.hive.HiveInterpreter</value>
<description>Comma separated interpreter configurations. First interpreter
become a default</description>
</property>
```

By removing the interpreters that aren't required, we restrict the users' access to the Data Lake, as per the policies of the company. To run Zeppelin in a multiuser environment, there are two possible options:

- Every user runs a Zeppelin server instance on his desktop that is only locally accessible by setting firewalls rules on the desktop
- Using docker containers as proposed in this link `https://hub.docker.com/r/epahomov/docker-zeppelin/`

We are not going cover these options in details as they are the beyond the scope of this chapter.

Testing our data pipeline

We have loaded the data into our Data Lake and configured the users and security in the system. We will now check if our system works as intended.

First, we verify if the table `t_custmaster` is accessible to the users in the roles of `acctmngr` (Account Managers). For this purpose, we will create a note in Zeppelin and set a valid user and password for Hive in the interpreter settings page. In the following figure, we can see that the user `lynda`, set in Hive interpreter settings, can run a map reduce-based Select query on table `t_custmaster`.

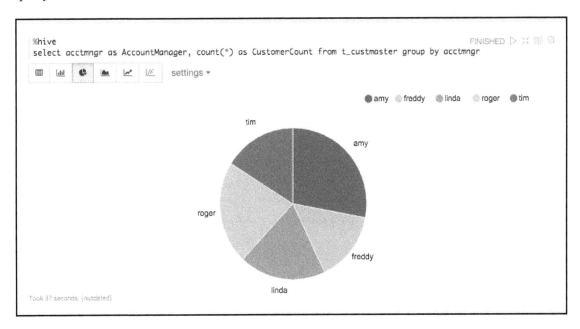

Figure 32 Zeppelin pie chart report for Account Managers

The Zeppelin note in *Figure 33* shows that the user `linda` can access all the columns in the table `t_custmaster` as a result of full access to all the columns granted in Ranger.

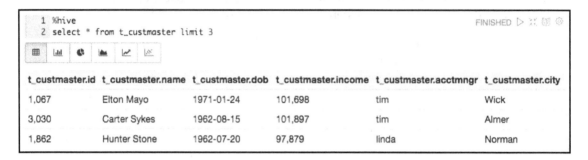

Figure 33 Accessing all the columns of table t_custmaster

After testing the access for users in the role of Account Managers, we will test the access for Analysts. Remember that Analysts do not have access to all the columns, so when we run select query on the column `t_custmaster.id`, then it fails with an error message as shown in the following screenshot:

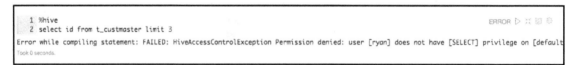

Figure 34 Ranger access control error message

However, when we run the select query on the other columns that are allowed to be viewed in Ranger, then we see the results as shown in the following screenshot:

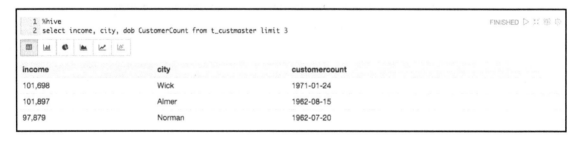

Figure 35 Query results when Ranger allows access to columns

Figure 23 shows that user `ryan`, in the role of analyst, can run a select query which requires map reduce to produce the results.

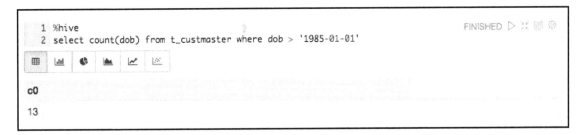

Figure 36 Running a query that requires map reduce

Now the testing of our data pipeline is complete. We have successfully loaded the client master data from our CRM system to a Hadoop-based data lake, set up security, and, with the help of Zeppelin, we have run queries while enforcing the data access control policies of Big Gains Inc. In this section, we covered running queries using Zeppelin. I recommend that you run similar queries using the Beeline tool to check where you should expect to find the same results.

Scheduling the data loading

After the data pipeline testing has been successfully completed, we will schedule the Sqoop data loader job so that, at a predetermined frequency, it can refresh the data in the Data Lake of Big Gains Inc. The simplest solution is to set up a cron job which will run periodically. We can wrap in a Sqoop command in a shell script and run it using cron.

Our Sqoop command is wrapped in a shell script named `clientmaster-loader.sh` located in the home directory of `hduser` as shown in the following code:

```
$ cat clientmaster-loader.sh
sqoop import --connect jdbc:mysql://localhost/customer --table T_CUSTMASTER
--username sqoop -password sqoop --split-by ID --hive-import --hive-
database default  --verbose --hive-overwrite --hive-drop-import-delims  --
hive-table t_custmaster --warehouse-dir /user/hive/warehouse
```

Replace the password in the script with the password you have set for the MySQL user.

Now, we can create a cron job by editing the crontab so that it runs at 1:30 A.M. every night. We do this as follows:

```
crontab -e
```

Add the following line:

```
30 1 * * * /home/hduser/clientmaster-loader.sh
```

Cron will automatically add a new schedule in the list of schedules and trigger the script when the time comes.

Cron is a valuable scheduling tool, however, if you have to manage multiple scheduled jobs to load data in Data Lake, then you should consider using a scheduling tool, whether open source, such as Oozie, or commercial, such as Autosys. These tools provide better administration capabilities, as well as improved logging, auditing, and retry functionality.

Refining the business requirements

You have now built the first version of a Data Lake for Big Gain. You demonstrated it to the senior executives of the company. They are impressed and they want to add more data to the Data Lake. This makes sense; a Data Lake with data from just one source—CRM—does not seem to be worth so much effort. So now the company comes up with the following new set of requirements:

- Allow Account Managers to see the stock portfolio of their clients
- Allow all the data lake users to view the daily stock prices.

Implementing the new requirements

We should design the security in such a way, that only the authorized users can access the data. The stock portfolio information of clients should be accessible to the Account Managers, but Analysts can only see the stock name and quantity but not the portfolio information of the specific clients. The source of stock prices is a feed from a public stock price feed service. This data need not be protected because it comes from a public source.

To implement the requirement mentioned above, we will first identify the data sources and design the approach to load them. The stock portfolio information will be delivered to us in a semi-colon-delimited file. This file is extracted from the portfolio management system once per month and provided to us as a text file. The following are a few sample rows from this file:

```
DATE;ID;SYMB;HOLDING
2016-05-20;1008;MSFT;515
2016-05-05;1003;MSFT;473
2016-05-16;1002;RHT;625
```

```
2016-05-30;1005;GOOG;236
2016-05-11;1005;MSFT;399
2016-05-18;1007;GOOG;681
2016-05-05;1008;GOOG;386
2016-05-16;1000;MSFT;711
2016-05-28;1003;GOOG;875
```

The first column represents when the stock holding changed as a result of a buy or sell transaction. The second column contains the client ID, which is the same as the client ID in the CRM system. The third column is the ticker symbol of stock held. The fourth column shows the units of stock held by the client. For the sake of simplicity, we will only use a few known stock symbols in our data, such as GOOG, MSFT, and so on.

In the previous section about Flume, we already explained how we can load data from Yahoo Finance into HDFS.

Loading the stock holding data in Data Lake

Let us define a new table in Hive which will hold the stock holding data. The DDL for this table is as follows:

```
CREATE TABLE `HOLDING` (
  `PORTFOLIODATE` date,
  `CLID` int,
  `SYMB` varchar(4),
  `UNITS` int
) ROW FORMAT DELIMITED FIELDS TERMINATED BY ';' LINES TERMINATED BY '\012'
STORED AS TEXTFILE;
```

The column structure of this table corresponds to the portfolio data file structure that we presented in the previous section. We will be receiving the portfolio information in the form of monthly data feeds. Portfolio data feed file samples have been included in the sample code provided with this chapter. The files are named as `data-Jan-2016.csv` and `data-March-2016.csv`. Using Hadoop file system commands, we will copy these files in the `/user/hive/warehouse/holding` directory where data files will be kept.

```
$ hadoop fs -put staging/* /user/hive/warehouse/holding
```

Once we have copied a file, we can run a select query from Hive to check if the loading has been successful. Now we have to encapsulate this script in a shell file so that we can run it as a monthly scheduled job. This shell script in its bare minimum form should do the following:

1. Check if the staging directory is not empty
2. Load the file in Data Lake
3. Clean the staging directory

A simple shell script for this purpose is as follows:

```
$ cat stockloader.sh
cd staging
if [ "$(ls -A .)" ]
then
hadoop fs -put * /user/hive/warehouse/holding
rm *
else
echo "no filename exists"
fi
```

You can put this script in cron tables to run at pre-scheduled intervals. You can also make this shell script smarter by generating error messages or alerts if the scheduled job fails due to some error.

Restricting the access to stock holding data in Data Lake

We have already restricted access to certain columns to the users in the role of Analyst in the previous sections of this chapter. *Figure 37* shows the settings in Ranger to restrict the access to a few columns in the table `holding`.

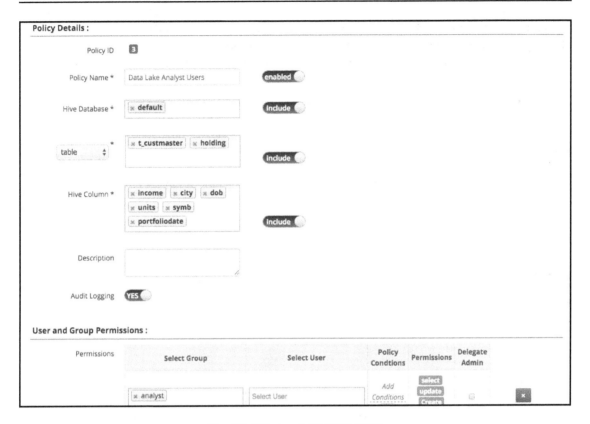

Figure 37 Restricting access to client ID field in Ranger

Testing the Loaded Data with Zeppelin

We can run a few queries on the table `holding` to see if the data has been loaded correctly. I have created a note in Zeppelin which shows the results of a query which joins the table `holding` and the table `t_custmaster`.

We will run the following query:

```
select  portfoliodate, name, symb, units  from holding as a, t_custmaster
as b   where a.clid = b.id and a.clid=1005  order by  portfoliodatedesc;
```

This query will show the transaction date when the client with ID 1005 has bought or sold stock, as well as the new stock position for a ticker symbol. By creating the join, we can also see the name of the client in the query. The results of running this as a Zeppelin note are shown in *Figure 38*:

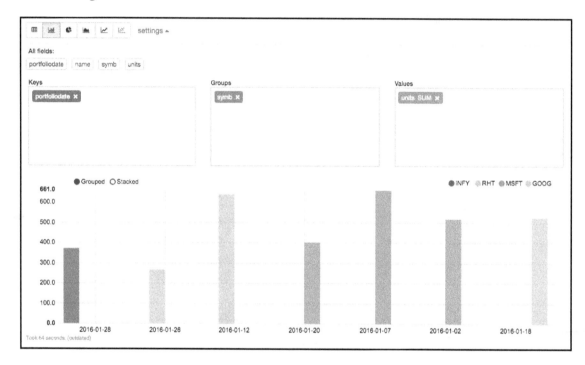

Figure 38 Transaction history of client by ID

By running the following two queries, you can verify whether the user `ryan` in the role of `analyst` can access only those columns which are permitted by the company policy.

```
select distinct symb from holding;
select * from holding;
```

The second query fails with an error. If you look in the audit reports of Ranger then you will find that this denial of access has been logged.

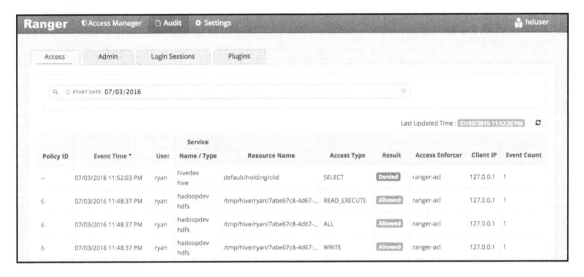

Figure 39 Audit report in Ranger logs denied access

Adding stock feed in the Data Lake

In this chapter, you were introduced to Apache Flume. We have selected Flume as one of the tools to implement the data ingestion tier of our data lake. To fulfill the new requirements of our Data Lake for Big Gains Inc., we need to provide the stock price information in the data lake. We will fetch this information from a web-based service as we have explained earlier in this chapter. However, at this time we are going to write the data fetched from the web-based service directly in the HDFS of out data lake.

Fetching data from Yahoo Service

The following script polls the Yahoo service at a regular interval as defined by the sleep time (5 minutes) and outputs the prices of four stocks in the specific format: (Elias, 2012)

```
$ cat stockfetcher.sh
#!/bin/bash
while true;
do
curl
"http://download.finance.yahoo.com/d/quotes.csv?s=RHT,MSFT,GOOG,INFY&f=d1t1
sa";
sleep 300;
done
```

This script writes the following text on standard output in a never-ending loop:

```
"7/7/2016","4:01pm","RHT",71.96
"7/7/2016","4:00pm","MSFT",51.38
"7/7/2016","4:00pm","GOOG",695.40
"7/7/2016","4:02pm","INFY",17.68
```

Configuring Flume

First, we define a configuration file to write the output of stock fetcher script in HDFS. This configuration file is called `hdfsloader.conf`. You can find this file in the code samples directory supplied with this chapter. Let us examine the contents of this file before we start using it:

```
# A single-node Flume configuration to read the output of a shell script

# Name the components on this agent
a1.sources = r1
a1.sinks = k1
a1.channels = c1
```

The preceding lines declare that in this Flume topology, we will have a source `r1`, channel `c1`, and sink `k1`.

```
# Describe/configure the source
a1.sources.r1.type = exec
a1.sources.r1.command = ./stockfetcher.sh
```

The preceding lines define that the source r1 is of type exec, which can execute a shell script and read its output. The shell script or the command associated with source r1 is the script stockfetcher.sh, which we have seen in action in the previous sub-section.

```
# Describe the sink
a1.sinks.k1.type = hdfs
a1.sinks.k1.channel = c1
a1.sinks.k1.hdfs.path = /flume/stockfeed
a1.sinks.k1.hdfs.filePrefix = feed-
a1.sinks.k1.fileType = DataStream
a1.sinks.k1.hdfs.writeFormat = Text
```

The preceding lines define the type of sink k1 as HDFS. It is associated with the channel c1. This sink will write data in the directory /flume/stockfeed. Note that the HDFS sink gives you many options to name the output directories and files based upon the timestamps. All of the HDFS sink escape sequences that generate a directory/filename are found here https://flume.apache.org/releases/content/1.4./FlumeUserGuide.html# hdfs-sink.

We have used a fixed directory name in this example:

```
# Use a channel which buffers events in memory
a1.channels.c1.type = memory
a1.channels.c1.capacity = 1000
a1.channels.c1.transactionCapacity = 100
```

The preceding lines define channelc1 as a type of memory-based channel.

```
# Bind the source and sink to the channel
a1.sources.r1.channels = c1
a1.sinks.k1.channel = c1
```

The preceding lines define the topology by linking source and sink together via a channel.

Running Flume as Stock Feeder to Data Lake

We will now run the Flume using the following command:

```
hduser:~/flume$ bin/flume-ng agent --confconf --conf-file
conf/hdfsloader.conf --name a1 - Dflume.root.logger=INFO,console
```

The preceding command will generate some logging info. If Flume is running successfully, then you will see that the data is getting written into HDFS at regular intervals. You can reduce the polling time in the shell script `stockfetcher.sh` to a few seconds if you cannot wait for 5 minutes. We can open the HDFS file browser to see if we have new files in the HDFS sink directory as shown in *Figure 40:*

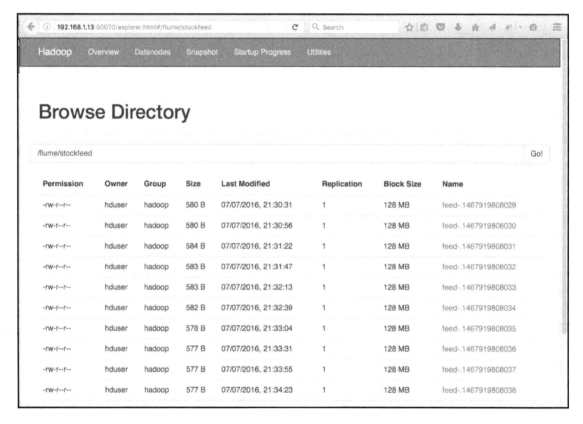

Figure 40 Stock feed files coming via Flume

You might wonder why we are creating so many small sized files using HDFS Sink. HDFS Sink gives you options to define when the file has to be rolled over based upon the file size or event count. This will let you configure the file size. You can read more about it in the Flume documentation.

Transforming the data in Data Lake

We mentioned in the beginning of this book that in the Hadoop-based data warehousing and data lake systems, we chose the **ELT** model, which stands for **Extract, Load,** and **Transform**. Transforming the data to make it suitable for some purpose is done in the Data Lake itself using Hadoop. Raw data is simply retained in the data lake for the future data-exploration purposes. Since the stock data has been picked up from a public source, we do not have to secure any part of it.

The first step in the transformation is building a temporary table in Hive to hold the data loaded in the Data Lake by running the following command in a Zeppelin note:

```
%hive
create external table temp_stockfeeds (col_value string)
STORED AS SEQUENCEFILE
location '/flume/stockfeed'
```

We have created a single string column table named `temp_stockfeeds`. This table is an external table where the data is stored as a SEQUENCEFILE, as well as in the HDFS directory `/flume/stockfeed`. Run a select query on this table; you will see an output similar to the following:

```
"7/7/2016","3:14pm","RHT",71.38
"7/7/2016","3:15pm","MSFT",51.190
"7/7/2016","3:14pm","GOOG",693.23
```

Now we have our data in the Hive table, but the columns should be extracted and put in the right format so that we can join this table with other tables. For example, we want to express dates in the YYYY-MM-DD format instead of what our stock feed service has provided to us. We do this transformation and column extraction using the following query:

```
SELECT
TO_DATE(from_unixtime(UNIX_TIMESTAMP(regexp_extract(col_value,
'[0-9]*\/[0-9]*\/[0-9]*', 0), 'dd/mm/yyyy'))) pricedate,
regexp_extract(col_value, '[A-Z]+', 0) symbol,
regexp_extract(col_value, '[0-9]+\.[0-9]+$', 0) price
from temp_stockfeeds
```

Let's try to understand the preceding query by focusing on the simpler parts first. The following fragment extracts the stock price using a regular expression which matches the last value in a row of stockfeed:

```
regexp_extract(col_value, '[0-9]+\.[0-9]+$', 0) price
```

Regex Tool

A great tool to build your own regular expressions is available here: `http://regexr.com/`.

The following fragment extracts the stock ticker symbol using regular expression and maps it to the column symbol.

```
regexp_extract(col_value, '[A-Z]+', 0) symbol
```

The following fragment first extracts the date string using regular expression and then converts it into Hive DATE data type using the `TO_DATE` function.

```
TO_DATE(from_unixtime(UNIX_TIMESTAMP(regexp_extract(col_value,
'[0-9]*\/[0-9]*\/[0-9]*', 0), 'dd/mm/yyyy'))) pricedate
```

The output of the `select` statement when run using Zeppelin is shown in *Figure 41*:

```
%hive                                                                          FINISHED ▷ ⠶ ▦ ⚙
SELECT
  TO_DATE(from_unixtime(UNIX_TIMESTAMP(regexp_extract(col_value, '[0-9]*\/[0-9]*\/[0-9]*', 0), 'dd/mm/yyyy'))) pricedate,
  regexp_extract(col_value, '[A-Z]+', 0) symbol,
  regexp_extract(col_value, '[0-9]+\.[0-9]+$', 0) price
from temp_stockfeeds
```

pricedate	symbol	price
2016-01-07	RHT	71.38
2016-01-07	MSFT	51.190
2016-01-07	GOOG	693.23
2016-01-07	INFY	17.660
2016-01-07	RHT	71.38
2016-01-07	MSFT	51.18
2016-01-07	GOOG	693.19
2016-01-07	INFY	17.6600
2016-01-07	RHT	71.38

Took 0 seconds. (outdated)

Figure 41 Stock feed transformation using Hive

If you want, you can define a separate table in Hive to hold the transformed data. Using the insert overwrite table command, you can copy the output of the preceding query in another table.

This brings us to the end of building the Data Lake as per our current business requirements. We have integrated client master data, client portfolio data, and stock feeds in the data lake. We also developed tools to fill the data in the Data Lake automatically.

Growing Data Lake

As the needs of the business grow, you should expect to integrate more data sources in the Data Lake. You will also be required to do more complex transformations. The need for tools in the insights tier might also grow. You might want to integrate Microsoft Excel or data science tools such as R or Spark in it. As the size and types of data source grow, you might have to build some kind of enterprise Meta Data dictionary to have a common understanding of what a column or data element in the Data Lake means. For example, if we have a column names stock price in the Data Lake, the users might ask questions such as whether it is the closing price or opening price. An Enterprise Meta Data Dictionary can disambiguate such terms.

In this chapter, we used a simple scheduling tool called cron. In the complex IT environment, you will need an enterprise grade scheduler which lets you run various ELT jobs, define dependencies among them, set up alerts in case of errors, and allows you to take corrective actions. The Hadoop ecosystem provides several tools to manage these aspects of data lakes such as Oozie.

Summary

In this chapter, we started with the basic building blocks of a data lake. We learned that a data lake has three tiers, namely an ingestion tier to ingest the data, a storage tier to store the data, and an insight tier to take business actions. A data lake needs solid operations facilities to secure the data, as well as to guarantee its timely availability.

A Data Lake is supposed to hold the data of the entire enterprise where solid data security is essential. We learned about Apache Ranger and how it creates the fine-grained security in Hadoop by controlling access to various tools in the Hadoop ecosystem with the help of a role-based access model.

We learned about Apache Flume, which lets you build a data ingestion system using the concepts of source, channel, and sink.

We also covered a very new tool called Apache Zeppelin, which eases the data access in Data Lake with the help of simple-web based notebooks that allow you to run HDFS commands and hive queries.

We built a data lake for a fictitious company, Big Gains Inc., where we integrated three different of data sources and built a security layer in Ranger to restrict the access to data. We also built the dashboards to demonstrate the capabilities of Apache Zeppelin.

In this chapter, you have been introduced to the basics of building a Data Lake. You can take this learning further by following the developments in the Hadoop community and the news from Hadoop vendors, such as Cloudera and MapR.

8
Future Directions

The Hadoop ecosystem is constantly evolving. As a result, it has many more tools to offer, but at the same time, alternative technologies are emerging to compete with and complement Hadoop. Hadoop exists to solve certain business problems. Before we suggest that Hadoop is the solution, we must know what the problem really is and whether it requires a technology as complex as Hadoop to solve it. Some problems can be solved by using traditional relational database management systems that are better understood and well tested in the enterprise. Hadoop and its ecosystem of tools introduce a significant dimension of complexity to your technology landscape, and that requires skilled people to operate.

A successful Hadoop implementation that delivers business value will be a collaborative effort between engineers and data scientists. If you have found the right skilled people and a problem that is right for Hadoop, then you will be setting up a Hadoop cluster, if it is not available already. This is by no means a simple task if you are in a tightly regulated corporate IT environment. You will have to arrange the budget and address security- and risk-related concerns before you can store useful data on the system for analysis. Cloud-based Hadoop services offer an attractive option to spin Hadoop clusters quickly as needed and lower startup costs.

When you build a Hadoop-based solution such as a Data Lake, you will find that Hadoop can coexist with other database systems that are suited for interactive queries and as reliable and performant backend databases for mobile and web applications.

Finally, you will also discover that the shift towards streaming analytics is driven by the needs of the business, which somewhat limits the role of Hadoop to just a tool for big data storage and the analysis of historical data.

In this chapter, we will cover four topics that are loosely coupled with Hadoop but are important to consider when you build a Hadoop-based solution. These topics are as follows:

- Hadoop solutions team
- Hadoop on Cloud
- NoSQL databases
- In-memory databases

Hadoop solutions team

The rise of big data technology-based solutions has given birth to a new role: the data scientist. Data scientists, just like other scientists, perform a number of experiments to generate new insights and prove a hypothesis right or wrong. Data scientists perform their experiments on big data by combining their knowledge of statistics, computer science, and mathematics in solving data science problems (O'Reilly Media Inc., 2013).

The role of the data engineer

This book has focused on building Hadoop-based solutions with the help of tools available in the open source ecosystem. We have covered how various tools can be selected, installed, configured, and programmed to build a solution. Typically, these tasks will be performed by a data engineer. The data engineer has a strong knowledge of a number of tools available in the big data ecosystem. Data engineers will build data pipelines, program ELT routines, and design queries. They will have the skills to deploy a Hadoop cluster and monitor an operational Hadoop cluster.

Data science for non-experts

Data science remains a very specialized discipline, but we also see the emergence of advanced analytics solutions that make data science tools accessible to non-experts. Generally, these tools require little or no programming knowledge to get started. Many such tools provide visual interfaces to enable users who are not data geeks to perform data analysis. We have seen one such tool in this book: BigML. Other examples are DataHero and DataCraker. Such tools allow you to apply analytics algorithms such as classification and clustering to datasets. However, the interpretation of results and recognition of patterns in the data remains a difficult task. Therefore, the involvement of expert data scientists becomes essential it's difficult for non-experts to evaluate the results.

From the data science model to business value

After experimenting with data, data scientists build a model that can be deployed in an operational process to deliver business value. When a model is ready, the focus shifts to the deployment, monitoring, and maintenance of the model. This job is performed by data engineers. The deployment, monitoring, and maintenance of a model can be automated with the help of automated deployment tools. The DevOps movement, which advocates building an automated deployment pipeline to promote your software artifacts in development, test, acceptance, and production environments, provides a solid technical and conceptual foundation, which can be used for the automated deployment of a data science model as well. The following quote sums up the role of the data scientist very well in an amusing way:

> A data scientist is someone who is better at statistics than any software engineer and better at software engineering than any statistician.

A good end-to-end Hadoop solution delivery team will have the right balance of skills. As an example, in an eight-member scrum team working on Hadoop solutions, four data scientists and four data engineers will be a good mix to get started. In this team structure, in order to deploy the model in production, the data scientists learn to work in close cooperation with data engineers, who have a good knowledge of scalable distributed systems, building data pipelines, and programming technologies available for Hadoop.

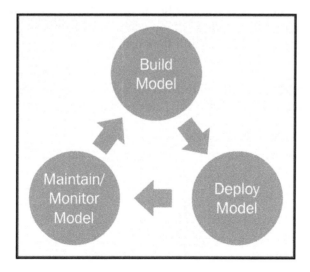

Figure 1: Data science model life cycle

Figure 1 shows a high-level view of the iterative process of building, deploying, and maintaining the model. By having data engineers and data scientists working closely together, these iterations can happen pretty fast. Keeping the data science team separate from data engineering team is not very effective because long communication paths will introduce the risk of building models that take too long to go into production.

Sometimes a model developed by data scientists has to be recoded in a production-friendly programming language. This can happen for a variety of reasons, such as recoding done in another programming language for better performance or security-related reasons. Data scientists prefer to experiment with a bouquet of software tools; many of them might not be supported on the production environment. For example, a data scientist might work with Python or R but the production environment might only support Java or .NET. Such recoding activities will be up to data engineers with a strong programming knowledge.

Despite the role of data scientists getting a lot of attention, the role of data engineers remains equally important in building a production-quality business solutions on Hadoop.

Hadoop on Cloud

Hadoop is a distributed system and it is capable of running over thousands of distributed nodes. Hadoop mega clusters with thousands of nodes are already in production. In this book, we developed solutions on a single-node cluster. Such a setup is good for learning but not sufficient for a production environment. Setting up even a modest three- or five-node Hadoop cluster may not be very feasible at home due to the cost of hardware involved. Arranging the budgets for a five-node Hadoop cluster in a company will require you to go through a budgetary approval process and then order the hardware, which can be a time-consuming process.

Hadoop on Cloud offers a good alternative to having a multinode Hadoop setup in your own data center or company premises. You can use Hadoop on cloud in two ways:

- Deploying Hadoop on cloud servers
- Using Hadoop as a Service

Deploying Hadoop on cloud servers

All cloud service providers let you provision standard Linux- or Windows-based servers by following simple steps. These servers come preinstalled with the operating system. You can set the number of CPUs, storage space, and so on during the server configuration process. After provisioning the servers, you can deploy Hadoop on them manually or using automated deployment tools such as Ansible. This option offers you maximum flexibility in terms of which version of Hadoop to use and which tools to use. You can choose the latest and greatest version of Hadoop to run on your cluster, which might not be the case when you use Hadoop as a cloud-based service. However, this also creates a significant amount of overhead in deploying and managing your Hadoop cluster. In this model, you will not be able to get the full benefit of additional tools available from vendors that are only supported for their flavor of Hadoop as a cloud-based service. For example, HDInsight comes with a user-friendly Hadoop deployment portal as shown in *Figure 2*:

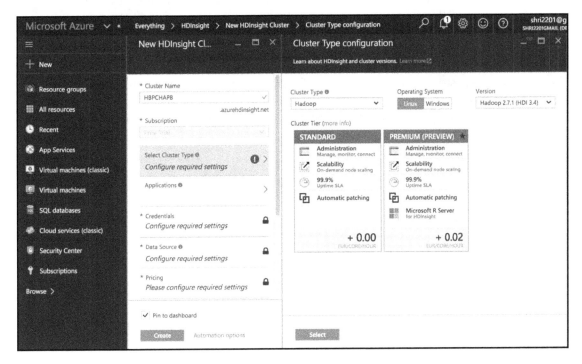

Figure 2: HDInsight deployment portal

Using Hadoop as a service

Amazon Elastic MapReduce (also known as Amazon EMR) from Amazon is Hadoop as a Service on Cloud. HDInsight is another Hadoop-on-cloud service. Microsoft delivers this service on the Microsoft Azure platform and it can provide Apache Hadoop, Spark, R, HBase, and Storm as a service. Hadoop on cloud-based services offers you all the benefits of Hadoop and limits your time and money investment risk in buying and setting up new hardware and software. These services also take away some of the pain involved in setting up and configuring Hadoop with installation utilities. In addition, these services offer you a pay-as-you-grow model, which allows you to scale up your cluster as your business demand grows rather than making a huge upfront commitment in hardware capacity.

In the on-premise Hadoop installation, you will use disk storage on the hard disk drives attached to your data node machines. In the service models of the Hadoop as a cloud-based service, you will find that compute and storage are two separate commodities and are billed separately based on the usage. When you pay for the compute service on the basis of the uptime of cluster nodes, it makes sense to shut down the cluster when you are not using it. Generally, cloud-based compute nodes provide ephemeral data storage, so when a Hadoop cluster is shut down, you lose the data saved on the cluster too unless you've saved your data on a separate storage service. Amazon S3 and Azure Blob storage are two examples of cloud-based storage services that provide durable data storage that can live beyond the lifetime of your Hadoop cluster. The following image shows the design of the HDInsight storage architecture (Gao, 2016):

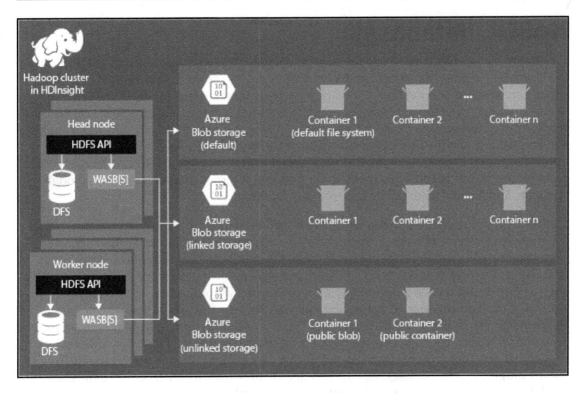

Figure 3: HDInsight storage architecture (Source: Microsoft Azure Website)

In addition to providing durable storage of data, storage services offer more advantages that are not available when you set up your own Hadoop cluster. You can find more information on the advantages of HDInsight storage here: `https://azure.microsoft.com/en-us/documentation/articles/hdinsight-hadoop-use-blob-storage/`.

For getting started quickly with a production-quality the Hadoop cluster, Hadoop as a cloud-based service is a very good option and is worth exploring.

NoSQL databases

Programmers and DBAs have used relational database management systems (RDBMS) for the last three decades. RDBMS systems have been used to build online transaction processing systems and data warehousing systems. The relational model of database design is well understood in the industry, where data is stored in tables in a structured format and relationships between the tables are maintained using the concept of keys. As a result of the exponential jump in the number of transactions taking place through web and mobile applications, having a scalable RDBMS that delivers high availability and performance at a reasonable cost has become gradually more difficult. Internet companies such as Google, Amazon, and Yahoo! were the first to face this problem.

Hadoop is one such system that took center stage in handling the massive volumes of data for analytic purposes. However, the requirement to process big data and offer superior performance and availability is not limited to analytical applications alone. Increasingly, web and mobile applications need a reliable and affordable database for several use cases such as processing transactions, managing web-based shopping carts, and quickly retrieving product catalogs. The growing popularity of continuous delivery principles requires teams to quickly iterate from requirements to deployment; this is another reason why NoSQL databases have become popular, because they offer a flexible or simple data model that does not require sophisticated data modeling and schema management. This means programmers can quickly build and deploy new features by modifying the data model as needed, without confronting the rigidity of relational data models.

To summarize, the following factors have contributed to the rise of NoSQL databases:

- Growing storage costs of massive volumes of data
- Growing costs of infrastructure to deliver high availability and performance
- Pressure to build and deploy software in short iterative cycles
- A variety of data types and query models for which relational tables are not the best suited systems

Types of NoSQL databases

NoSQL database management systems can be divided into four types:

- **Wide column stores**: In wide column stores, each row in a table can have a varying number of columns. Columns can store different data types and may be very large in number. Cassandra, Amazon Dynamo, and HBase are examples of such databases. Such databases are optimized for queries over large datasets.
- **Key-value stores:** In a key-value store, each record is associated with a key and value. For example, a value can be a single attribute such as the zip code, but it can also be a full address recorded in XML form. Some key-value stores will allow you to specify the type of data stored in the value. Redis, Riak, and BerkelyDB are some popular key-value stores.
- **Document databases**: Document databases store and retrieve records in document format, which can be in XML, JSON, or BSON. The stored documents will have self-describing schemas. Document databases provide a rich query language to query the attributes contained in the self-describing schema. MongoDB, CouchDB, and Mark Logic are popular Document Databases.
- **Graph database**: Graph databases store information in nodes and edges. Social networks and networks of suppliers and customers are examples of problem domains that can be modeled better with a graph than with other approaches. Nodes in a graph can represent the entities and edges can represent the relationships among nodes. Apache Giraph and Neo4J are popular graph databases.

Common observations about NoSQL databases

We can make some common observations about the characteristics of Hadoop and other NoSQL databases (Sadalage, 2014):

- A flexible data storage schema
- The ability to run on a cluster built on non-proprietary hardware
- Strong support from the open source community
- Built with the needs of web, mobile, and data crunching applications in mind

NoSQL databases rely heavily on data replication to deliver high availability and resilience to random failures. Data replication is a tunable parameter that can be set depending upon the need of the application. Sharing is another technique used by NoSQL databases to improve the performance and resilience of the system.

NoSQL databases give a lot of flexibility to application programmers when it comes to finding the right balance between the data consistency of reads and the performance of writes. At the same time, they make application logic complex, to deal with the unwanted side-effects of a lack of data consistency.

CAP theorem

 You can learn more about the topic of data consistency in NoSQL systems by reading about the CAP Theorem: `http://robertgreiner.com/214/8/cap-theorem-revisited/`.

NoSQL databases often lack support for distributed transactions and transactions spanning multiple records.

Hive provides an SQL-like language to query the data stored on HDFS. Another NoSQL database management system, Cassandra, also offers an SQL-like language to query and insert data. However, it should be understood that SQL support in these systems is merely a layer on the top of the underlying file structure, unlike in RDBMS where it is natively supported.

Having a good knowledge of one or more NoSQL database management systems is definitely useful when you build Hadoop-based solutions.

In-memory databases

Throughout the evolution of distributed technologies, engineers have been trying to push them to their limits. Earlier, people were looking for faster, cheaper ways of data processing; this need was satisfied when Hadoop was introduced. Everyone started replacing their ETLs with Hadoop-bound ecosystem tools. Now that this need is satisfied and Hadoop is used in production by numerous companies, the need arose to process data in a streaming manner; this gave rise to technologies such as Apache Ignite, which we will cover in the following section.

Apache Ignite as an in-memory database

In this book, we've generally used HDFS as the storage medium for massive volumes of data. In-Memory Databases, such as Apache Ignite, offer an alternative to the disk-based data storage common in HDFS and other relational database management systems. To understand the differences, let us first examine the differences between data storage in HDFS and other RDBMSes.

HDFS is an essentially a network- and disk-based data storage system. Relational databases also make heavy use of networks and disks to store data though their architecture differs significantly from the HDFS architecture of data storage.

Fetching data from disk is a relatively slow process as compared to how fast a CPU can process the data. Before a CPU can process the data, it should be loaded in the RAM of the computer. When the data is shuffled or transported between the data nodes in Hadoop, the transmission of the data over the wire can introduce a delay in processing.

If loading the data takes time, then the CPU will have to wait before the data arrives for processing. In batch analytics, these differences may not be visible to the end users, but in interactive web and mobile applications, slow response can negatively affect the customer experience.

To speed up the processing, RDBMSes make use of in-memory buffers for frequently accessed data. The data stored in the buffers is a subset of the data stored on the disk drive. Algorithms such as the **Least Recently Used** (LRU) algorithm evict the data from the buffer when it is not accessed and flush it to the disk. Similarly, to speed up write processing, a write in-memory buffer is used, which regularly flushes the data to the disk. This ensures that the client programs and the users who use them do not have to wait for the disk write to finish.

In contrast with disk-based databases, in-memory databases keep all the data in the RAM of the computer instead of keeping a subset of data in the buffer in the RAM. The price of RAM has fallen to a small fraction of what it was a decade ago. As a result, it has become affordable to fit large databases in RAM. Just like HDFS and Hadoop MapReduce, in-memory databases such as Apache Ignite provide both data storage and compute features.

Apache Ignite is an in-memory database that is a high-performance distributed database management system. It can be used as a fast key-value store, distributed computing system, and data stream processing system. Apache Ignite can run on a cluster of nodes where the data can be replicated in the RAMs of various nodes to provide fault tolerance. The performance of Apache Ignite can be several times faster than disk-based database management systems such as HDFS and Oracle. Apache Ignite bridges the gap between the **Online Transaction Processing** (**OLTP**) and **Online Analytical Processing** (**OLAP**) worlds. By using a single Apache Ignite database, you can run both analytical and transactional workloads on the same system. Apache Ignite provides full ACID support for transactions, which makes it an attractive choice for building OLTP systems.

Apache Ignite can run as a layer on top of existing databases systems such as Oracle or HDFS. In such a scenario, we can get the benefits of the in-memory capabilities of Apache Ignite and using a disk-based database as a backup storage. Apache Ignite supports distributed computing patterns such as map-reduce and fork join, which can perform parallel computations on a cluster of computers.

Apache Ignite is a Java-based system that runs on JVM. It provides APIs in several programming languages such as Java, C++, and .NET.

In most new databases such as Hadoop, Cassandra, or Redis, full SQL support is limited. Apache Ignite provides full ANSI-99 SQL support. This is a very attractive feature for developers and DBAs who are much more familiar with SQL-based queries. Apache Ignite can use aggregation and grouping functions in SQL. It also supports distributed SQL joins.

Apache Ignite as a Hadoop accelerator

Apache Ignite can be used as an in-memory accelerator for Hadoop, as shown in *Figure 4*. Apache Ignite comes with an in-memory filesystem known as **Ignite File System** (**IGFS**), which is 100% compatible with HDFS. It also has an in-memory version of MapReduce. When Apache Ignite is deployed as a Hadoop accelerator, it can deliver a performance that is as much as 100 times faster than disk-based map-reduce. Using Apache Ignite as a Hadoop accelerator is a simple plug-and-play functionality. It does not require any complex integration or programming. It is compatible with open source Hadoop and other commercial versions of Hadoop, such as Hortonworks, Cloudera, MapR, Apache, AWS, as well as any other older Hadoop 1.x version or Hadoop 2.x distribution.

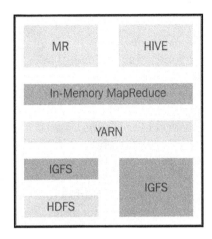

Figure 4: Apache Ignite as a Hadoop accelerator

Apache Spark versus Apache Ignite

In this book, we have already covered Apache Spark. Apache Spark is an open source engine for fast data analytics. Apache Spark is also an In-Memory computing solution targeted towards analytical applications. Apache Ignite is more suitable for building an OLTP solution.

Apache Spark loads data from disk-based database systems into RAM for processing. When the processing is finished, it will not keep the data in RAM but it will discard it. Apache Spark itself is not a database. Apache Ignite is a database. It will keep the data in its RAM even when it is not required for processing or when the processing is over. Apache Spark is based on **Resilient Distributed Datasets** (**RDD**), which it builds by reading data from the disk. It performs actions or transformations on the RDD. Apache Ignite is a key-value store where operations can be performed on the stored data using a programming language such as Java.

Summary

In this chapter, we covered some topics that are useful in building Hadoop-based solutions but not directly related to the main theme of this book. We explained that building a Hadoop-based solution involves a team work, where data engineering and data science skills are represented adequately. We covered how cloud-based Hadoop reduces the upfront investment and time-to-market for Hadoop-based solutions. Hadoop as a cloud-based service is available from Amazon and Microsoft. NoSQL databases play an important role in building web and mobile applications. Often, a Hadoop-based data pipeline will have to be integrated with NoSQL databases. Finally, we covered how In-Memory databases are changing the nature of analytics, transaction processing, and stream processing to provide actionable business insights faster.

This book has given you several practical examples of how we can use Hadoop to solve business problems. We covered several commonly used tools from the Hadoop ecosystem to build solutions. We are pretty certain that the business problems that you will solve using Hadoop are going to much more complex than the problems presented in this book. This book has built a solid foundation for you to be an expert Hadoop solution developer and architect.

Index

www.ingramcontent.com/pod-product-compliance
Lightning Source LLC
Chambersburg PA
CBHW062107050326
40690CB00016B/3232